Listening to Popular Music
Or, How I Learned to Stop Worrying and Love Led Zeppelin

Theodore Gracyk

The University of Michigan Press   Ann Arbor

Copyright © by the University of Michigan 2007
All rights reserved
Published in the United States of America by
The University of Michigan Press
Manufactured in the United States of America
⊛ Printed on acid-free paper

2010   2009   2008   2007   4   3   2   1

A CIP catalog record for this book is available from the British Library.

Library of Congress Cataloging-in-Publication Data

Gracyk, Theodore.
     Listening to popular music, or how I learned to stop worrying and
  love Led Zeppelin / Theodore Gracyk.
        p.   cm. — (Tracking pop)
     Includes bibliographical references (p.   ) and index.
     ISBN-13: 978-0-472-09983-2 (cloth : alk. paper)
     ISBN-10: 0-472-09983-3 (cloth : alk. paper)
     ISBN-13: 978-0-472-06983-5 (pbk. : alk. paper)
     ISBN-10: 0-472-06983-7 (pbk. : alk. paper)
      1. Popular music—Philosophy and aesthetics.   I. Title.   II. Title:
  How I learned to stop worrying and love Led Zeppelin.

  ML3877.G72   2007
  781.64'117—dc22   2006032063

Listening to Popular Music
Or, How I Learned to Stop Worrying and Love Led Zeppelin

TRACKING POP

SERIES EDITORS: LORI BURNS, JOHN COVACH, AND ALBIN ZAK

In one form or another, the sonic influence of popular music has permeated cultural activities and perception on a global scale. Interdisciplinary in nature, Tracking Pop is intended as a rich exploration of pop music and its cultural situation. In addition to providing much-needed resources for the ever-increasing number of students and scholars working in the field of popular culture, the books in this series will appeal to general readers and music lovers, for whom pop has provided the soundtrack of their lives over the past fifty years.

For my parents, who put up with a lot of music they hated

Popularity is not, as many seem to think, a specialty of strings of obvious phrases built on a simple rhythm. That music is *popular* which arrests people's attention and, when heard again, compels their recognition; not that whose highest success is momentarily to tickle their ears.

—Edmund Gurney, 1880

Contents

Acknowledgments

I would like to thank John Covach for his immediate support for this project when I mentioned it to him. Had he been less enthusiastic, this would have been another one of those projects that sits for years on my hard drive, half-finished.

This book also reflects the kind help, support, and advice of a number of friends and scholars. I would particularly like to extend my thanks to Philip Alperson, Ralph von Appen, Bruce Baugh, Wayne Bowman, Lee B. Brown, Magdalene Chalikia, Stephen Davies, David Goldblatt, Athena Gracyk, Kathleen Higgins, Bill Irwin, Andrew Kania, Justin London, Renée Lorraine, Elizabeth Nawrot, Alex Neill, Bennett Reimer, Carlos Rodriguez, Joel Rudinow, and Robert Stecker. In most cases, our conversations and exchanges directed my thinking. (It's remarkable how the simplest exchange will sometimes redirect an argument in an entirely fresh direction.) Some directed me to valuable research sources. Some gave me detailed feedback on parts of the manuscript. Others invited me to write essays for their own projects, and those essays contributed to several of the chapters.

I very gratefully acknowledge and thank the three anonymous readers whom the University of Michigan Press secured to read and comment on the book as it developed. Their advice, together with that of Chris Hebert, was enormously useful to me.

I thank the editors and publishers who have kindly granted permission to reprint work appearing, in revised form, in this book. The original publication information is as follows.

"Valuing and Evaluating Popular Music," *Journal of Aesthetics and Art Criticism* 57, no.2 (Spring 1999): 205–20; "Popular Music: The Very Idea of Listening to It," is from *Bridging the Gap: Popular Music and Music Education,* edited by Carlos Xavier Rodriguez. Copyright © 2004 by MENC—The

National Association for Music Education, 2004. Reprinted by permission; "Music's Worldly Uses," in *Arguing About Art: Contemporary Philosophical Debates,* ed. Alex Neil and Aaron Ridley, 2nd ed. (London: Routledge, 2002), 135–48; "Does Everyone Have a Musical Identity? Reflections on *Musical Identities," Action, Criticism, and Theory for Music Education* 3, no. 1 (May 2004), http://www.siue.edu/MUSIC/ACTPAPERS/v3/Gracyko4 .pdf.

Finally, I thank Minnesota State University Moorhead for providing one semester of sabbatical leave, during which I completed my first version of the manuscript.

Introduction
Aesthetics and Popular Music

Despite my subtitle, this is not a book about Led Zeppelin. Susan Fast has already written that book: *In the Houses of the Holy: Led Zeppelin and the Power of Rock Music*. What's more, I am not offering any sort of music criticism, biography, or autobiography. Instead, this book concentrates on the idea that popular music has an aesthetic dimension, and everyday engagements with popular music are concerned, in part, with aesthetic value.

At the same time, I really have *learned* to love Led Zeppelin, and it is one of several personal examples that I use to clarify technical ideas and arguments. But my examples of popular music are merely examples, and each one could be replaced with any number of other ones. Popular music embraces a staggering range of sounds and practices, and examples are offered with the assumption that readers will substitute their own examples for each of mine.

Part 1 offers my detailed characterization of, and support for, the claim that popular music aesthetically enriches lives. Unfortunately, any discussion of aesthetic value generates objections based on the elitism of traditional aesthetics. A great deal of interesting scholarship on popular music arises from the insight that we value music as a social practice. As a subdiscipline of cultural studies, broadly defined, many studies of popular music explicitly dismiss the importance of the music's aesthetic dimension.[1] Claims about aesthetic value are regarded with great suspicion, as being unavoidably elitist and Eurocentric. Drawing on recent arguments by sociologists engaged in cultural studies and philosophers interested in broadening the field of aesthetic experience, I make a case that popular music studies has no essential conflict with philosophical aesthetics. Agreeing that music is always social practice does not demonstrate that music is *only* social practice.[2]

Part 2 challenges conceptions of aesthetic value that regard popular culture as a second-rate domain of aesthetic value. Where earlier chapters defend aesthetic theory against criticisms rooted in sociological accounts of culture and communication, these middle chapters recognize a counterbalancing need to defend popular music against prejudices bolstered by traditional aesthetic theory.

Part 3 explores related issues that arise at the intersection of aesthetic and communicative uses of popular music. Aesthetic interest does not preclude symbolic interaction. Attending to the cultural location of music does not require a suspension of aesthetic discrimination, and aesthetic experience does not require transcending the socially and politically local dimensions of lived experience.

Obviously, I will have to do some work to clarify what I mean by "aesthetic value," for otherwise there is no substance to the claim that many people are interested in popular music for its aesthetic value. But that topic is merely the gateway into another, more controversial one. *Should* we look to popular music as a source of aesthetic enrichment? Or, if one prefers a roughly equivalent question, is popular music a legitimate source of aesthetic value? From the perspective of traditional aesthetics, there is concern that the world of popular culture is aesthetically impoverished. From the perspective of sociological accounts of popular culture, there is concern that aesthetic value is a red herring, directing attention away from what is really at stake in popular culture.

These questions and concerns emerge from a shared, broad agreement that popular music and serious music are distinct fields of cultural production and consumption. So they should not be subjected to the same standards. But what is being assumed here? How does a cultural distinction obliterate the relevance of aesthetic evaluation?

Taken at face value, the divide between high and low—between serious and popular—suggests that each field operates according to distinct norms. But this observation is a relatively trivial admission, as harmless as Aristotle's presupposition, twenty-four centuries ago, that distinct standards apply to comic theater and tragedy. We would have to build in many additional assumptions before we would conclude that comedies should not be subjected to aesthetic evaluation. A parallel situation holds for music. To the extent that explicit standards directly apply, why would anyone think that Beethoven's symphonic compositions should be evaluated according to standards appropriate for jazz improvisation, or vice versa? Any given genre of music requires listeners to apply culturally acquired skills and capacities. Anything but a completely superficial and naive response requires a listener's grasp of contingent standards of merit.[3]

One way to grant the aesthetic merit of widely diverse cultural products—to endorse tragedy and comedy, or both Beethoven and the blues—is to distinguish between universal aesthetic standards and the universal human impulse to respond aesthetically. The standards may be localized and variable. Yet the fact that we always *have* standards may be an important fact about human life.[4]

For example, Aristotle thinks that tragedy is "higher" than comedy. However, he does not assign aesthetic value to tragedy in order to deny it of comedy. Similarly, the chilly beauty of Miles Davis's *In a Silent Way* (1969) does not arise from adherence to Viennese classical sonata form. Only the most rigidly elitist of music lovers supposes that because Beethoven's music rewards aesthetic evaluation, Davis's does not. Seeing an analogous situation, I wonder why the divide between high and low—between Verdi's *Rigoletto* at New York's Metropolitan Opera and the Beatles appearing on the *Ed Sullivan Show*—encourages the false dilemma of reasoning that aesthetics belongs with the "high," so it doesn't apply to the "low."[5]

Coming at the high/low divide from the other direction, there is an entrenched *popular* suspicion of applying "high culture" concepts to popular music. For instance, consumers and producers of popular music remain leery of terminology and concepts borrowed from music theory or analysis.[6] Most people are still like John Lennon, who made fun of a music critic who identified the aeolian cadence at the end of an early Beatles song.

> LENNON: . . . But the basic appeal of the Beatles was not their intelligence. It was their music. It was only after some guy in the *London Times* said there were aeolian cadences in "It Won't Be Long" that the middle classes started listening to it—because somebody put a tag on it.
>
> PLAYBOY: *Did* you put aeolian cadences in "It Won't Be Long?"
>
> LENNON: To this day, I don't have *any* idea what they are. They sound like exotic birds.[7]

Notice Lennon's opposition of "intelligence" and "music." As a result, Lennon seemed unable to conceptualize the links between a song like

"Help" and the musique concrète of "Revolution 9." In this respect, Lennon bought into the assumption that people cannot hear his music for what it is if they intellectualize it by putting a fancy "tag" on it. Instead of erasing the divide between high and low, popular culture has internalized the distinction: many listeners use the distinction between "rock" and "pop" as another way to divide high from low, while others make parallel distinctions among rock bands by opposing art and commerce.[8]

Recall my basic question: Should we look to popular music as a source of aesthetic enrichment? This one led to a closely related question: Don't the obvious differences between serious music and popular music mitigate the importance of aesthetic value in the production and reception of the popular? And I have suggested that this question invites another: Among the many differences we might cite, which ones are supposed to reduce the relevance of aesthetic value when we listen to popular music? So it isn't just a question of whether we should attribute aesthetic value to the popular. It is also a question of why anyone thinks that it is possible to engage meaningfully with popular music without doing so.

My approach balances two ideas. First, "higher" and "lower" levels of musical culture operate within a single, common set of background preconditions for aesthetic response. Second, popular music is like all other music in this way: each genre requires listeners to apply culturally appropriate skills and capacities. Evaluation demands local standards of merit, including aesthetic ones. These standards reflect numerous historical contingencies. Taken seriously, this observation reminds us that current "country music" demands something very different from listeners than did 1950s honky-tonk. The genre has changed so much that country legend Merle Haggard recently said, "I don't even consider myself country anymore. . . . What they're calling country is about as country as downtown New York!"[9] Funk of the 1970s has little in common with 1990s hip-hop that samples it. Joni Mitchell fans who enjoy her jazz-influenced *Mingus* album (1979) may respond with bewilderment to the jazz that inspired her, including the Charles Mingus album *Mingus Ah-Um* (1959). If we cannot reduce the appeal of all popular music to just one value, we cannot expect a listener to derive much aesthetic value from unfamiliar genres. One of the purposes of this book is to explain why reduction to a single, all-encompassing standard is tempting but erroneous.

I suspect, however, that most people believe in such a standard, and they believe that it informs their own listening. As David Hume argued more than two hundred years ago, our ongoing failure to pin down this universal standard does not override our "common sense" commitment to it.[10] So why is it so hard to shake the belief that all music is good or bad in the same way?

A major culprit is that our "education" in popular culture is more or less invisible to us. In the same way that someone raised in Minnesota hears the vocal accent of someone from Alabama or Massachusetts but does not hear her own accent as a regionalism, our everyday music sounds natural and therefore right. Forgetting that competence reflects years of experience, proficiency with a few styles of popular music encourages us to make a hasty generalization about our cultural competence regarding all of popular music. There is a corresponding tendency to assume that others are deprived if their tastes are different. "I think the popular music has gone truly weird," complained former Beatle George Harrison shortly before his death.[11] "It's either cutesy-wutesy or it's hard, nasty stuff. It's good that [Beatles music] has life again with the youth." In 2000, the Beatles had experienced a fresh wave of popularity, this time due to the compilation album *1*. Adolescents who knew little of the Beatles' music purchased many of the millions sold. Harrison's rhetorical contrast—promoting the Beatles' music by denigrating other popular music—illustrates Pierre Bourdieu's observation that "when they have to be justified, [tastes] are asserted purely negatively, by the refusal of other tastes."[12]

Although our listening habits are culturally influenced, my argument presupposes that both *musicality* and *aesthetic interest* are universally human capacities. Properly understood, there is little controversy about this proposal, particularly concerning musicality.[13] Musicality is as basic as our capacity to balance upright and walk. It parallels our capacity to sort complex visual phenomena so that we effortlessly see most objects as distinct from one another, and from their general background. Some people are physically or visually impaired, yet no one thinks that the basic activities of walking and seeing are fundamentally contingent capacities, on a par with the ability to stay in tune when singing and to recognize Led Zeppelin when their music comes on the radio.[14] Common capacities are culturally adapted in diverse ways. But these capacities need not aim, as Hegel proposed, at a final consummation at the level of art. One of my working hypotheses is that we can make sense of our desires and evaluations concerning popular music without assuming that it is, or even aspires to be, art.

If musicality is a universally human capacity, then perhaps the normative stance toward music—the basic impulse to evaluate it—is, too. And if *aesthetic* discrimination informs listening to a Beethoven piano sonata and a jazz improvisation, then perhaps aesthetic discrimination is simply a part of our basic musicality, so that it also operates (subject to "local" development of appropriate expectations) when listening to Chuck Berry, Patsy Cline, and David Bowie.[15] This proposal is elaborated over the course of this book.

Discussion of this possibility has been stifled from two directions. Until recently, the interdisciplinary field of aesthetics was dominated by whichever issues seemed most relevant to making sense of the rapidly evolving standards governing the world of art. Aesthetics was either silent about, or hostile to, popular culture. So I will challenge the dogma that popular music is aesthetically impoverished, "music for an anesthetized market" and "the dregs of musical history."[16]

A very different paradigm was adopted for studying popular culture. There is now a broad consensus that popular culture is best examined from a social science perspective. Consequently, most analyses of the popular occur within a framework demanding evaluative neutrality about any aesthetic standards that apply to the consumption of popular music. But there is no neutrality about aesthetics: "aesthetic approaches per se are incompatible with studies that treat music as socially constructed."[17] I will challenge this view.

Aesthetic values are not incompatible with other values.[18] Aesthetic values generally *enhance* other value. To this degree, George Orwell (author of *1984* and *Animal Farm*) was on to something when he said, "Every artist is a propagandist in the sense that he is trying, directly or indirectly, to impose a vision of life that seems to him desirable."[19] Orwell was thinking about novels, rather than paintings or modern poetry, but if we change "impose" to "suggest," then what he says about novelists is probably true of most popular musicians. Most of them want to communicate a vision of life to a large audience. But they cannot impose that vision, for the "mass" audience is not a passive one. The popular musician who recognizes this will try to offer an aesthetic enticement to attend to the vision. "There are a lot of people who don't really see me anymore; they just see this idea they have of me, and they want a bit of it," complains Bono, U2's vocalist. "But I know there's other people who are still into the music [and] it's the music that's special, not the musicians."[20]

In trying to articulate why "the music" is "special," I face the methodological problem of what music to discuss. Study of popular music is now an established academic field. It continues to grow and thrive in spite of (or perhaps even because of) a failure to agree about the meaning of *popular* in *popular music*. It is widely understood that at least four distinct concepts of the popular are at work here.[21] First, there is music that is widely liked, generating a standard that classifies music as popular or unpopular according to how many people actually endorse it. Adopting record sales as a criterion of the popular, Lou Rawls, Bing Crosby, and Cher are as important as Madonna, Nirvana, and Muddy Waters. Stylistically similar music that fails to attract an audience is not popular and, perversely, we might question whether Skip James and Yoko Ono made popular music.[22]

Second, the popular is thought to be the broad cultural field occupying the "low" side of the distinction between high and low cultures.[23] This criterion produces a shifting target, as the culturally low moves, over time, to the privileged high side. Think here of both Louis Armstrong and the Beatles, and contrast their musical apprenticeships in seedy clubs in red-light districts with their eventual positions as the recipients of serious musicological scrutiny.[24]

Third, we can recast Yoko Ono and blues singer Skip James as popular by modifying our first criterion to include all music that is intended to be widely accepted. In short, popular music is accessible music. Increasingly, that means music that is intended to be commercially profitable as a product.[25] Now we include almost all music that circulates as commercial culture and mass entertainment. This generates another shifting standard, because music ceases to be popular when only an elite has access to it. For example, most of the commercially recorded music of the twentieth century is no longer "in print." Copyright law prevents its free circulation, and copyright holders have no commercial incentive to allow it to circulate. Gradually, thousands of western swing and polka band recordings cease to be popular music. Conversely, isolated oral traditions that would normally count as popular no longer do so, for they fall outside of the commercial framework. Similarly, many rock groups, primarily in the genre of punk, resist commercial expectations and adopt strategies to maintain marginality.[26]

Fourth, a number of analyses turn the third criterion on its head by restricting the popular to the culture that people actually produce for themselves. It must be "by" rather than "for" the common person. This criterion requires either a mode of production outside of the prevailing capitalist framework—suddenly our folk tradition and anticonsumerist punk are authentically "popular"—or consumers who transform and subvert commercial products through active consumption. Thus, listening is popular if the listener sings scatological lyrics to a hit tune. But the music of Frank Zappa does not count as popular if it is being analyzed in the context of research on Zappa intended for presentation at a musicology conference.

At the very least, we face distinct criteria of popular as mass, popular as folk, popular as counterculture.[27] Worse, in actual practice a great deal of music is simply ignored. Anahid Kassabian warns that we misrepresent the full scope of popular music when we reduce the popular to whatever people *consciously* choose to hear. Contemporary life overflows with "musics that are always there, beyond our control, slipping under our thresholds of consciousness."[28] This music includes the soundtracks of movies, television shows, audio books, and sporting events. Aural wallpaper fills most public space. Purses and coat pockets suddenly erupt with music installed as personalized ring tones of cellular telephones. In recent years, the predominant music "education" of many adolescent males is the numbingly repetitive soundtrack music that accompanies video games.

In short, "popular music" designates what philosophers call an open concept. No one expects precise criteria for using the phrase, and its scope of application continues to expand and contract.[29] I will make no attempt to define or limit it. At the same time, I am an American academic writing in English at the beginning of the twenty-first century, in a cultural context where the musics heard by most people are created, distributed, and consumed as recorded music. In this context, most popular music circulates as mass art, designed to be readily understood by a listener who possesses little or no formal music training.[30] With this in mind, the majority of my examples of popular music fall squarely in the genre of rock music. Yet I have not entirely neglected country music, blues, and hip-hop, and some arguments involve extended discussion of earlier popular musics. I have tended to use examples that are relatively well known, that remain commercially available (and thus readily available for listening), and that have been subjects of academic study or, at the very least, have been extensively discussed in the popular music press.

Part One
Aesthetics without Elitism

1. Separating Aesthetics from Art

Imagine an aesthetic (if the word has not become too depreciated) based entirely (completely, radically, in every sense of the word) on the pleasure of the consumer, whoever he may be, to whatever class, whatever group he may belong, without respect to cultures or languages: the consequences would be huge.

—Roland Barthes, *The Pleasure of the Text*

The Question of "Art"

P. T. Barnum made a fortune promoting popular entertainment. But when fame and fortune did not translate into cultural respectability, Barnum decided that he was willing to risk enormous sums of money in a project that would associate his name with "high artistic powers."[1] He was tired of being known for such popular attractions as midgets, minstrel shows, fake mermaids, and staged buffalo hunts in New Jersey. So he hired a European opera star, Jenny Lind, for an extended concert tour of the United States. Lind signed a contract for 150 concerts. But she risked nothing. She would not sail for America until Barnum deposited her guaranteed minimum earnings in a London bank.

Barnum's publicity machine went into overdrive to sell Lind's concert tour to the American public. She became the centerpiece of a larger media campaign to link Barnum with morally uplifting material. He renovated his principal New York business, the American Museum, and reopened it mere weeks before Lind's arrival, advertising it as a place where amusements were selected to "train the mind of youth to reject as repugnant anything inconsistent with moral and refined tastes."[2] Lind was advertised as "goodness personified."[3] In a scene that has strong modern parallels in the American outbreak of Beatlemania in 1963, Lind's arrival in 1850 drew a crowd of perhaps thirty thousand to the docks of New York City. The clamor for Lind allowed Barnum to hold a public auction for tickets to her New York debut (a practice recently revived by an equally savvy self-promoter, the singer Madonna). In the wake of so much hype, "the musical performances, tumultuously received as they were, formed only an anticlimax."[4]

Tracing the gradual development of the divide between popular and "high" culture, Lawrence Levine treats Lind's American concert tour as evidence that opera was once a form of popular entertainment.[5] However, the situation was already far more complicated than that. Barnum made no secret of the fact that he brought Lind to the United States because she represented art. His gamble was that promotion could transform a celebrated artist into a celebrity. He succeeded. In the words of a contemporary news report, Lind became "the most popular woman in the world."[6] Here we see the disanalogy between the Atlantic crossings of Jenny Lind and the Beatles. Ed Sullivan did not bring the Beatles to the United States in order to bask in the aura of their "artistic powers." The four boys from Liverpool did not yet have any such reputation. They were charismatic performers of pop songs. "I Want to Hold Your Hand" did not have the cultural status of Lind's showpiece aria, "Casta Diva," from the opera *Norma*. Felix Mendelssohn and Giacomo Meyerbeer wrote concert showpieces tailored to Lind's vocal range. But Aaron Copland and Leonard Bernstein never composed songs for the Beatles. At the start of the 1960s, the decade in which the Beatles remade popular music, the divide between high culture and popular entertainment was as firmly established as it had ever been. However popular a musician might become, no promoter would follow Barnum's lead and invest a fortune in the belief that art music could reach the top of the pop charts.

The great irony is that now, retrospectively, a chorus of voices proclaims that some popular musicians of the 1960s were artists all along, and their music is art. Receiving their own volume in Phaidon Press's 20th-Century Composers series, the Beatles are placed on an equal footing with Maurice Ravel and Benjamin Britten. Since my aim is to explore and defend the aesthetic value of popular music, it might be assumed that I endorse this trend. I do not. In the same way that Barnum sold Jenny Lind to the public by ignoring music and emphasizing her philanthropic generosity and moral goodness, calling popular music "art" praises it for all the wrong reasons. We can, and should, confirm the aesthetic value of popular music without any appeal to the increasingly contested concept of art.

Here is an example of what we should resist. Concluding a short book about the Beach Boys' album *Pet Sounds*, Jim Fusilli proposes that "in the not-too-distant future, 60s pop music will have been all but forgotten, the songs no more a part of the daily landscape than are the hits of the early twentieth century today."[7] Yet he also claims that because *Pet Sounds* is "the finest album of the rock era," it will be "perhaps one of fewer than a dozen that will be valued for its depth of expression and musical sophistication long after we are gone."[8] Why is Fusilli so confident that, in a future period when 1960s pop music is irrelevant, *Pet Sounds* will be highly valued? Because, he says, it is a great work of art.

> *Pet Sounds* opened a new world for me, one that reveals itself through art, which, in turn, illuminates the real world around me. . . . I recently read, for the first time, the poem "The Lost Darling" by Lydia Sigourney. Do you know it? It's marvelous, and it's heartbreaking. . . . [You] confront a work of art and it speaks to you and suddenly the world is no longer the same. Maybe you're walking through the Art Institute of Chicago and you come upon Antonio Mancini's "Resting" [and] your life is changed. It is nothing like it was before the work of art became part of you.[9]

Fusilli proposes that *Pet Sounds* possesses this same combination of beauty, emotional lucidity, and capacity to transform lives. It will stand the test of time. It is, therefore, a work of art.

In contrast to an older tradition of celebrating some popular music as folk art, treating commercial popular music as full-fledged art is relatively new. Few claims were made about the art status of jazz prior to the 1950s. In 1968, rock critic Jon Landau identified and attacked an emerging trend of rock musicians positioning themselves as artists, promoting their songs and albums as works of art. Unfortunately, Landau's criticisms rely on the old stereotype that art is intellectual and contrived, whereas popular culture is visceral, immediate, and "authentic."[10] Landau seems to have been more or less ignorant of what was taking place in the art world of the 1960s and early 1970s. Roughly simultaneous with the appearance of Landau's book of rock criticism, artist Chris Burden had himself crucified to the roof of a Volkswagen, a well-publicized performance piece that generally provokes an immediate, visceral response. Even then, Landau's position was an oversimplification of real-world art practices.

So what should we say in response to those who associate aesthetic merit with art status? The association is more than a marketing strategy. It reinforces influential challenges to aesthetic explorations of popular music. Dick

Hebdige's hugely influential book *Subculture: The Meaning of Style* taught a generation of theorists how to approach the intersection of youth subcultures and popular music. Reference to aesthetic appreciation and musical taste are dismissed as an attempt to recast popular art into "timeless objects, judged by the immutable criteria of traditional aesthetics" (that is, to mistakenly treat popular culture as high art).[11] Hebdige thinks that aesthetic value deprives popular music of the immediacy and relevance that matters to its audience.

I grant that traditional aesthetics ignores many issues that come to the fore in popular culture. But just as Landau ignored the variety of practices flourishing in the art world, Hebdige overlooked the wide range of positions being defended under the interdisciplinary umbrella of aesthetics. In the wake of a century of modern and postmodern art, few art theorists or philosophers believe that artistic value and aesthetic value are tightly intertwined.[12] As artists self-consciously blur the border between the art world and "real life," it becomes increasingly clear that artistic and aesthetic values are frequently at odds with traditional aesthetic theory.[13] Furthermore, a growing number of aestheticians reject the relevance of immutable criteria for artistic excellence. These issues are highlighted by a "new aesthetics" that emerged in the 1960s. A summary of the new aesthetics is provided later in this chapter.

Although not every mention of aesthetic value implies endorsement of traditional aesthetics, I share the worry that we distort important truths about popular culture if our only standard for aesthetic merit is derived from the model of fine art.[14] So it is worrisome that the fine art model is increasingly employed in nonacademic discourse about popular music.[15] For example, at the same time that I read Fusilli's book on *Pet Sounds,* I bought two other books in the same series, J. Niimi's *Murmur* (about an R.E.M. album) and Bill Janovitz's *Exile on Main St.* (about a Rolling Stones album). Both books baldly claim that they deal with great works of art. "If *Murmur* is great art—which we agree it is, since you bought this book," Niimi says, it must reach beyond the local to address "universal notions."[16]

There is no great problem with saying that *Pet Sounds, Murmur,* and *Exile on Main St.* are "art" if the term is being used in a merely classificatory sense, as a description that confers no value. In that case, "art" might be understood to include any artifact made with some concern for its aesthetic features, in the way that allows so many non-Western and prehistoric artifacts to count as artworks.[17] This classificatory use of the term *art* is sometimes challenged on the grounds that art is a problematic cultural construction. I will set that problem aside and return to it later in the chapter. Here I want to concentrate on problems that arise when music is classified as art in order to recommend it as especially valuable. Used in this dual way, as both classificatory and honorific, the label *art* is no more helpful than using the broad category of "tool" to rate two randomly selected tools. Which is a better tool, a can opener or a door stop? Which is a better tool, a flashlight or a toilet plunger? What pointless questions! The answers depend on what you need to accomplish. Similarly, it seems silly to expect that we can compare all music to all other music by treating it all as art.[18]

Pet Sounds and Traditional Criteria for Art Status

I will spend some time examining the idea that *Pet Sounds* is art. Doing so provides focus for reflecting on the reasons that we value popular music. It also sets the stage for my argument that popular music's aesthetic value is independent of the music's status as art.

For anyone unfamiliar with *Pet Sounds,* here is some pertinent history. In the early 1960s, the Beach Boys were America's most popular musical group playing in a rock and roll style. Their first regional success came in 1961, with a song about surfing on an independent record label. Their 1962 move to Capital Records led to a string of chart-topping records. While there is nothing very special about their earliest songs, what is special, at least for pop music in 1962, is the sophistication of the vocal harmonies. The voices were arranged by Brian Wilson, who wrote or cowrote most of their material. But Wilson's ear for trio, quartet, and quintet vocal harmony does not explain everything. There is the additional fact that two of Wilson's brothers were his partners in harmony, and they had been singing together for years. Brian Wilson crafted harmonies for voices he knew as intimately as he knew his own.

The themes of the songs also contributed to their popular success. Frequently dismissed as trivial fare about surfing, cars, and girls, the lyrics focused on adolescent life in Southern California at a time when the United States was enamored with that place as a "new west," a land of continuing opportunity. Today, a Beach Boys song like "Fun, Fun, Fun" seems little more than just another lightweight, up-tempo song about cars and girls. But it takes on more weight in the context of the Chuck Berry song "Promised Land," in which a "poor boy" takes a trip to California, the new promised land. Harmony vocals aside, Berry was an important influence on the Beach Boys; their first national hit, "Surfin' Safari," was rewrite of a Chuck Berry song.

Just before Christmas, 1964, the Beach Boys boarded a flight from Southern California to Houston, Texas, where they were scheduled to perform. Almost immediately after takeoff, Brian Wilson became distraught. He cried and screamed for much of the flight. Refusing to continue traveling with the group, he returned to Los Angeles. He informed the Beach Boys that he would no longer tour or participate in live performances. The group promptly hired a replacement for touring purposes, freeing Brian to concentrate on writing songs and on the increasingly sophisticated process of crafting pop hits in the recording studio.

A new working pattern evolved. By the summer of 1965, the other members of the Beach Boys came to the studio merely to add vocals and harmonies to instrumental tracks recorded in their absence. On July 12, thirteen of the best session musicians in Los Angeles created the elaborate backing track for a traditional song, "Sloop John B." Brian was not the main advocate of recording it, and the track was set aside while Wilson worked on his own material. The Beach Boys finally added vocals to "Sloop John B" in late December, one day short of the anniversary of Brian's ill-fated flight to Houston. In April 1966, he released his first solo recording, the single "Caroline No." When it failed to generate strong sales, "Sloop John B" was quickly released as a Beach Boys single. It sold well. The next Beach Boys album, *Pet Sounds,* sequenced the two recordings as the closing songs on the two sides of vinyl (a sequence that reversed the industry practice of beginning album sides with hit songs).

When Fusilli argues that *Pet Sounds* is a work of art, he is sophisticated enough to observe that not everyone agrees. In its favor, he observes that *Pet Sounds* radically altered Paul McCartney's thinking about popular music and, consequently, changed the course of the Beatles' career. But Fusilli also notes that British pop fans more warmly embraced the album than did Americans. When it was new, the album violated expectations of what the Beach Boys should sound like and the topics they should sing about. Anticipating this problem, the record label increased the album's marketability by insisting that it include their biggest recent hit, "Sloop John B." Thematically, it clashes with everything else on the album.

Finally, Fusilli allows that he was like other Beach Boys fans and took some time to recognize its greatness: "It would be foolish to say my life changed the moment I heard *Pet Sounds,* and it would not be true. Back then . . . it was all about the hits. . . . But once I started exploring the moods of the songs and listening to the words, I began to understand that this piece of music was unlike anything I'd heard before."[19] So the art status of *Pet Sounds*—its capacity to transform lives—is not based on the claim that *everyone* who listens will be transfixed by it. There may be special obstacles for those who enjoy the Beach Boys' earlier music. So Fusilli suggests that its merit is based on a distinction between the easy pleasure of "hits" and a less accessible value.

But why should we grant that this reduced accessibility is related to art status? The explanation constitutes one of five points advanced to confirm that *Pet Sounds* is art.

First, it is widely held that artworks are autonomous things that belong to a world unto themselves. Fusilli calls it a "new world," different from the "real world." As Preben Mortensen summarizes this idea, art "should be appreciated and interpreted in a manner that does not relate it to political and social issues, or to the context in which art is produced and consumed."[20] Second, there is the closely related idea that art has a universal appeal that transcends place and time. Future generations will ignore most twentieth-century popular music, but *Pet Sounds* will endure. *Pet Sounds* will cast its spell despite the audience's general ignorance of *other* Beach Boys music, of the Caribbean elements of "Sloop John B," of the Latin rhythms and percussion in the title track, of the jazz borrowings in "I Just Wasn't Made for These Times," and of the relative daring of the harmonic modulations in many of the songs. Third, Fusilli cites the album's originality, and assigns credit for it to the group's guiding genius, Brian Wilson. (Several critics argue that *Pet Sounds* is better understood as Brian Wilson's first solo album than as a genuine Beach Boys album. In making the same point, at least one writer mistakenly credits Wilson with all of the album's lead vocals.)[21] Fourth, the experience of art involves feelings of awe, wonder, and a suspension of the ordinary. Fifth and finally, art combines emotional lucidity and intensity. Great art alters our perception of the world. It does so by emotionally transforming the audience. In short, art expresses emotion in an act of genius, thereby transcending its sources and ensuring its universal accessibility.

Despite my personal admiration for *Pet Sounds,* I will make a case that this cluster of five ideas is incoherent. I will also call attention to the fact that these ideas have histories. Relatively few people pay attention to the complex histories of terms that do the cultural work they want done. But we cannot understand these criteria unless we explore some of that history. It turns out that several of the criteria were proposed independently, as *competing* ideas about art.

Beginning with the idea that only a few cultural objects stand the test of time, how likely is it that future audiences will be in a position to admire *Pet Sounds*? The answer depends on whether future listeners know mostly the same things that we know about music—"know" in the active sense of having experienced similar music and having formed similar listening habits.

Fusilli is a professional music critic, and he patiently outlines the harmonic construction of each piece on *Pet Sounds*. Consider the complexity of the song "God Only Knows," which sounds as if it is set in A major. The song is actually set in E major, and a reoccurring B-minor triad gives the melody an odd, wistful feel. Now consider a pivotal moment in the song:

> Brian came pretty close to writing himself into a dead end. There's really nowhere to go coming out of the bridge, which modulates to G major from D major but ends with a D major–A major–B minor pattern. Thus, when the song returns to D major, it must do so from the B minor, which is kind of static change, particularly when the next chord is a B minor with only a slight variation in the bass.[22]

Brain Wilson masks the dull sequence at this crucial transition between song segments by overlaying a "startling glissando" of three harmonizing voices, so that the entrance of the solo voice at the verse sounds like a fresh beginning. "There is," writes Daniel Harrison, "no moment in rock music more harmonically and formally subtle than this transition."[23]

Yet admiration for such moments depends on a listener's familiarity with a general family of song structures and harmonic sequences. It presupposes an ability to locate the bridge, to follow the chord progression in the instrumentation, to grasp which measure constitutes the beginning of the verse, and to contrast these elements with the independent construction of the vocal element. Someone familiar only with strophic song, common in blues and folk music, would not understand sectional contrast (verse into chorus into bridge, returning to verse). Such a listener would be puzzled by the bridge passage and would not properly anticipate the moment at which the new verse begins. There would be no recognition of the problem at the conclusion of the bridge passage, and so no admiration of the "subtle" solution provided by the voices. In order to admire this moment in this song as a solution to an aesthetic problem, listeners must evaluate it in the musical context of its production. This, in turn, requires a knowledgeable listener, one who does *not* admire "God Only Knows" from a position of ignorance about other, similar music.

As distinct from simply *liking* some music, *admiring* a piece of music presupposes an appropriately experienced listener and not just anyone, anywhere responding to a (supposedly) autonomous sound construct. It is a mystery how anyone expects *Pet Sounds* to be recognized as admirable in a future in which 1960s pop music is all but forgotten. *Pet Sounds* will impress future listeners only if those listeners are knowledgeable about similar kinds of music. I will expand on this point in my discussion of the conceptual demands of listening, in chapter 3. For now, it is sufficient to note that a second claim for the music's art status—its supposed universality—is at odds with the presumption that the hearer is familiar with a culturally specific manner of constructing songs. Furthermore, it is only against a very specific cultural backdrop that the controlling vision constitutes genius, as a contrast to artistic strategies that have become ordinary and too familiar.

Another problem about art status arises when we reflect on the music's expressive dimension. *Pet Sounds* presents a unified theme, providing "cohesiveness, a conceptual unity in musical texture as well as in lyrical content."[24] Brian Wilson has said that the theme is "growing up and the loss of innocence."[25] But the theme is more specific than that. The album is a song cycle about romantic love. It emphasizes the sad maturity that comes with the inevitable transition from naive devotion to heartbreak. Harrison summarizes it as "a complex treatment of love and loneliness, moving between these two with an attitude that itself alternates between naïve fantasy and budding cynicism."[26] Recognition of this theme therefore makes the presence of "Sloop John B" baffling except as a crass commercial move (introducing yet another standard idea about art; art is diametrically opposed to commerce). "Sloop John B" is not a song about romantic love. It's a song about conflicts among some men during a commercial sailing voyage. It belongs to *Pet Sounds* only because it is sonically of a piece with the rest of the album, its backing track arranged and recorded toward the beginning of the *Pet Sound* sessions.

Two problems now emerge. The criterion of genius does not apply very well to *Pet Sounds*. Furthermore, if its status as a work of genius requires comparing it with other music, such as the Beach Boys' previous recordings, then the criterion of genius contradicts the idea that its universal appeal rests on its being an autonomous, self-contained object of appreciation.

Many critics take two distinct claims—that *Pet Sounds* is the product of genius and that it is heartbreakingly expressive—and merge them. The album is more than a technical achievement; Brian Wilson's growth as a studio producer is an extension of the fact that the song cycle arises from and expresses his own personal difficulties. For example, several critics note that the chorus of "Caroline No" derives from earlier, more autobiographical lyrics. It was written about a girl Wilson knew, Carol Mountain, and the original line was "Carol, I know." Other lines derive from cowriter Tony Asher's feelings for a girl that he had known. Wilson combined these elements into an expression of his emerging regret that the passing years were altering his relationship with his wife, Marilyn. Because these multiple sources are successfully integrated in this act of genuine self-expression, "Caroline No" makes an important contribution to the album's art status.

This yoking of genius and personal expression is so common that it is generally accepted as common sense. But the template of this story comes to us from nineteenth-century doctrines that arose as a challenge to earlier theories of art. If we go back a bit further, to the Renaissance, we find an earlier notion of genius. It celebrates superior representational skill rather than heightened emotional expression.[27] Within the field of music, earlier models of expression had little or nothing to do with self-expression.

Even as recently as the final decade of the eighteenth century, artistic genius had nothing to do with personal expression and everything to do with providing unexpected stylistic innovations that became models for imitation by subsequent artists. Immanuel Kant conceived of genius as the mysterious, natural gift for finding new "rules" for an established art medium.[28] In the absence of genius, art is dominated by routine conventions, and it lacks the imaginative play that distinguishes art from other modes of communication.

Unfortunately, Kant's writings are selectively read. Many people get to his assertion that "fine art is the art of genius" and conclude that Kant, as the fountainhead of modern aesthetics, has claimed that each and every work of art requires a display of genius. But that is not his doctrine. What he actually says is that fine art requires genius in a way that craft and science do not. But what is true of the category is not true of every instance. Most works of art are mannered, highly derivative, or "soulless." In any particular case, genius is just as likely to produce "original nonsense" as significant communication.[29] So the presence of genius is not sufficient to make something art.

For example, Pink Floyd fans tend to regard founding member Syd Barrett as the group's resident genius. Yet only the most devoted fans think that his solo albums merit attention. Their minimal coherence appears to be the work of Pink Floyd guitarist David Gilmour, not Barrett. In the second stage of Pink Floyd's history, Roger Waters emerges as the controlling genius and, again, the music suffers as soon as Waters stops collaborating with others—evidenced both by his solo career and by his final album with Pink Floyd, *The Final Cut,* which is more or less a Waters solo album.

At best, genius is a mechanism for explaining the fact that art has a history of successive styles. Because Kant invokes genius to account for unpredictable changes of direction, he recognizes that most art is not the product of genius. Genius is reserved for exceptional cases, as art's path to progress (a genius gives a new rule to art, a rule that is not determined by what the artist has previously found in art when developing skills with the artistic medium). This eighteenth-century doctrine of genius is basically a doctrine of autonomous creativity, not a criterion for art status. Taking it for granted that music is an art form, Kant recognizes every musical composition to be art. But few composers qualify as geniuses.[30]

Ignorant of the fact that different eras have proposed different standards for artistic genius, it is a simple matter to regard *Pet Sounds* as a work of genius on expressive grounds. Brian Wilson is a genius for doing one valuable thing particularly well, namely, expressing his own emotions and, in the process, expressing yours and mine: "*Pet Sounds* resonates within us because it was already a part of us, an echo of the story of our lives."[31] This way of thinking about genius evolved from nineteenth-century priorities in art, and it culminates in the expression theory of art. A particularly insightful version is R. G. Collingwood's *The Principles of Art.*[32] Following a long tradition of distinguishing art from what is merely enjoyable or entertaining, Collingwood wants to dismiss most examples of each art form as something less than real art. To be art, music must express the artist's emotions. When it successfully does so, Collingwood believes it will express those of the composer's peers, as well.

Ironically, Collingwood condemns popular music as necessarily inferior, as a calculated attempt to entertain. We do the same when we treat *The Best of the Beach Boys* as a great collection of songs that is insufficiently cohesive to rise to the level of art. The general theory of expressive genius was originally a reactionary attack on the expanding commercialization of art and culture.[33] If art is the expressive product of genius, deciding that something is art requires recognition of it as something rare and particularly valuable. Entertainment music simply could not count as art, and its lack of genius could be used to make the case against it.

If we say that *Pet Sounds* is special and fundamentally different from the Beach Boys' earlier music, we prioritize one among several models of genius. We endorse the personal self-expression that characterizes romanticism, rather than the eighteenth-century model that made genius so central to fine art. In contrast to expression theory, the eighteenth-century concept of genius places no restrictions on the content or meaning of great works of art. For example, Friedrich Schiller's account of genius assigns no importance to content. Form alone matters.[34] The nineteenth-century's gradual emphasis on expressive content can be read as a backlash against this excessive formalism.

The problem, then, is that expression theory is being used to support the claim that Brian Wilson is a genius, which is then used to classify the album as art. A theory of art is adopted without considering the alternatives, and it is mixed together with elements of conflicting accounts of art. It is also assumed, without additional argument or explanation, that art status demonstrates great value. The older, eighteenth-century model assigns art status to every painting, poem, and musical work without assuming that they cross some minimal threshold of aesthetic value. I have explored some of this historical background to show that selective borrowing from aesthetic theory can be more trouble than it is worth. But these points do nothing to challenge the aesthetic value that *Pet Sounds* has for listeners culturally positioned to appreciate it. The lesson, I hope, is that we should separate questions about the aesthetic value of popular music from questions about its status as art. So where do we go if we grant that *Pet Sounds* is expressively valuable, and thus aesthetically valuable, without its having to be a work of art? Do we really need to claim that its aesthetic value is an enduring, intrinsic value?

Returning to the specifics of *Pet Sounds,* notice that an endorsement of expression theory undercuts the appeal to artistic autonomy that is supposed to give it enduring value. However, as David Novitz so neatly summarizes it, the autonomy thesis tells us that "our understanding and evaluation of [art] should not concern itself with matters extraneous to the work."[35] The life of the artist is one such extraneous matter. If proper appreciation of *Pet Sounds* requires or is enhanced by recognition that the emotions expressed in the songs reflect Brian Wilson's life and outlook, then its value stems from a concern with something beyond, or extraneous to, *Pet Sounds.*

Similarly, "Sloop John B" is completely at odds with the album's unifying theme. Setting it to one side—blaming its presence on record company executives, and thus excusing its disruption of the album's thematic integrity—is yet another extraneous consideration. "Sloop John B" is set aside based on special pleading: its presence depends on someone besides Brian Wilson. Unfortunately, so does the song "I Know There's an Answer," which he presented to the group with a different set of lyrics, "Hang On To Your Ego." But the other members of the group resisted those words. The point of the song was obscure and the title phrase might be taken as a reference to hallucinogenic drugs. Vocalist Mike Love suggested new words for the chorus. The finished song integrates more smoothly with the *Pet Sounds* theme than did Wilson's original. But if we ignore "Sloop John B" and embrace "I Know There's an Answer," we do so on aesthetic grounds. If we evaluate it by reference to Brian Wilson's genius, we would reject both songs and not just "Sloop John B."

Here is another objection to applying multiple ideas about art to *Pet Sounds.* Expressive genius is valuable when the art of genius allows us to express, vicariously, our own emotions. As such, the value of the work depends on something more than its brilliant formal construction. The music's form, its design, must be in the service of emotional expression, and the emotion that is expressed must be one that has not previously received an adequate expression. Otherwise, there is no basis for linking innovation with expression. But what is original about the themes treated in *Pet Sounds?* What is present that is not already present in the popular understanding of Shakespeare's *Romeo and Juliet?* But if we downplay innovation and allow that the value of *Pet Sounds* partially derives from a standing interest in the themes expressed, then we run up against the fact that many people are disturbed by the expression of certain themes. Any emphasis on what it expressed—on the content expressed—becomes a barrier to appreciation. I'll return to this topic in the next chapter.

Perhaps a more recent theory of art would support the claim that *Pet*

Sounds is art. Instead of expecting a musical work to simultaneously satisfy several distinct criteria, we might adopt the far more plausible idea of the disjunctive theory of art. Instead of satisfying multiple criteria (A and B and C and D), something is art if it satisfies any one of several traditional criteria (A or B or C or D) for being art.[36] However, there is very good reason against certifying *Pet Sounds* in this manner. The disjunctive theory of art offers no guidance in distinguishing between better and worse Beach Boys albums. The threshold requirement for obtaining art status is now so low that being a work of art confers no special merit. If Shakespeare's plays are works of art because they involve imaginative, narrative representations, then so is any Christmas pageant performed by kindergartners. Were we to adopt criteria according to which *all* music is art, then designating *Pet Sounds* a work of art does not elevate it above other Beach Boys albums, such as *Little Deuce Coupe* and *15 Big Ones*. *Art* would be a classificatory term without any honorific force. Each cynically commercial repackaging of their hit songs is as much a work of art as *Pet Sounds* is.

What emerges from this discussion of art criteria and *Pet Sounds*? Art status is claimed for a specific piece of commercial, popular music, in order to assign it a higher status than is typically assigned to such music. But this appeal to art status incorrectly assumes that there are characteristic differences between art and nonart that confer value on art. Furthermore, it requires a use of "art" that denies the art status of most music.

However, the concept of art has a long history, and no one *aesthetic* value has consistently been employed as a criterion for art status. The ordinary concept of art is so open, and covers so many different kinds of things, that we should be suspicious of anyone who claims that art status depends on a narrow range of value-conferring criteria.[37] If we want to praise popular music for providing a valuable aesthetic experience, we should set aside the issue of its art status and address its aesthetic value. But first I want to address barriers to doing so.

The Problem Generalized

If music critics and ordinary listeners do not always take the time to explain their criteria for evaluating music, philosophers are waiting in the wings to offer various models of evaluation. Influenced by the democratic impulses of pragmatism, Richard Shusterman makes a strong case that "works of

popular art do in fact display the aesthetic values its critics reserve exclusively for high art."[38] If we can establish that maligned genres of popular
culture include examples of high aesthetic merit, then we can set aside the
established distinction between high and low music and endorse its sociocultural legitimacy as art. But here again, the strategy is to elevate *some* popular culture to the level of art.

Unfortunately, I've just argued that a high degree of "aesthetic quality"
does not demonstrate that we are dealing with works of popular *art*. Such
arguments prove both too little and too much. *Pet Sounds* might reflect the
aesthetic values normally reserved for "serious music," music as high art, but
that demonstrates nothing about its relationship to high art. After all, the
aesthetic merits of natural objects and environments are unrelated to their
status as works of art. The aesthetic value of the Grand Canyon does not
make it a work of art. A high degree of aesthetic quality does not guarantee
value as a work of art, popular or otherwise.

On the other hand, the argument tries to prove too much. It tries to
show that popular music meets standards of excellence set by its detractors.
But anyone whose musical world is not restricted to popular music knows
that this is dishonest. "We were literary; it wasn't like we were rejecting
high culture," says critic Ellen Willis about the first rock critics. "We just
saw that the way we experienced rock 'n' roll was not the same as the way
we experienced Beethoven or whatever."[39] Shusterman knows this, too. In
many cases, he observes, popular music "is dedicated to the defiant violation
of [high art's] compartmentalized, trivializing, and eviscerating view of art
and the aesthetic."[40] In short, we know that some popular music meets
some of the standards of excellence recognized by traditional aesthetic theory. But it usually satisfies another set of standards, inimical to those traditional standards. This position makes the "art" value of popular music a
mere accident—it is rather like preparing a sumptuous meal and then
finding, when challenged, that it coincidentally conforms to the standards of
nutrition that its detractors have denied it.

Nor would it help to say that popular music isn't merely art, but is postmodern art that challenges "high modernist conventions of aesthetic
purity."[41] If the idea is that modernism defines the aesthetic of fine art—
which, I've argued, it doesn't, since many people endorse nineteenth-century romanticism rather than modernism—and if good popular music vio-
lates those standards, then the notion of art status is beside the point. It does

not help to say that some popular music "warrants particular attention by suggesting fruitful ways to rethink the very nature of art."[42] If popular culture redefines art, doubting elitists can simply respond that this is an attempt to appropriate the honorific implication of the term *art* while cutting it free from the normal concept of art.

Nor does artistry make a thing art. There can be artistry in flower arranging, leading to arrangements of considerable aesthetic value; I do not conclude that my local florist creates works of art. Flower arranging is a traditional form of art in Japan, but my local florist does not participate in that tradition. If we have learned anything from contemporary philosophy of art, it is that two things may be perceptually indistinguishable, yet only one will be informed by the weight of tradition and theory that makes it a work of art.[43] Art status requires correct placement within an artistic category or genre that will influence its aesthetic character.

Because different musical categories are dominated by different aesthetic values, specific values cannot be required as a general criterion for saying that a particular piece of music is or is not valuable as art. The paintings of Jan Vermeer are valued for their restrained beauty, their narrative power, and their allegorical subtlety. The paintings of James McNeil Whistler are not. It does not follow that Whistler's paintings are flawed, or not art (although his contemporaries often thought so, as evidenced by his libel action against critic John Ruskin). Nor would Whistler's paintings be better works of art for sharing the same aesthetic properties as those of Vermeer. It's been said that Gustav Mahler's contemporaries were appalled by his liberal use of pastiche, irony, and sentimentality. Today's audiences feel quite at home with Mahler. By analogy, it is largely irrelevant whether *Pet Sounds,* hip-hop, or heavy metal possesses the sorts of aesthetic qualities that are typical of the best classical music.[44]

Because different styles may generate the same aesthetic properties by different musical means, the capacity to appreciate one style of music will not necessarily make it easier to appreciate others. As I argue in chapter 3, this fact also limits our ability to establish criteria for evaluating particular categories of music. The Band's *Music from Big Pink* is an aesthetic landmark in the context of late 1960s rock music, so much so that Eric Clapton's admiration for it encouraged him to disband Cream, but that does not count against the real merits of Cream's *Wheels of Fire.* Not every 1960s rock album is aesthetically good in the same ways.

Finally, we must be wary of the trap of supposing that only complex, challenging music has real aesthetic value. Arguments that privilege classical music or specific genres of popular music by highlighting the most complex cases seem overly reliant on such an assumption. Yet simplicity and directness can also be of value, and we find "artistic" achievement when such aesthetic qualities are embodied in appropriate means.

The economy and simplicity of Ernest Hemingway's nonfiction prose does not indicate a corresponding aesthetic poverty in Hemingway's short stories. Early in the rock era, critic Robert Christgau remarked, "The reason rock has engendered such rhapsodic excitement . . . is not merely that if offers so much, emotionally and intellectually and physically, but that it does not at first appear to do so."[45] R.E.M.'s "Everybody Hurts" and Bob Dylan's "Knockin' On Heaven's Door" are direct and simple. They do not parade any structural complexity, yet they display a mastery of their means of expression. Furthermore, the combination of simple elements can take on a surprising power. The virtues of simplicity are too often ignored, especially when we start comparing works of art. Chad Taylor, guitarist for the band Live, identifies Neil Young as his favorite guitar player. But Taylor's admiration is not directed at Young's virtuosity: "He is so limited, but there's something beautiful about that kind of simplicity in rock & roll."[46]

For similar reasons, I am suspicious of Simon Frith's belief that all music listeners endorse music as "good" when it strikes them as "unusual, unusual because it cannot easily be explained away in terms of everyday social practice, as a matter of class or commerce or functional routine."[47] Pursuing the strategy that we saw applied to *Pet Sounds,* Frith points to transcendence as the common denominator of aesthetic evaluations of both popular and serious music. Aesthetic success is the music's "disruptive cultural effect," its instrumental capacity "to free us from everyday routines, from the social expectations with which we are encumbered."[48] I grant that sometimes it is that. But sometimes it's not. Ornette Coleman's *Free Jazz* would certainly transform the dance floor at a wedding reception, shattering the routine flow of the event. But almost no one in that context will say that Coleman's music is "good." Even if Frith thinks that we achieve "transcendence" whenever we transform our relationship to ordinary social expectations, this way of putting things assumes too strict a dichotomy between everyday function and aesthetic merit.

Pierre Bourdieu and the Sociological Critique

We stand to lose more than we gain—obscuring far more than we elucidate—when we assign selected popular music to the field of cultural production known as "art." Because it's historically too late to erase the honorific implications from that label, a better move is to show that aesthetic theory is not restricted to art, that aesthetic theory is not coextensive with a theory of fine art, and that aesthetic value is not equivalent to artistic value. Most people have significant aesthetic experiences with things they do not consider art.

Such considerations encourage the conclusion that the gulf between art and popular culture leads to two competing aesthetics, one for high culture and one for low. This sharp bifurcation of aesthetics has been strongly encouraged by Pierre Bourdieu's criticisms of Kant's aesthetic theory. Deservedly, Kant serves as the primary example of traditional aesthetics. With major books on reason, ethics, and aesthetics, Kant self-consciously promoted Enlightenment values. His theories are frequently dismissed as a supporting pillar of Eurocentrism. Bourdieu attacks his views as "the expression of the sublimated interests of the bourgeois intelligentsia."[49] However, Bourdieu also argues that aesthetic theory cannot be applied to popular culture. We seem at an impasse: we don't want to apply traditional aesthetics to popular music, but we have no alternative waiting to take its place.

It is no accident that Kant, the prime mover in securing the intellectual legitimacy of philosophical aesthetics, serves as the great bogeyman to be challenged when we question aesthetic theory. If one hasn't studied Kant or become informed about the competing interpretations of his aesthetic theory, Bourdieu's criticisms seem substantial. He begins by documenting the degree to which traditional aesthetics endorses a disinterested, formal stance toward fine art. Bourdieu conducted an empirical study of 1,217 French adults. Among other things, he asked them to choose three favorites from a short list of music that included Bach's *Art of the Fugue* and Strauss's "The Blue Danube" waltz. Bourdieu found that Bach appeals almost exclusively to listeners with higher levels of education, privileged social origins, and attendant social status. In short, "the aesthetic disposition" that endorses Bach is a class-based disposition. The privileged class endorses music that is formally challenging and expressively undemonstrative. It encourages disgust toward facile, sensuously gratifying music. Increased cultural capital appears to correlate neatly with a Kantian "primacy of form over function."[50]

By treating an acquired competence as a natural response, high culture generates a cultural standard for identifying and disparaging those who lack a socially sanctioned taste for fine art. Pretending that the rewards of art are thoroughly aesthetic and thus immediately available to everyone, aesthetic theory posits a seemingly neutral standard that demonstrates the "barbarism" of the masses.[51] In other words, by ignoring the fact that everyone must *learn* how to listen to music, elite taste appears natural. On this view, classical music is better than Led Zeppelin, and opera diva Maria Callas is a better singer than Robert Plant. (If we differentiate between high, middle, and low, Plant may rank as a better singer than a "pop" star like Kelly Clarkson or Britney Spears, but Callas is still at the top.) What they *sound* like is more or less beside the point. For the disinterested, elite listener, the value of music has little or nothing to do with listening. Its value is the platform it offers for evaluating the tastes, and social standing, of other listeners. Art is primarily valuable as a "weapon in strategies of [social] distinction."[52]

One consequence is that aesthetic intolerance is particularly strong among professional educators. One composer who also teaches music offered the following display of elite taste:

> The great classics, of course, have been time-tested and sifted through millions of people. . . . But people come up and say to me, "Can you play 'Stairway to Heaven'?" A Led Zeppelin tune I'm sure you know. Well, yes, I can play it but why in God's name would I ever want to, and why would you like it?[53]

Similarly, the academic journal *Psychology of Music* still publishes research on music education that posits a preference for popular music as evidence of a failure of music education.[54] As Bourdieu predicts, a comparison between two cultural fields is used to map a distinction in preferences, which is, in turn, used to dismiss those with the less cultured taste.

But is aesthetic intolerance the inevitable result of Kant's aesthetic theory? Take a cursory look at Kant's seminal book on aesthetics, the *Critique of Judgment*. Kant's theory of aesthetic judgment occupies most of the book. His primary example is finding a rose beautiful. His theory of fine art, a theory about certain cultural objects, occurs at the end, as a poorly integrated afterthought.[55] As Carl Dahlhaus insightfully warns, "To avoid gross misunderstanding, the judgment of taste analyzed by Kant must be distinguished from the judgment of art, from art criticism. According to Kant, the work of art is not exhausted by being an aesthetic object."[56] Ignoring this point, Bourdieu's summary of the Kantian aesthetic derives entirely from the "Analytic of the Beautiful," the opening twenty-two of sixty sections. Although Bourdieu says that he is challenging Kant on "taste and art," he ignores what Kant actually says about art.[57] Within those early sections, Kant denies that artifacts can and should be evaluated without thought about their intended function. A rose might be appreciated with a pure aesthetic judgment, but a painting, a church, or a poem is appreciated with an impure, dependent judgment (dependent, that is, on the purpose it serves).

Ironically, Kant argues that instrumental music—the most formal of arts—offers little "culture" to the mind. Consequently, music "has the lowest place among the fine arts."[58] Maria Callas has higher status than Led Zeppelin, but mediocre poetry is culturally superior to both. Kant's account ranks genres, not particular artworks, and thus songs have more value than absolute music. As a result, both Callas's performance of the opera *La Sonnambula* and Led Zeppelin's "Stairway to Heaven" are ranked higher than Bach's *Art of the Fugue*. Bourdieu's map of cultural rankings does not line up very neatly with Kant's aesthetic theory.

Kant's theory of taste attempts to specify the basic grounds of aesthetic *experience*. That is, he identifies universal conditions for having the subjective mental states that constitute the distinct experiences of beauty and sublimity. One is hard pressed to find any practical guidance for the task of evaluating specific works of art or for ranking objects according to their possession of beauty or sublimity. Yet, following Bourdieu's lead, most challenges to traditional aesthetics are framed as challenges to Kantian disinterest. Although this is not the context to show it, I think that most of what is challenged as "traditional aesthetics" did not come together in a standard doctrine until a century after the publication of Kant's *Critique of Judgment*. The main targets are nineteenth-century aestheticism and twentieth-century justifications of modernist painting and literature.[59]

Two final points about Bourdieu are pertinent to popular music. First, he doubts that it is meaningful to talk about popular "art." He denies that we can formulate an aesthetic theory adequate to popular consumption. Second, important aspects of his research have not been replicated in similar investigations, suggesting that his findings are peculiar to French culture in the 1960s.

The first point seems to be a quirk of Bourdieu's system of key terms. Art is the focus of elite social practices. Practices are defined in terms of a framing *habitus* or socially conditioned scheme of perception. Because the fine art habitus is the "negative opposite" of the popular habitus, there cannot be shared values. Where elite taste is governed by one practice, popular taste is too heterogeneous to unify in a theory.[60] The problem here may be Bourdieu's own habitus, which takes Kantian disinterest to be the central concept of aesthetics. We get a very different result if we stress Kant's idea of aesthetic experience as any sense perception that encourages a free play of imagination and understanding.[61] This description provides a model of aesthetic response that applies equally to popular and serious music.

For example, consider one of my favorite songs, John Prine's "Angel from Montgomery." The first words are "I am an old woman named after my mother." I understand the meaning of these words. I also understand that Prine is a man, not a woman. In Samuel Taylor Coleridge's famous description, the whole thing will seem stupid unless I engage in a "willing suspension of disbelief." Prine is playing a role. I have to imagine that a woman is relating her life story to me. Many writers have made this point in different ways. Here is David Cantwell's version:

> Insistence upon a singer's "authenticity" is commonplace today, but it misunderstands how art works. It especially underestimates the art of the singer. Art is artificial, it's human-made, and even art that is what we call realistic is capturing not what is real but an illusion of the real. . . . When we demand authenticity of what is essentially inauthentic, we disrespect the singer's art.[62]

Challenging the misplaced vogue for "authentic" country music, Cantwell means "art" in a merely classificatory sense that applies to all singing. To the degree that musical taste requires a listener's imaginative engagement, there is no difference between listening to Maria Callas and John Prine.

The second point is that the social fields that shape French tastes may be very different from those found elsewhere. Bourdieu claims that more cultural capital translates into narrower tastes. The elite class "likes"—or pretends to like—less pleasurable, more complex, and less accessible cultural products. These features exaggerate the gulf separating the elite from the masses.

Recent studies conducted in the United States have replicated two of Bourdieu's findings. People with high-status occupations are the most likely to listen to classical music. Many people justify their own tastes by insulting the music and musical tastes of other people. However, other patterns conflict with a sharp divide bewteen high and low taste. Above-average education and social status are linked to significantly *broader* musical tastes, not narrow tastes. Musical narrowness decreases with education. Listeners in the highest occupational groups are the least likely to be snobs, the most likely to enjoy both elite and nonelite musical forms, and the most likely to endorse multiple types of nonelite music. The narrowest tastes tend to be among those with less education and the lowest occupational status. These listeners are the most likely to listen exclusively to one and only one style of music, and they are the most insistent about the undesirability of music they dislike. In other words, someone with a college degree and a white-collar job is more likely to listen to an eclectic mix of music, and might equally enjoy Bob Marley, Maria Callas, and Miles Davis. An unskilled laborer who never finished high school is more likely to listen to country music or heavy metal while actively disliking everything else.[63]

Researchers found limited patterns of elite taste linked to a dislike of nonelite music. In the United States, country music fits the pattern that Bourdieu found in France. Elite listeners tend to regard it as a lower form and tend to dislike it. Another study examined more variables and found that country music is not unique in this way. High-status people actively dislike low-status music when it is closely associated with the least educated audiences. Four genres stand out in this regard: heavy metal, country, gospel, and rap. In the United States, more education results in nonexclusive musical tastes and a flattened cultural hierarchy, yet tastes do not entirely escape class distinctions.[64]

The evidence that many listeners endorse both serious and popular music challenges the idea of mutually exclusive listening practices. Why was Bourdieu convinced that elite listeners reject all nonelite music? Examined more closely, his account of highly exclusive musical tastes does not make much sense. As we saw, his general contrast between elite and popular taste hinges on a corresponding emphasis on form and function. (To sharpen this distinction, he ignores Kant's category of dependent beauty.) Because the questionnaire that he administered lists no popular music, Bourdieu's primary evidence about popular music is lower-class approval of the "The Blue Danube" waltz.[65] But he failed to document the attitudes of elite listeners concerning popular music.

Among the examples offered in the questionnaire, two operas come closest to satisfying his general description of what "low" audiences enjoy about "low" forms: they offer spectacle, narrative, and identification with *representational content*. Like Bach's *Art of the Fugue*, "The Blue Danube" was written as instrumental music. It cannot be more popular due to representational content. However, "The Blue Danube" is much simpler than the *Art of the Fugue*, and thus more immediately accessible and pleasurable. But if simplicity and identification with content are the features that attract nonelite listeners, the Beatles should never have surpassed Herman's Hermits in the British pop charts. With their increasing emphasis on formal experimentation and corresponding obscuring of represented content, *Sgt. Pepper's Lonely Hearts Club Band* and *The Beatles* (the "White Album") should not have been popular successes. I will return to these issues in chapter 2.

Despite my reservations, I endorse Bourdieu's attack on aestheticism, the doctrine that the aesthetic dimension of culture trumps all other ways of valuing it. At the same time, most cultural products (and this includes collectively designed environments) have an aesthetic dimension that can, is, and *should* be assessed. In some situations, other modes of value can and should take precedence. I suspect that I am not alone in finding most performances of the national anthem of the United States to be musically unpleasant and somewhat grating, particularly when poorly trained voices fail to rise to and hold the high notes. But this aesthetic evaluation does not justify a change of anthem, nor public disrespect—covering one's ears, for example—when it is sung. There are many situations in which our knowledge of the relevant social values provides a reason to put up with what we would reject aesthetically. But there are also everyday situations in which the primary focus is the aesthetic dimension. With Bourdieu, I resist the idea that the best explanation of this importance is a fine art aesthetic. Against Bourdieu, I see no need to polarize aesthetics into two camps, each the negative opposite of the other.

Of course, Bourdieu offers merely one of many sociological critiques of traditional aesthetics. So what have I accomplished? Freed from the specifics of his account, we find that many of these other critiques repeat the charge that aesthetic theory was historically important in defending the values of fine art. Therefore, any sympathetic treatment of aesthetic evaluation is a "reactionary response" that cannot help but "serve vested tastes and vested interests."[66] Furthermore, because "the traditional agenda of aesthetics is tied to appeals to universal consensus that eliminates the possibility of political struggle over discourse, aesthetic approaches per se are incompatible with studies that treat music as socially constructed."[67] One sociologist says that the fundamental problem is that aesthetic theory ignores the degree to which all "criticism and evaluation are ideological." Aesthetics is "an intellectual practice [that] takes as its subject-matter artefacts and works which have been produced as the 'great tradition' by the ideological practices of particular groups in specific social conditions."[68]

In other words, exploration of aesthetic value is so inescapably bound to the history of fine art that aesthetic values just *are* fine art values, which are, in turn, elite values. On this view, I am on solid ground in challenging the assertion that *Pet Sounds* is art, but I try to build on shifting sand when I go on to endorse its aesthetic value.

In response, we might note that although aesthetic theory has a great deal to say about art, it is difficult to find a theory of art that defines art in terms of aesthetic value.[69] In the past fifty years, aesthetics has followed the art world in emphasizing the conceptual and the social while de-emphasizing the aesthetic. For example, George Dickie's institutional theory of art is one of the most debated accounts of the last half-century, yet Dickie explicitly formulated it as an alternative to aesthetic accounts. To some extent, attacking aesthetic analysis on the grounds that doing so presupposes elite values of fine art is rather quaint, as if I'd mentioned that I drive a Ford and you assumed that it was a Model T.

Yet there is merit to the sociological critique. As an interdisciplinary field of inquiry, aesthetics *has* been dominated by the general presumption that its primary concern is defining fine art—the very reason it has downplayed aesthetic experience and aesthetic value. But this is hardly news within aesthetics. Books on aesthetic theory have been pointing it out and attacking it since John Dewey argued that aesthetic value is an organizing principle of everyday life, not just a matter of paintings in museums. Coming at the same issue from a different perspective, Friedrich Nietzsche challenged the Kantian tradition for its excessively narrow understanding of what constitutes aesthetic appreciation.[70]

Furthermore, the charge that aesthetics is unduly centered on Eurocentric high culture has encouraged exploration of non-Western aesthetics. The result is unequivocal: aesthetic discrimination is central to the cultural practices of every group examined. For example, Crispin Sartwell's *Six*

Names of Beauty explores a basic aesthetic concept in six different cultures. Within the broad sweep of Western culture, the ancient Greek ideal of *to kalon* is a source for, but does not match precisely, the relatively modern concept of beauty. Yet there are closely related standards in such diverse languages as Japanese *(wabi-sabi)*, Navajo *(hozho)*, Sanskrit *(sundara)*, and Hebrew *(yapha)*. In passing, Sartwell briefly discusses the centrality of *ase* in the Yoruba aesthetic of West Africa.[71] Although he does not highlight the similarity, the Yoruba concept is strikingly similar to the definition of beauty offered by Thomas Aquinas in the Middle Ages. Yet the Yoruba concept did not arise within the economic and educational settings that is identified as "the" aesthetic response.

Similarly concerned about the narrowness of traditional aesthetics, Shusterman advises that we already possess the necessary tools for cleaning house: "Notions of aesthetic experience that . . . embrace context, content, interest, and function have been common in theories of art from Aristotle through to the pragmatist aesthetic of today."[72] Examined carefully, few of the canonical texts of "the great tradition" prove to be myopically focused on artworks. Kant, for one, discusses both carpets and jokes as occasions for aesthetic judgment. A carpet can be appreciated aesthetically. Appreciating the humor of a joke is no less aesthetic than admiring the beauty of a rug. Suppose we follow Kant's lead and think about an example that combines both of those things.

Everyday Aesthetics

Ethan and Joel Coen's 1998 film *The Big Lebowski* starts with a failed attempt by two thugs to recover money from Jeffrey Lebowski. The attempt fails because they have gone to the wrong residence. Lebowski, who prefers to be called "the Dude," has no money. Memorably portrayed by Jeff Bridges, the Dude tries to explain that they have the wrong person. Angered by this lack of cooperation, one of the thugs vandalizes the living room carpet. This act irritates the Dude far more than the physical violence he's suffered, and his search for retribution sets off the rest of the screwball plot.

Why, Lebowski is asked several times, is he making such a fuss about a rug? Because, he patiently explains, "it really tied the room together."

In the context of the movie, this line is hilarious. It is not funny that a rug should tie a room together. What's funny is that we don't expect this character—his place is a pigsty and he shops at the grocery store while wearing an old bathrobe—to have an aesthetic sensibility.

This example illustrates an important point, and it does so in two distinct ways. First, the line is not intrinsically funny. The line is made funny by the particular situation. Second, it reminds us that rugs really do "tie" rooms together. The Dude does not value the rug for its own sake, as a discrete object for aesthetic appreciation. He values it for the way it interacts with the rest of the room and for the resulting environmental transformation.

In an important way, Lebowski's rug is like his statement about the rug. Although a rug and a statement are very different sorts of things, both can be aesthetically valuable. But neither is *by itself* (autonomously) the object of the evaluation. Their aesthetic appeal depends on their presence in a particular context. In these and in many other cases, the aesthetic properties that we value (the humor of the line, the integration of the living room) do not exist apart from our awareness of *"situations* in which experiences occur."[73]

We can generalize this insight about aesthetically valuable objects and situations. When something is aesthetically valuable, some of its features will strike us as more relevant than others will. Suppose we select one of those features and isolate it. Arnold Isenberg offers the example of a curved line that accounts for the success of a painting.[74] Suppose we reproduce the line, by itself, on a blackboard. The presence of the line will not transform the blackboard into an equally beautiful thing. The isolated line may look insipid. (Perhaps, like Lebowski's rug, the line is aesthetically significant for the way that it ties the painting together.) The aesthetic quality of each feature depends on its interaction with other features.

The importance of context frustrates attempts to offer decisive reasons why something is aesthetically good or bad. When we cite reasons, we single out particular aspects or properties of the admirable object or situation. The Beach Boys song "God Only Knows" is all the more lovely and moving for the subtle transition out of the bridge. *Pet Sounds* is unified by its expressive journey from exuberance ("Wouldn't It Be Nice") to regret ("Caroline No"). But, as I suggested throughout my discussion of *Pet Sounds,* these reasons do not generate universal aesthetic standards. Muddy Waters's song "Feel Like Going Home" would not be enhanced by the addition of a bridge passage with a subtle transition. Nor do I want a Muddy Waters album to follow the emotional path of *Pet Sounds*.

Any particular feature is aesthetically good or bad, better or worse, by virtue of its participation in a certain context. We learn to evaluate different things in relation to different *scopes* of context. The fine art tradition has gradually developed its own environments and attendant behaviors for viewing art. In a standard "museum" model for experiencing art, viewers attend to one perceptually isolated object at a time. Art museums encourage this isolation of attention by hanging all paintings at eye level, some distance apart, on a neutral background. (Yet even here, Paul Ziff reminds us, not every painting is best seen from the same distance. Some are best viewed by stepping back, others by moving very close.)[75] In the concert hall, classical music lovers sit very still and remain silent during the performance—like the paintings, the music should have no perceptual competition. People learn not to applaud during the short silences between musical movements: the whole piece is experienced before anyone responds. The "proper" bodily dispositions facilitate a "distanced" contemplation of the aesthetic object. The fine art habitus encourages a nonparticipatory, distanced response.

Ironically, one of the most famous examples of aesthetic distance is Edward Bullough's discussion of experiencing fog while on a ship at sea.[76] The fog is not an object, but an environment surrounding the traveler. In many cases, aesthetic rewards derive from our experience of an overall environment, not an intense focus on a single object. A well-developed Japanese aesthetic centers on engagement with weather, including fog.[77] Arguing that we cannot understand aesthetic engagement unless we come to terms with such experiences, both Tom Leddy and Arto Haapala offer the example of a daily walk to work.[78] During some parts of a walk, our aesthetic appreciation is object focused. At other times, the aesthetic effect is holistic, and all of the senses are employed as we respond to the total environment.

Both writers stress that the aesthetic effect is largely a matter of repeating the walk on a regular basis. (We must not forget that every situation has a temporal dimension.) As Haapala emphasizes, a neighborhood is perceptually and thus aesthetically very different when it is experienced as something strange, foreign, or new. Everything is experienced as special—and this quality of being special has been taken as a model for all aesthetic experience. Experienced as something familiar, as a "home" environment, the same streets and buildings are experientially safe. Many features fade into a perceptual background against which a few features emerge as salient, as favorites, or as personally meaningful. Our general sense of attachment is no less valid, Haapala argues, than is the "distanced" feeling that is regarded as evidence that one has had a successful experience with a work of fine art. The two modes of experiencing a neighborhood are aesthetically satisfying in different ways.

The variety of nonelite response demonstrates that the distinction between an art aesthetic and an "everyday" aesthetic does not coincide with the distinction between high and low culture. A fine art aesthetic prioritizes disorientation and transcendence over ongoing, immersed attachment. However, an aesthetic experience does not have to be extraordinary in order to be worthwhile.[79] Recall Frith's claim that music is regarded as "good" only if it is regarded as unusual and special. Even if he does not call it "art," Frith straitjackets popular music with a fine art aesthetic. Transcendence is not always the point. Sometimes we are more interested in a routine musical experience than in a life-changing one. We often use popular music because its predictable familiarity makes us feel at home, and at home with one another. We put on a favorite recording of Christmas music to set the mood for trimming the tree, request "our song" from the DJ at the wedding reception, or go for a morning run listening to the same mix tape every day.

Suppose we downplay the aesthetics of fine art that emerges when we liken the Beach Boys' *Pet Sounds* to the artworks in the Art Institute of Chicago. Suppose we embrace an aesthetic theory that is equally concerned with jokes, carpets, walking through a familiar neighborhood, and everything by the Beach Boys, not just *Pet Sounds*. Arnold Berleant seems to have been the first to call this approach "the new aesthetic." Others prefer the label *everyday aesthetics*. Whatever we call it, we do not have to choose between the fine art aesthetic and the everyday aesthetic. We want a characterization of aesthetic value that embraces both.

We must be careful about the idea that human culture produces artifacts with aesthetic properties. Not every artifact is an individual, material object. Our lived environment is another, more pervasive artifact. When we recognize that environments offer aesthetic rewards, we need an aesthetic that puts greater emphasis on *experiences* than on *objects*. If the traditional analysis of the aesthetic attitude emphasizes a disinterested contemplation of a distinct object, the new aesthetic directs us to look for aesthetic rewards in any directed awareness of a situation. We should expect to find aesthetic value in any appreciative perceptual experience. Music profoundly colors every environment in which it participates. Therefore any situation involving popular music can be evaluated aesthetically.

Music's capacity to transform environments has consequences for the way that we think about the connection between aesthetic properties and aesthetic value. Aesthetic properties do not simply belong to stable objects. They are perceptual features of objects, situations, or events that anyone cites as directly contributing to—or detracting from—the aesthetic value of an experience. While I am not particularly fond of Led Zeppelin's "Dazed and Confused," many of its live performances have a sublime quality that arises from the sustained intensity of a lengthy performance of it. (A *brief* song tends to be brutal and exhilarating, as is the case with so much of the early music of the Ramones. But brevity lacks the grandeur of the sublime.) In and of itself, the length of a song is neither aesthetically good nor bad. But the distinction between a *long* piece of music and a *sublime* one presupposes the difference between nonaesthetic and aesthetic categorization. "Long" can be verified without attempting to appreciate the perceptual experience—we can determine that a performance of "Dazed and Confused" in Paris in 1971 is a long one simply by noting that it clocks in at slightly more than eighteen minutes. But we can only tell that the performance is sublime—rather than tedious—by listening to the whole thing. In contrast, Led Zeppelin's "Hot Dog" is goofy fun. On *In Through the Out Door,* the band sounds like they're having fun playing it, and it is fun to hear. Saying the song is fun in either of these ways praises it, even if "fun" is almost never used as an aesthetic predicate in the world of serious art.[80]

Aside from a few evaluative labels such as *beautiful* and *ugly,* many descriptions have both aesthetic and nonaesthetic uses. *Powerful* can be non-aesthetic. The Grateful Dead's 1973–74 sound system, nicknamed the Wall of Sound, was *physically* powerful in terms of the decibels it produced. Whether any of the music played through it was *aesthetically* powerful can only be determined by listening to the music. The aesthetic use of the term *powerful* emerges when it is used to support an aesthetic evaluation. This insight opens up the range of features that we identify as aesthetic properties.[81] The range of terms employed aesthetically in everyday life is enormous.

Taking stock, we conclude that aesthetics is no longer confined to thinking about art. Broadening our horizons, we find that aesthetic uses of terms are directed at both everyday objects and lived environments. Aesthetic uses of terms refer to positive or negative features that make an experience more or less valuable as the experience that it is.[82] These features ground appreciative experience of an object or event and make the experience worth appreciating.[83] Pulling these ideas together, we can say that popular music is aesthetically valuable when it contributes aspects of an aesthetically valuable experience. *Any* experience becomes aesthetic when the person having the experience evaluates it as such, as an experience worth having or not. Allan F. Moore observes that, no matter what type of music is involved, "the reason we (communally) go out of our way to experience music is *simply in order to have been part of the experience that was that music. It is thus, at root, the experience which is subject to interpretation.*"[84] My argument is that interpretation of "the experience" will leave out something vital if it ignores aesthetic value. To pursue an experience because it *is* an experience is the hallmark of the aesthetic.

Besides broadening the scope of what counts as aesthetic, another advantage of this approach is that aesthetic value is not necessarily in competition with functional value. Someone who walks to work may or may not do so for aesthetic reasons. If someone walks to work simply because it's convenient and never evaluates the experience it affords, the walk lacks aesthetic value. Similarly, people play music for nonaesthetic reasons. Someone who plays the car radio solely to stay awake while driving is not listening for aesthetic reasons. But when a business provides background music to influence the behavior of both employees and customers, one basis for the selection is aesthetic: music with an undesirable tempo and loud volume might be stylistically unpleasant for the customers, poisoning the experience.

Music's transformation of the driving experience can be aesthetically valuable, too. In endorsing the idea that aesthetics is a matter of how we evaluate experiences, we have to resist the fine art disposition to focus on isolated objects. When "Sloop John B" or "Wouldn't It Be Nice" comes on the car radio, there's no reason to pull over to the side of the road to listen with undivided attention. Such rapt attention is a specialized mode of experience and not a necessary condition of aesthetic appreciation.[85] We should worry less about *Pet Sounds,* the musical work, and think more about what it means to appreciate the different experiences it informs.

2. Clearing Space for Aesthetic Value

I just play music. Some people try to make too much out of it. Just listen to it and enjoy it.
> —Kurt Cobain, *Hit Parader*

The 1990s thus saw a boom in the academic Madonna business—the books! the conferences! the courses! Scouring compulsively through all this material, I couldn't tell whether Madonna was a good singer (as well as a skilled media operative); whether she was an engaging dancer (as well as a semiotic tease); whether I'd actually want to play her records and videos as well as read about them.
> —Simon Frith, *Performing Rites*

Interpreting Songs

On a recent afternoon, I gathered up some administrative paperwork and headed down the hall to a department office where I expected to find the student worker who was assisting me. She had gone to fetch the afternoon mail, so I waited for her. Like so many people confined to an office, she had a radio on, providing a musical background to her work. Naturally, she'd left the radio playing while she ran her errand. As I entered the office, a new song started in the background. As with most background music, I only half-listened. After a minute, I found myself humming along to Bruce Springsteen's hit song from 1984, "Dancing in the Dark."

As I left the building a few minutes later, it occurred to me that the catch phrase at the end of the song's chorus ("even if we're just dancing in the dark") was an interesting metaphor for responding to popular music. The song expresses frustration, but I realized that I didn't know how to interpret the phrase "dancing in the dark." Dancing in the dark is romantic. But Springsteen seemed to mean that dancing in the dark is engaging in an activity, or a whole life, that has no clear direction or purpose—you're moving, but you can't see where you're going. It struck me that this metaphor also applies to a great deal of interaction with popular culture.

Consumers move with and are moved by it, appreciating the experience it offers without knowing what larger purpose or consequences it may have. In treating "Dancing in the Dark" as a metaphor for listening to popular music, I take it that the metaphor is not entirely negative. No one wants to be "in the dark," yet darkness can enhance the sensation of dancing.[1] Deprived of sight, we become more alive to the physical sensations of our movements, and of each other.

There is an older, different song with the same title, with lyrics by Howard Dietz and music by Arthur Schwartz. It was written for the Broadway musical *The Bandwagon,* later adapted into a movie vehicle for Fred Astaire. This earlier song clearly links dancing to romantic love. The lyrics express the idea that love provides a reason to live, giving meaning to our otherwise perplexing and fleeting existence. This message is conveyed both by the slow, dreamy music, and by the lyrics, which are mostly about hearing music and dancing to it. In one couplet, the phrase "we can face the music together" sets up the title phrase, "dancing in the dark."

Springsteen's lyrics are not so tightly integrated. His "Dancing in the Dark" is a rambling dramatic monologue over the basic pop song structure of verse-chorus-verse-chorus-bridge-verse-chorus-coda. The music is aggressively up-tempo and suited to the dance floor of a club. Synthesizers color the background with surging figures that would, in earlier decades, be horn parts. Guitar eventually enters the arrangement, thickening the texture and reinforcing the forward motion. Complaints dominate the verses: "I ain't getting nowhere just living in a dump like this." In the third verse, Springsteen's narrator moves beyond complaining. For the second time, the language suggests he's addressing a woman, whom he addresses as "baby." He wants to make it clear that he hasn't been inviting her pity: "Come on baby the laugh's on me." He's been making the point that he needs someone to jolt him out of his rut; perhaps the woman he's addressing will be the one, and will offer him some encouragement: "Come on now baby gimme just one look." He's making it clear to her that he's available: "this gun's for hire."

There is nothing in the lyrics to "Dancing in the Dark" that makes the verb *dancing* specifically relevant. Given the content of the monologue, the song would work just as well if the phrase was replaced with "even if we're just laughing at ourselves." However, there is a nonverbal way that the "dancing" line pays off. The recording concludes with an instrumental sequence of some thirty seconds. Clarence Clemons's saxophone appears for the first time, supplying a relatively relaxed, swinging line that suggests, musically, that the couple is dancing.

In both Springsteen's song and the earlier one, "dancing" is a metaphor for a relationship between a man and a woman. In contrast to Dietz's lyrics, Springsteen's character says nothing that suggests dancing is an act of redemption. A new relationship is desired, but it is with the knowledge that it might not last. If the song is about coping in the face of purposeless, repetitive action, Springsteen's song expresses the very idea with which Theodor Adorno condemns the consumption of popular music. Alienated from jobs and meaningless work, we seek meaning and release in popular entertainment. But popular music cannot help us. "Its stimulations are met with the inability to vest effort in the ever-identical," Adorno warns. "This means boredom again. It is a circle which makes escape impossible."[2]

Springsteen's "Dancing in the Dark" is particularly interesting for being the initial single released to promote his *Born in the U.S.A.* album (1984), the biggest-selling album of his career. The last song written for the album, it was expressly written to *be* the album's lead single. The remainder of the album is dominated by "rock" music, but the unwavering dance beat and synthesizers identify the "Dancing in the Dark" single as "pop," not "rock"—perhaps "a little further" toward pop, said Springsteen, than he wished.[3] Remove Springsteen's vocal, and the track sounds far more like Prince's *Purple Rain,* another hit album of 1984, than anything else on *Born in the U.S.A.*

Dave Marsh, a rock music critic and Springsteen biographer, downplays the sound of the record. He observes that Springsteen initially resisted the emphasis on drums and synthesizers. Marsh directs attention away from the musical arrangement and attributes the song's power to its personal authenticity: the song "summed up Bruce Springsteen's life in that moment. It was exactly what the album needed. But it was also far, far more—the most directly personal excavation Bruce had extracted from himself since 'Born to Run,' a song whose intimacies ran bitter and deep."[4] We seem to have returned to the doctrine of expressive genius. Yet when Springsteen wrote it, band member Steve Van Zandt certainly did not hear it as "deep." He regarded "Dancing in the Dark" as a "mistake" and recommended its removal from the album.[5]

Aided by a promotional video, the popularity of "Dancing in the Dark" translated, as intended, into strong album sales. But for the casual record buyers who owned none of Springsteen's earlier albums, the opening moments of *Born in the U.S.A.* must have offered a shock. The album begins with the title track. Although drums and synthesizers also dominate it, the music of "Born in the U.S.A." is in a different style from "Dancing in the Dark." The album's lead single turns out to be a sonic fluke, not much like anything else Springsteen had, or has since, done.

Famously, "Born in the U.S.A." became entangled in the politics of the presidential election campaign of 1984. Conservative columnist George Will attended a Springsteen concert and was impressed by the rapport between Springsteen and his blue-collar audience. In September, Will wrote a political column extolling Springsteen's masculinity, work ethic, and "affirmation" of American life, and asserting that the audience responds because "his message affirms the right values."[6] One week later, President Reagan made a campaign visit to New Jersey, Springsteen's home state, and the president proposed that Springsteen's values were Reagan's values: "America's future rests . . . in the message of hope in songs so many young Americans admire: New Jersey's own Bruce Springsteen. And helping you make those dreams come true is what this job of mine is all about."[7] Springsteen addressed Reagan between songs during a live performance a few days later. Springsteen wondered aloud which of his songs appealed to the president and he surmised that Reagan didn't listen to the bitter, politically charged songs of the *Nebraska* album.

Springsteen became concerned that many Americans besides President Reagan misunderstood the relatively clear message of the song "Born in the U.S.A.," hearing it "simply as a homage to America."[8] But this way of describing the situation, saying that people have consistently misunderstood it, assumes that one interpretation is better than others are.[9] Springsteen himself certainly thinks so. "I mean, 'Born in the U.S.A.' is not ambiguous," he complains. "You just have to listen to the verses."[10] What is significant here is that Springsteen does not think that his interpretation is privileged because it is *his*. There is no appeal to authorial intentions. He thinks that one interpretation is privileged because it makes better sense of the complete text. The chorus of "Born in the U.S.A." might sound like flag-waving, but the verses do not sustain that interpretation.

Within cultural studies and popular music studies, interpretive disagreement is seldom treated as a case of one group correctly understanding the song and a second group misunderstanding it. Instead, disagreement displays contested meanings, and popular culture is regarded as a forum for working out underlying social conflicts. From this perspective, no authorial intention or other mechanism can fix or fully determine the meanings and values of the songs and performances, so there is no point in saying that the Reaganites misunderstood the song. They merely miscalculated the political consequences of their appropriation of it.

In the arguments that follow, I remain neutral about whether either reading involves misunderstanding, or whether one reading constitutes a better interpretation. I will simply concede that, within popular culture, meanings always remain to some degree open-ended. Songs are designed to function as symbols for a broad audience, so that their ongoing presence in a society requires constant redeployment and reinterpretation. They "may represent different things for different audiences and in different contexts."[11] The phrase *dancing in the dark* illustrates this point. It furnishes the title to two songs, written a half-century apart. But we should not assume that it means the same thing each time. The phrase is used somewhat differently in each case. And the lesson can be extended from smaller to larger units, from uses of the *phrase* to uses of each *song*. There is no reason to suppose there is only one use. Meanings multiply as uses do. In the context of American politics, a song like "Born in the U.S.A." has multiple meanings.

However, does the admission that no group can plausibly claim to have the definitive interpretation, the "correct" one for all listeners in all contexts, undercut the proposal that different groups might share agreement about the music's aesthetic value? Does it refute the hypothesis that the broad "community" of Springsteen fans is unified as much by aesthetics as by politics? A formalist aesthetic says that its merit is independent of the many things "Born in the U.S.A." is taken to say about the United States in the 1980s. The song's aesthetic appeal might explain why audiences disagreed about its political content, and not the other way around. Music fans thought that it was worth disputing about, in a way that was not true for a thousand other songs released in 1984, and this evaluation by the audience made it a ripe target for political appropriation.[12] Without assuming that the *Born in the U.S.A.* album is a work of art, could it be the case that some measure of its aesthetic value transcends politics, and that this is a positive aspect of this music?

Many prominent voices in popular music studies express deep reservations about any distinction between aesthetic and nonaesthetic value. Our primary orientation toward the world is one of active interpretation. We respond to meanings, and anything that was formerly labeled "aesthetic" value is really a case of being concerned with meanings. Combine this proposal with the idea that all meanings are essentially contestable, and we arrive at an argument that there cannot be any shared, distinctively aesthetic interest in popular music.

I am not convinced that the first idea, concerning the interpretation of content, supports the second, concerning the irrelevance of aesthetic value. I will spend the bulk of this chapter examining these points.

First, I identify the reasoning that moves us from an account of interpretation to a claim about aesthetic value. Taken at face value, it seems to be a change of subject, as if one person asks, "Why don't you like this kind of cheese?" and receives the answer, "Because of the war in Iraq." The two topics are unrelated until we supply some further assumptions: the cheese is French, France did not support the United States, and the person is boycotting French products. Likewise, a doctrine of interpretation does not undercut aesthetic value unless we supply relevant background assumptions. Second, I argue that the background assumptions ignore or distort relevant cases of valuing popular music. Overall, I argue that aesthetic rewards often encourage us to go "dancing in the dark," getting us to embrace things that we barely, or only partially, understand. In the consumption of popular music, decisions about aesthetic merit often precede and create an interest in social codes and practices, generating attachment to some things that would otherwise disturb us.

The Social Relevance Thesis

To summarize what is at issue here, consider the reading that Susan McClary and Robert Walser supply to a cartoon in which two musicians read a review of their recent show.[13] The musicians respond to the music review by asking, "Yeah, but do we kick butt?" McClary and Walser propose that the musicians are puzzled because the reviewer fails to address "what is really at stake in the tunes." But what is at stake? As I read the cartoon, the puzzled musicians want to know whether the reviewer assigns aesthetic success or failure to their performance. McClary and Walser think that they want to know whether their music contributes to the ongoing reconstruction of semiotic codes in a way that organizes the time, pleasures, and bodies of listeners in a progressive social project. Perhaps the fictional musicians *were* aiming at something of that sort—such goals are so broad that they can be equally attributed to self-professed Marxists, such as the Clash or New Model Army, and the Carter Family, whose early advertising for live performances assured audiences, "The Program is Morally Good."[14]

But in the absence of compelling evidence to do so, why assign such intentions and expectations to *all* musicians? After all, some musicians explicitly deny that they have any such goals. As a fan of African-American music, Brian Jones (one of the founding members of the Rolling Stones) remarked, "If you ask some people why they go for R&B you get pretentious answers. . . . for me it's merely the sound. . . . It doesn't express damn-all to me, really. . . . But I like the sound."[15] One might reply that Jones was simply not *conscious* of his interest in the collision of African-American and British values. But why not take him at face value? Aren't *some* musicians more interested in exploring a world of sound than in the social dimensions of those sounds? Avoiding live performance after a disastrous 1974 tour, ex-Beatle George Harrison suddenly staged a dozen performances in Japan at the end of 1991. What prompted his return to the stage after seventeen years? Harrison seems to have done it because Eric Clapton offered to play lead guitar if Harrison would perform, and Harrison valued the opportunity to play music with Clapton: "it gives me goose bumps," said Harrison, "every time the [guitar] solos come and Eric follows me!"[16] In other words, the decision to perform live again was settled by aesthetic considerations. Even scandalously "political" performers have been known to urge the audience to judge the music aesthetically, as when Madonna points to the "best" songs she's written, her ballads: "[I expect] for people to just enjoy the music, purely and simply. . . . What I expect is just for people to appreciate my music, and lyrically maybe understand where I'm coming from."[17]

If the pursuit of aesthetic value is one among several reasons to make music, it may be one of several reasons to listen. In what follows, I defend a distinction between listening for aesthetic and listening for nonaesthetic reasons, and I will suggest that both are important when listening to popular music. In place of a model that depreciates or erases the aesthetic in favor of the social and political, I suggest that they frequently and fruitfully interact.

To more precisely identify the target of my criticisms, let's call it the social relevance thesis. This view proposes that each listener's musical taste reflects that listener's social, historical, and institutional positions. Aesthetic concerns cannot be isolated or distinguished "from other areas of social life."[18] The true force of the social relevance thesis is its role in organizing a cluster of linked proposals, which adherents employ as a general model of how social practices influence evaluations.

I have no quarrel with the foundational assumption that individuals are always socially situated. This point supports the plausible conclusion that aesthetic responses are socially situated (an idea that I explore in chapter 3). Musical taste always reflects contingent instrumental values made relevant by a listener's social position.[19] This point also explains why different groups favor different styles of music and different performers. But from here, proponents of the social relevance thesis move to the less defensible claim that any value that listeners assign to the music reflects contingent meanings and associated values.[20] Because they also believe that proponents of aesthetic value regard such value as necessary (noncontingent) or autonomous (noninstrumental), they regard aesthetic value as irrelevant to what actually takes place when someone prefers country music to reggae or, within the genre of country, prefers Garth Brooks to Willie Nelson.

Setting aside cases of completely subjective and idiosyncratic response, the social relevance thesis says that each positive evaluation reflects the listener's assessment of the presence of symbolic aspects that "speak to" that listener, contingent on a preexisting endorsement of some cluster of social codes, practices, and discourses.[21] Because communication is necessarily social, Raymond William cautions, "we have to replace the specializing category of 'the aesthetic' . . . by the radically different vocabulary of 'the dominant', 'the associated', and the 'subordinate'."[22] In George Lipsitz's version of the same idea, specific musical tastes always "reflect important social statements and experiences that seem only incidentally related to the music itself."[23] In other words, popular songs are fundamentally symbols, and their aesthetic dimension is irrelevant.

In aesthetics, the idea that music is always or primarily valued for what it represents is known as aesthetic cognitivism. It prioritizes the cognitive (where the emphasis is on what one thinks and believes) over the aesthetic (where the emphasis is on perceptual processes) as the only value shared by all "good" works of art, literature, and music. In the most plausible modern formulation, cognitivism holds that "art is most valuable when it serves as a source of understanding."[24] Successful works of art are "vehicles for the exploration and elaboration of certain human ideals, religious devotion [in architecture] being an obvious example."[25] Delete references to art and artistic value from this doctrine, expand it to a doctrine about all cultural symbols, and we have the social relevance thesis.

So, whatever its label, what is wrong with this account of aesthetic value? My primary concern is that it inescapably binds together meanings and values. I will challenge the problematic claim that *every* evaluation of every piece of music (including "aesthetic" evaluation) can and should attend to social and political values. For starters, we must ask how, exactly, a judgment about social position translates into "aesthetic" approval. The account assumes, John Guillory observes, that each listener interprets a "work" and responds to whichever values are understood to be present in it, "as though the work were simply the container of such values."[26] So a listener makes a positive evaluation of "Born in the U.S.A." only if she endorses the specific values she finds expressed by it. Conversely, she makes a negative evaluation only if she does not endorse what she finds. Her controlling interests arise from—and position her within—a social code and related body of discourse.

In the previous chapter, I challenged the universal value of *Pet Sounds* by noting that an interest in the album's theme of romantic love places a limitation on its appeal. If a listener does not endorse romantic love, or if a listener does not endorse the specific ideas about love that the songs are taken to express, then that aspect of *Pet Sounds* becomes a liability instead of a positive feature. So it might seem that my argument already endorses the social relevance thesis. But I support a less sweeping proposal. A listener's recognition of the aesthetic value of *Pet Sounds* shares an important similarity with her recognition of its theme of romantic love: both are influenced by her familiarity with a range of other texts, both musical and nonmusical. In that sense, *both* aesthetic and nonaesthetic responses to *Pet Sounds* can be expected to vary for social reasons. However, my criticisms of the transcendent, universal aesthetic value of particular cases do not deny the general importance of aesthetic value.

Because the social relevance thesis links each individual to one or more social groups, the thesis easily extends to cases where different groups arrive at conflicting interpretations and, thereby, at conflicting tastes. Here, public disputes about "good" music are always interpreted as conflicts between competing social codes and practices. "The question of values," Guillory observes about this perspective, "does not emerge at all except in the circumstance of contestation."[27] For example, Walser argues that "smooth jazz" saxophonist Kenny G is less important for the fact that millions love his music than for the intense hatred directed at him, crystallizing arguments "about what jazz has been, is, and should be."[28] On this view, aesthetic evaluations—"His music is beautiful" or "Her music is boring"—should be expected to clash, because they will vary according to various listeners' contingent needs and interests. Walser argues that nothing useful comes from trying to decide whether one group has more competence with respect to this music, or has a better justification of its evaluative claims. Rather than take sides or to arbitrate between competing evaluations, responsible scholarship about popular culture treats evaluative disputes as starting points for investigating how and why tastes arise, and what those tastes betray about various listeners.[29]

My main problem with the social relevance thesis is that none of this demonstrates that aesthetic concerns cannot be distinguished from other bases for evaluation. After all, my participation in almost every activity has a sociocultural explanation. Consider the distinct activities of voting in a municipal election and reading a daily newspaper. Underlying sociocultural patterns explain why I am so much more likely to do these things than are the students I teach, yet that does not blur real differences between voting and reading a newspaper. Similarly, I know that there are social and historical explanations for my aesthetic preferences. But this admission does not prevent me from distinguishing aesthetic evaluations from other decisions made about music, books, movies, performances, and other popular culture texts. When I decide that Springsteen's *Born in the U.S.A.* album is weaker than *Nebraska,* I can maintain this evaluation in the face of my awareness that, in terms of politics and message, the two albums are cut from the same cloth.

An obvious response will be launched against my distinction between aesthetic and nonaesthetic evaluations. It will be objected that I am making too much of the fact that some people, myself included, engage in aesthetic evaluations. Aesthetic responses are "historically specific products of social relations and practices,"[30] and because I have learned to apply aesthetic discourse to my interactions with a wide variety of cultural symbols, I extend that discourse to *Pet Sounds,* Bruce Springsteen, and other popular texts. Furthermore, this objection continues, my positive evaluations of these examples reflect further contingencies: where I grew up, what I was exposed to, my gender, my social position, and so on. So my response proves nothing about how *most* people respond to popular music. There is no reason, concludes the objection, to think that most people adopt an "aesthetic" stance toward popular texts.

Although this kind of challenge is frequently raised against the importance of aesthetic evaluation, it immediately backfires as a reason to favor the social relevance thesis. The objection holds that all discourse is contingent. Granting that, it follows that every analytical framework employs a discourse that is historical and contingent. If the contingency of aesthetic evaluations counts against them, then a sociological perspective on culture must be rejected, too. If someone replies that the social sciences, history, and economics have genuine objects for study, distinct from their evolving discourses, then the same can be claimed about aesthetics. At best, the charge that aesthetic evaluation reflects a historically contingent and ideological discourse reminds us that our theories are theories. Theories are always subject to revision in the face of ideological pressure and from the stubborn way that the objects of our theorizing frequently refuse to conform to our theoretical models. The fact that every account is flawed does not prove that none is more accurate than any other.[31] If the historical contingencies shaping aesthetic evaluations are a reason to be cautious about the scope of my claims, then the social relevance thesis must face a parallel difficulty.

In summary, the social relevance thesis is important because it has erased considerations of aesthetic value from the study of popular culture and popular music. But the thesis has empirical ramifications, and we can and should evaluate it on that basis. Specifically, the thesis denies that someone will assign a high value to a particular song, performer, or performance while simultaneously indifferent to, unclear about, or negative toward whatever is expressed. This denial provides us with a test of this thesis. We can also look at cases where the thesis is employed, and ask whether it adequately links musical preferences to listeners' extramusical social practices.

Dutch Teens and the Excess Problem

One of the most sustained attempts to confirm the social relevance thesis is Wilfred Dolfsma's account of why Dutch teens became so enamored with

American rock and roll in the 1950s and 1960s. Instead of focusing on subcultures and subcultural preferences, Dolfsma examines a relatively homogenous population of Dutch youth at the key moment when that group "decides" to embrace or reject rock and roll. He wants to demonstrate that economics fails to explain this decision because economic explanations ignore the degree to which patterns of consumption reflect value deliberations. Because Dolfsma is an economist and is attempting to explain social theory to economists who routinely ignore it, his book is a particularly lucid explanation of the assumptions that dominate sociological accounts of popular culture. Consequently, he is also willing to highlight problems that arise within such an account.

Dolfsma usefully distinguishes between two levels of value, which he designates VALUES and values. The central problem is to explain how VALUES (strongly held, widely shared sociocultural convictions) translate into values (the importance placed on a specific thing or relationship).[32] VALUES correspond to any "content" that people attribute to music. These include "matters of justice, beauty, love, freedom of will, social standing and behavior, and personal identity." Furthermore, these change over time, as when personal freedom became more important for teenagers than it had been. But VALUES are mediated by social institutions, which involve groups of people engaging in common behaviors in similar situations, and where participating individuals understand and explain that behavior in common ways.[33] If VALUES remain constant while institutional context changes, new values will emerge. Institutional change also creates tension between values and VALUES, and VALUES may adjust. Musical taste, involving any activity that assigns value to music, is most closely linked to VALUES surrounding social standing and personal identity. So if a style of music or a particular artist gains or loses popularity, it is explained by reference to institutional change, change in VALUES, or both.

Against this backdrop, Dolfsma focuses on a small number of questions. Which VALUES and institutions changed in Dutch society during the 1950s and early 1960s? How did these changes reshape the social identities of Dutch teens? Finally, why did this encourage them to value Bill Haley, Elvis Presley, Ricky Nelson, and other American rock and roll performers? In short, what accounts for "the advent of pop music," particularly American pop music, in the Netherlands at a time when the music did not become popular in neighboring Belgium?[34]

Dolfsma's conclusions are consistent with the social relevance thesis. He proposes that the Dutch adolescent audience gravitates to American popular music when "showing a liking for it" emerges as "the most effective way in extant circumstances" to express common VALUES.[35] By listening to and buying recordings of American rock and roll, "and subsequently talking about this music with your friends, you could show yourself to be an autonomous and independent person [relative to Dutch adults], and you showed you had the VALUES that mattered."[36] It is important to notice that Dolfsma does not treat listening as the most important activity for translating VALUES of autonomy and independence into the valuing of Haley and Presley. The most important thing, he contends, is the listener's opportunity to *display* VALUES to peers by talking about the music. Teens consume music by talking about the music. In Dutch life at the time, listening to the music and talking about the music are relatively distinct activities. Listening takes place at home, usually alone. Listening has some immediate value in showing adults that one has independent likes and dislikes, distinct from "adult" expectations.[37] But the primary value is that the music offers listeners a means "to relate to each other in relation to others, within *and* between generations. Pop music is bought for *whom* it represents."[38]

The significance of Dolfsma's study is that he recognizes a need to integrate two levels of explanation. The goal is to explain why the audience was attracted to a limited range of music, given the broader range of music available to them. On the one hand, it is important to document that the audience held VALUES that distinguished them from other groups, such as Dutch adults and Belgian and German teens.[39] Besides autonomy and individual freedom, such VALUES included newness, vitality, creativity, and youth itself. For the Dutch, American and English cultural products had already acquired the necessary association. On the other hand, it is necessary to show that institutional changes played some role here. How did American music become available at just this time, and in a manner that made it an effective means to express this set of VALUES? Dolfsma concentrates on changes in Dutch radio broadcasting during the period in question. Had radio-broadcasting practices remained static, American rock and roll would have been too obscure to be useful. Had things been less static, the music might have been too familiar or officially endorsed, at which point it would no longer represent what teens wanted to express.

A crucial factor for Dutch youth was their access to a weekly radio program, initiated in 1949, that played the top ten records of the American hit parade. Because the show was already established, "Hitparade" offered some American rock and roll when Dutch radio otherwise played none. In 1957, Pete Fellman, the show's producer and host, was forced to quit the program when he created a conflict of interest by taking a paid job with a record label. (The government tightly controlled Dutch radio, and stations were not allowed to play anything that might have been supplied by a record company.) By 1957, two other Dutch programs played American popular hits, and these shows continued in the wake of Fellman's forced departure. Furthermore, Dutch radio and the Dutch music press were initially hostile to such music, and Dutch teens understood them to endorse a more traditional set of VALUES.[40] In the Netherlands, therefore, American rock and roll arrived as a scarce commodity that was clearly not valued by dominant (adult) society.

To hear more American music, many Dutch teens listened to "pirate," commercial radio stations. Broadcasting from the North Sea, Radio Luxembourg offered a limited amount of pop programming with a Dutch disc jockey. Additional programs were broadcast in Dutch when another "pirate," Radio Veronica, appeared in 1960. Soon, there were more. Despite relatively poor radio reception, many Dutch teens also listened to military radio, Allied Forces Network, which played some rock and roll for soldiers stationed in Europe. Afraid of losing its audience to the commercial stations, Dutch radio gradually incorporated more and more American and British music as the 1960s progressed.

Dutch music magazines were never subject to the same degree of government control as radio, and the magazines reported some of what was happening in American music. So Dutch teens were able to read about—and grasp the VALUES of—a great deal of music that they had to go to some trouble to hear. As a result, the clashing VALUES of competing radio stations and programs encouraged the development of a new institution among increasing numbers of Dutch teens, the practice of listening to the radio at the specific times when American and English popular music was available. Because Dutch social customs limited the extent to which friends got together in homes, Dutch teens institutionalized the practice of listening to rock and roll music alone. But many also reported that they did not want others present when listening. Given their limited access to the music they valued most, they did not want to be distracted by the presence of their friends. Only afterwards, when they saw their friends again and could talk about it, would the music gain its primary value as an expression of their generation's VALUES.[41]

I have gone into detail about these findings because the Dutch experience of rock and roll offers a relatively simple version of what happened in so many other places. In most countries, rock and roll became popular more rapidly and it happened in culturally more complex settings, making it very difficult to isolate and examine the explanatory factors. (For example, the Dutch audience did not have to grapple with issues of race in quite the way that Americans did.) If anything validates the social relevance thesis, the Dutch experience does so.

However, in the course of his study, Dolfsma discovers two things that the thesis does not explain. First, why was *music* institutionalized and valued in this way? For the purposes music served in the 1950s and early 1960s, it was no better than any number of other cultural products that expressed equivalent VALUES. Dutch teen interest in Elvis Presley might have stopped right there, as a brief fad.[42] In fact, very few Dutch teens understood the meanings of the lyrics until translations appeared in music magazines. Arguably, American rock and roll was ill suited to function as anything more than a passing fad. Dolfsma recognizes that although American rock and roll did the job, the social relevance thesis does not really explain what happened.

Facing this sort of issue, many theorists of popular culture argue that specific meanings are beside the point. "Meaning" has very little to do with represented content. What matters is the *active use* to which the music is put.[43] Thus, dance music means freedom to adolescent girls who, by dancing in clubs, use it to escape repressive gender expectations.[44] As long as a group uses a particular style of music in an institutionalized manner, it symbolically represents important VALUES, and their endorsement of that style (their valuing it) is explained by the social relevance thesis. However, the equation of meaning and use does not explain what Dolfsma observes, for he discovers considerable "valuing" that does not fit any pattern of active use.

Dolfsma's second discovery, then, is an explanatory gap. Put simply, the amount of time that Dutch teens invested in rock and roll was excessive for the value actually created. Very little of their engagement with music ever translated into an engagement with their social environment. Let's call this the excess problem.[45]

> For its [Dutch] audience, pop music was more than simply a means of creating distinctions. If it were only that, listening to the faint broadcasts in English, which nobody really understood, by Radio Luxembourg, [or] the Allied Forces Network (AFN), . . . for example, would not be necessary. Listening to the few programs on official Dutch radio stations would suffice. Why spend long hours in the evening or at night listening to the radio, hoping to hear new records, when many did so alone and did not talk about it much in detail with others? There has to be something attributed to pop music by its audience.[46]

The interview subjects could not articulate what this "something" is. Dolfsma concludes that fans "*experienced* pop music as being intrinsically valuable." In other words, in addition to its value as a focal point for interaction with peers and adults, fans experienced the music in a special way. Quite literally, the experience of it was found to be worthwhile for its own sake. Social distinctions might motivate listening, but it motivates neither this amount of listening nor the strong desire to listen alone, free from social distractions.

Notice that the proposed solution to the excess problem invokes a standard description of aesthetic experience: "People *experienced* pop music as being intrinsically valuable."[47] So people listen to music for two distinct reasons. They listen because they value it as an expression of their VALUES, and because they value the experience of listening. In other words, the Dutch teens' efforts to learn enough to participate in discussions of music had an unintended consequence. The teens soon wanted to hear the music because their *experience* of that kind of music had become something they valued for its own sake. In short, they found that they liked some of the music, apart from their valuing it as an aspect of their social identities.

Once one becomes familiar with the excess problem, it is easy to spot it in many accounts of the reception of popular music. But when the person giving that account is strongly committed to the social relevance thesis, the excess problem is glossed over or suppressed. The consequent silence about aesthetic value makes for some puzzling explanations. Bakari Kitwana's recent book, *Why White Kids Love Hip-Hop,* is an interesting example.

Formerly the executive editor of *The Source,* a best-selling music magazine devoted to hip-hop music and culture, Kitwana's title neatly encapsulates his project. Like Dutch kids listening to American rock and roll, the popularity of hip-hop with white suburban Americans invites explanation. Much of the book is devoted to debunking myths about the so-called mainstreaming of hip-hop. Setting that aside, Kitwana's explanatory model mirrors Dolfsma's trio of VALUES, institutions, and values.

Kitwana sets the stage by arguing that increasing numbers of Americans find themselves alienated from "mainstream" American values, and this alienation arises from the failure of economic and educational institutions. This sense of alienation encourages a shift to alternative values and institutions. Hip-hop music expresses these new values.

> The globalization of the economy, a changing pop music scene and a declining sense of white privilege were all factors in the rise of white youth obsession with hip-hop, but there were others. A fourth societal change that paved the way for white American youth's engagement with hip-hop was the institutionalization of aspects of the civil rights movement's ideology.[48]

Hence, hip-hop music becomes popular with whites who recognize that they have more in common with African-Americans than was endorsed by "the old racial politics." Ultimately, participation in "hip-hop culture" is valued as a way to participate in a new American (and, increasingly, international) dialogue about white privilege and racial inequality. In short, recognition and positive evaluation of the music's role in institutionalizing a "new racial politics" translates into a high value for hip-hop music.

Although it contains no original sociological research, Kitwana's book is personalized with numerous profiles of individuals who value hip-hop. He discovers that many fans are attracted to the music long before they grasp how it immerses them in a dialogue about race.

> Like those who had identified with hip-hop about a decade earlier, many young whites who fell in love with hip-hop around [the mid-1990s] identify hip-hop's creative, engaging music as their initial attraction. Jeremy Miller told me, "I think there is something about the music that if you get it, it doesn't get any better. . . . I think the white kids into it now really feel the power in the music in the way it's put together."[49]

In several cases, Kitwana reconstructs the personal histories of fans and discovers that, as Miller claims, a passion for the music opens the door to an interest in racial politics. The music is endorsed first, and the "values" are worked out afterwards. When they become fans, most listeners are too young and inexperienced to grasp the symbolic content.[50] Hence, their early listening is similar to that of the Dutch teens who listened to pirate radio in a foreign language. Both involve excessive behavior that is not explained by the social relevance thesis. Yet Kitwana does not elaborate on Miller's proposal that the "engaging" quality of the music explains its appeal.[51]

Here is a more subtle case of the same difficulty. When Robert Walser devotes a book to heavy metal and names it *Running with the Devil,* taking his title from a Van Halen song, he establishes his credentials by revealing that he is a heavy metal fan. "I became interested in exploring heavy metal because I was drawn to the music. . . . I was attracted to heavy metal by specifically musical factors."[52] But, he explains, this means he was attracted to a "historically constituted and socially constructed" position within a larger "social system of values and practices."[53] He appears to be saying that his attraction was independent of any aesthetic value he found when experiencing the music. Walser concludes that any evaluation undertaken "in the absence of a specific context" of use is a retreat to personal likes and dislikes; thoroughly subjective, such evaluations require no overarching explanation.[54]

But is the social relevance thesis the only useful assumption when interpreting the data supplied to Walser by heavy metal fans? Summarizing the data, he finds that "musicians and fans alike tend to respond primarily and most strongly to musical meanings."[55] His evidence? According to a survey about their listening, a plurality of heavy metal fans direct the most attention to the music, the next group attends to both music and lyrics, and only a small minority focuses primarily on the lyrics. But the list of choices supplied to the fans does not confirm that they are responding to musical *meanings,* at least not in the sense demanded by the social relevance thesis. The fans indicated a strong interest in guitar solos and "powerful drums & bass."[56] This answer can be taken to point to their *aesthetic* interest, which may or may not be related to favored meanings. However, Walser has blocked that possibility with his framing argument that because musical meanings are historically constituted and socially constructed, aesthetic value is of marginal relevance. But if aesthetic responses are also historically and socially situated (as I argue in chapter 3), then Walser has unfairly overlooked a possible aesthetic explanation for why some fans are so attracted to guitar solos, as *aesthetic* highlights of heavy metal.[57]

Let's take stock. Proponents of the social relevance thesis assert that a positive evaluation reflects a listener's assessment of the presence of symbolic aspects that "speak to" that listener, contingent on a preexisting endorsement of some cluster of social codes, practices, and discourses. The single best explanation for the appeal of popular music is that it gives public voice to strongly held, shared convictions. From this perspective, aesthetic value explains nothing, for it postulates a kind of value that is indifferent to the representation of other values. However, the excess problem suggests that this explanation does not always apply. Listeners' recognition and endorsement of represented values is insufficient to explain their patterns of listening. Aesthetic interest in the experience of music easily explains these cases. While some popular music is highly valued in a manner consistent with the social relevance thesis, in other cases it seems to be valued for offering listeners an aesthetic experience. By itself, the social relevance thesis does not explain why so many people assign a high value to popular music.

The Interaction of Politics and Aesthetics

So far, I have suggested that the social relevance thesis should be supplemented by the proposal that musicality is a universally human capacity, and it involves an interest in music's aesthetic features. Aesthetic theory might explain some of what sociology does not. However, this way of putting it suggests that there are two competing values, social relevance and aesthetic appeal, which remain completely independent of one another.[58] Perhaps they do not have to remain completely independent. The two value orientations may interact in interesting ways.

It is clear that we do not keep them completely compartmentalized. If they sometimes compete, then they must sometimes interact. For example, they interact whenever we associate music with undesirable values and conclude that it cannot have value as music: Dutch teens refused to listen to the "light music" that government radio directed at them, prominent American politicians dismiss hip-hop as "barbarous," and many teenagers practice nonconformity by refusing to listen to whatever their peers endorse.[59] One music critic has written in some detail about his adolescent rejection of any music that did not sufficiently distinguish him from others.

I was about 16 years old, my hormones were growing mutinous, and the expected social pose was to reject everything your parents considered cool. . . . My initial method for creating a new identity was to associate with music that felt weird for weirdness' sake. I didn't want to be branded as just another well-adjusted, normal kid in town; I wanted to be mysterious, vague, difficult to approach and hard to read. I didn't want to listen to the same things my peers did, for fear of being just another face in the Led Zeppelin–worshipping crowd.[60]

These cases illustrate one direction of interaction: nonaesthetic values influence musical choices. But is there significant interaction in the other direction? Don't aesthetic choices influence nonaesthetic values?

Some of the stories about becoming interested in hip-hop suggest that aesthetic interest might generate an initial interest in music, paving the way for a heightened interest in what the music represents. What are we to make of cases where a listener has no clear understanding of a song and likes it anyway?[61] Should we say, with Walser, that those who value songs without understanding them are valuing them for trivial, personal reasons? Or do we treat this evasion of politics as itself political, as an appropriation of a political stance formerly reserved for high culture?

We do not want to dismiss such listening. For one thing, it often directs future listening. Poet and musician Patti Smith recalls her early responses to different styles of music. Consider her memory of hearing Little Richard when she was a child: "I didn't know what I was hearing or why I reacted so strongly. . . . It was something new and though I didn't comprehend what drew me, drawn I was. Drawn into a child's excited dance. That was 'Tutti Frutti,' so alien, so familiar. That was Little Richard. That was for me the birth of rock and roll."[62] But rock and roll was not the first music that that she loved. "When I was a child, I loved opera, loved Puccini. I loved Maria Callas," recalls Smith. "I didn't understand what it was about—I didn't understand Italian, obviously—but the sound, the concentration and perfection of the sound, would just take me soaring."[63] A few years later, Smith had a very similar response to Bob Dylan: "When 'Like a Rolling Stone' came out . . . I didn't know what Dylan was talking about in the song. But it didn't matter. It needed no translation. It just made you feel like you weren't alone—that someone was speaking your language."[64]

The common thread in Smith's admiration is that it did not depend on any particular assignment of meaning. She directs us to music's combination of aesthetic features and its ineffable sense of significance. Given that she had a similar response to both high culture and 1950s rock and roll, it is unlikely that her awakening interest in music was identical with her interest in extra-musical values she saw in it. Notice that her story is similar to that told by some of the hip-hop fans. Kitwana invokes the social relevance thesis, yet his explanations do not always "connect the dots" in the appropriate way. Like Smith, many of his listeners became fascinated by the music before they understood themselves as situated within the appropriate institutions. They did not assign value to particular cases on the basis of identifying with institutions and their associated values. Furthermore, they did not engage with it by conceptualizing it as "art" (i.e., as material that was socially sanctioned as autonomous and subject to appreciation without consideration of the political). So there are several things we can learn from cases of valuing popular music that are not explained by the social relevance thesis.

First, a listener does not have to *identify with* any associated values in order to value music. A basic human interest in music and aesthetic value would explain the widespread popularity of music that has not successfully conveyed "political" meaning to large numbers of those who listen to it.[65] Some of this might be an unschooled, naive attraction to music, as with Smith's childhood response to Little Richard and Maria Callas. Frank Sibley argues that we would not develop adult aesthetic sensibility and a corresponding critical discourse if we did not begin with naive childhood appreciation.[66] The social relevance thesis assumes that "educated" listening always attends to associated values at the expense of appreciative experience. However, there seem to be many cases where appreciative listening is independent of associated values.

Second, I suspect that most people never outgrow the practice of valuing some music apart from whatever it communicates. Obvious cases include any song that becomes widely popular while its content escapes the audience. I do not mean cases like "Born in the U.S.A.," where two groups disagreed with each other while establishing agreement within each group. The interesting cases are songs for which broad consensus never gets established, or for which listeners simply do not care—or cannot tell—whether the song expresses the broader kinds of values that they, as listeners, already endorse. I will discuss several cases in the next section.

I am not simply pointing out that we sometimes value songs aesthetically, without any concern for what they mean. We also face a normative question. Is this kind of listening valuable? Should we encourage the "aesthetic" mode of consumption? I think so, and not merely because so many people value such experience. The aesthetic mode of consumption is also valuable *instrumentally,* as a gateway into the world of content that makes popular culture vibrant and interesting, as a sphere of life in which values become contested.

Suppose listeners evaluate a song but are indifferent to or unclear about its meaning. Suppose they like it, but don't understand it. The song is about something—it expresses dominant or subordinate group values, but many listeners find its reference and significance unclear, or a matter of indifference: "the object is temporarily depragmatized and dereferentialized."[67] Dick Hebdige claims that popular culture works by means of "hidden messages inscribed in code on the glossy surfaces of style."[68] But the more hidden they are in a particular case, the less likely it will be that social relevance adequately accounts for why a song is (or is not) popular. As a matter of fact, this may be the initial status of most popular songs. Four decades of empirical research consistently say that, somewhat like judging a book by its cover, most people evaluate the *music* of popular music before understanding the lyrics.[69] Most popular music has lyrics, and these are an important means for conveying content and values. Yet the *music* is designed to reward listening in advance of a decision about the song's subject matter. As a general rule, only music with appealing "glossy surfaces" merits sufficient attention and cognitive resources to develop relevance to the listener's social, historical, or institutional position. When listeners respond but do not care or cannot tell what the message is, the response is what we broadly characterize as aesthetic.

One failure of traditional aesthetics has been the denial of an instrumental value for aesthetic interest. In contrast, I think that aesthetic interest can create an interest in, *and an empathy with,* points of view that we would quickly repress when operating with the kind of response that is required by the social relevance thesis. I am proposing that we can turn traditional aesthetics on its head: listening for its own sake can be desirable for encouraging interest in subject matter that challenges our existing interests.[70] There is something useful to be gained from listening aesthetically, without concern for the music's social implications. It does not follow we must endorse the old idea that music listening should always remain pure and free from any consideration of content. Aesthetic interest can get us to relax our inhibitions and can sustain approval for popular music that confronts our current sense of identity. Becoming attached to songs in this manner is a kind of dancing in the dark, but the activity may nonetheless make sense and have considerable value.

The Case of "Bohemian Rhapsody"

Consider the 1992 movie *Wayne's World*. One of its highlights occurs four minutes into the movie, as Wayne Campbell (Mike Myers) and several friends pack themselves into a small car in order to cruise the streets of Aurora, Illinois. Wayne chooses music for their drive: "I think we'll go with a little 'Bohemian Rhapsody,' gentlemen." The song, by the rock group Queen, had been immensely popular when it was released in 1975. In 1977, the British Phonographic Industry named it the best British single for the period 1952–77. Rereleased as a British single in 1991, it entered the British charts at number one. But "Bohemian Rhapsody" did not have quite the same status in the United States. In 1992, when *Wayne's World* was released, the song was largely ignored in America: because it is six minutes long, even "classic rock" radio stations had stopped playing it. It is a safe bet that most of the target audience for *Wayne's World* did not know the song, and its inclusion (and appeal) cannot be explained by an appeal to nostalgia.

Wayne's tape begins in the middle of the song, well past the lyrics that provide the song's narrative. This incorporation of the *edited* song is significant because it forces the film's audience to respond to its presence in the scene without the "commentary" of lyrics. The music stops when Wayne stops the car to pick up another friend, who crowds into the back seat. The song resumes. All five gleefully sing along to the lyric, "Beelzebub has a devil put aside for me!" For a moment, the song seems to confirm Walser's decision to discuss heavy metal under the title *Running with the Devil*.

An instrumental passage suddenly unfolds. Dominated by a powerful guitar riff, a wave of music bucks and weaves like a wild stallion. With perfect synchronization, the five friends thrash their heads up and down to the music in euphoric delight. Then the car stops so that Wayne can admire a Fender Stratocaster guitar in a music store window. Back in the car, the song resumes at the coda. A mournful guitar line accompanies the closing lyric, "nothing really matters to me." But we know that this line does not express Wayne's feelings, because it has just been undercut by his longing for a new electric guitar.

The image of the boys rocking their heads to the music is the film's one great merger of music and visual image. Their behavior is choreographed joy. The music synchronizes their response—we see that they are responding appropriately to something that they, and we, can locate in the music. The music encourages them to let down their adolescent cool and be silly.

The sequence is constructed to heighten a viewer's identification with Wayne and his primary sidekick, Garth (Dana Carvey). Up to this point, Wayne and Garth are objects of humor. But because almost everyone who likes popular music will like this music, their unbridled enthusiasm for the instrumental passage of "Bohemian Rhapsody" creates empathy for Wayne and Garth. They may be losers, but the rightness of their response shows that they know what's good. Ironically, the film's director originally objected to the music. The characters of Wayne and Garth are fans of hard rock and heavy metal music, but Queen was now understood to be a "pop" band. So the director worried that the song would not properly express values endorsed by Wayne and Garth. However, Mike Myers insisted that "Bohemian Rhapsody" fit the scene, and the song was used despite its seemingly poor fit to the imagined circumstances.

What interests me about this prominent use of a few parts of "Bohemian Rhapsody"—particularly the passage highlighting Brian May's guitar—is that their (and our) delight is independent of any particular interpretation of the song. The film uses only fragments of the song, and from those fragments we cannot guess what the song is about. The limited lyrics border on nonsense. But if the song's meaning and subject matter are unclear, then what it represents cannot explain its attraction. At the same time, the music appeals to most listeners.

The most significant point to be made about this use of "Bohemian Rhapsody" is that our delight in the music is not a self-contained engagement. It spills over into associated experiences. Our inability to compartmentalize auditory and visual streams is crucial to the general experience of film. Responses to soundtrack music influence judgments about a film's visual and narrative dimensions.[71] In *Wayne's World,* we like the music and we see that Wayne and Garth like the music, so when they thrash their heads in time to the music, it is hard to resist endorsing Wayne and Garth. (It is also difficult to resist moving with them.) Yet, four minutes into the film, we hardly know what we have just endorsed. In general, aesthetic rewards can create a powerful approval of a text in advance of otherwise interpreting it.

Exposure of popular music in movies and television advertisements often stimulates interest in that music, stimulating sales. Thanks to "Bohemian Rhapsody," the soundtrack for *Wayne's World* was a major hit. Yet these sales are frequently based on exposure to a mere thirty seconds of music. The use of Nick Drake's song "Pink Moon" in a 2000 Volkswagen commercial resulted in more music sales in a few months than Drake's three albums had sold in the previous twenty-five years. Similarly, the Clash's biggest hit, "Should I Stay or Should I Go," resulted from its use in a television commercial for blue jeans. In all three cases, most people who purchased the songs and listened to them discovered that they got more than they bargained for. In the same way that Springsteen's "Dancing in the Dark" does not prepare the average record buyer for most of *Born in the U.S.A.*, "Should I Stay or Should I Go" is one of the few Clash songs that is not overtly political. Imagine the surprise of someone buying a Clash album for its inclusion of "Should I Stay or Should I Go." The choices—either *Combat Rock* or a "greatest hits" set—are dominated by songs featuring strong critiques of dominant Western values. New audiences will not discover these themes until after they've embraced the music. As the songwriters and performers no doubt intended, captivating music may translate into receptivity to a song's subject matter. Without the seduction of the music, Bruce Springsteen and the Clash would limit their message to those already disposed to agree, a phenomenon known as preaching to the choir.

In the case of Nick Drake, those new listeners exposed themselves to one of the most intense performers in popular music. With Drake, the surprise is how the haunted quality of "Pink Moon" can be repeated, song after song, compounding the emotional intensity while rejecting any concessions to a listener's expectations for variety and entertainment. Moving one's hand over a flame is one thing; holding it there for an extended period is something else. Thirty seconds of "Pink Moon" accompanied by the commercial's pastoral images does not prepare anyone for the desolation of "Know" or "Black Eyed Dog."

In *Wayne's World,* "Bohemian Rhapsody" is heavily edited. Listeners who buy the soundtrack or the collection *Classic Queen* will discover that it is a campy pastiche of styles. As for subject matter, its nihilistic narrator kills a man for no reason and then resigns himself to execution and subsequent damnation. The initial dramatic monologue gives way to outrageous juxtapositions of music and words, so the song veers from melodrama to nonsense. Its over-the-top choral passage mocks opera and includes a smatter-ing of different languages. It seems to mock everything, including its own nihilism. Its chief appeal is not subject matter but its own musical delight. The song becomes so silly and outlandish that listening to it is like taking a ride on a roller coaster. It is enormous fun, and people like it so much that they hardly care what it is about.

Taken as a whole, "Bohemian Rhapsody" is notoriously difficult to understand. The impression that there is something to understand, and that it is *worth* understanding, is a result of valuing it aesthetically. Listeners respond to what Roland Barthes calls *signifiance,* to the text's sheer *intention-ality,* more than to the artist's intentions. But if listeners do search for the intentions behind "Bohemian Rhapsody," interest will fall on Freddie Mer-cury, the song's writer, arranger, and vocalist. If the song expresses Mer-cury's vision, it seems to signify Mercury's refusal to apologize for his own "crime" of homosexuality. The song can be understood as an extended metaphor for coming out of the closet. (Mercury died from AIDS between the filming of *Wayne's World* and the film's release.)

Wayne and Garth might be surprised to find that their cruising ritual centers on an anthem of gay pride. I doubt that the others in the car would be so open to the musical choice if Wayne had prefaced the music with the remark, "Gentlemen, let's go with some anthems of gay pride to get our-selves ready for the club scene." I am not making the point that everyone will somehow magically empathize with gay men and AIDS victims when they bob their heads to "Bohemian Rhapsody." But if they do come to know that the song expresses the worldview of a gay man, then they have already imaginatively entered into a worldview that may be richer and more complicated than they bargained for. Like someone who falls in love with a house and buys it without investigating the condition of the roof and plumbing, Wayne and Garth have unknowingly placed themselves (and us) in the position of having bought into something that may have unexpected consequences. Similarly, some heterosexual males among the millions of sports fans who regularly chant Queen's "We Will Rock You" and "We Are the Champions" might be equally surprised about the pleasure they derive from a gay artist.

My proposal is that once we become aesthetically interested in the music, we have already assigned value to the music and thus to whatever else the music communicates. Once we find aesthetic merit in such texts, we are more tolerant of their subject matter when they turn out to be something that we would reject as an affront to our current sense of identity, had it been our main concern. Having had a valuable experience with some elements of the song, few people can maintain a wall between those aspects and the others to which they are so seamlessly bound. (The flip side is the danger that we will also endorse ideas and behaviors that may have a harmful effect, a danger that led Plato to advocate censorship of poetry and music in Books II and X of *The Republic*.)

Elsewhere, I call this the "spoonful of sugar helps the medicine go down" defense of aesthetic value.[72] Unless we have an overriding prejudice against politically relevant songs, we can see that many songs are noteworthy for getting audiences to expose themselves to messages—even to sing along with messages—that they would otherwise avoid. Aesthetic features secure attention to subject matter, but in a way that integrates aesthetic and non-aesthetic codes. Many writers point out that music's representational capacities are limited and ambiguous compared with literature, painting, and other art forms. The meaning of a musical design must be clarified by some kind of text. Yet the text's subject matter is not necessarily an *appendage* to the music. "Bohemian Rhapsody" combines outrageous vocalizing with muscular guitars to suggest that masculinity and homosexuality are not incompatible. In each case, aesthetic properties and subject matter interact, so our perception of musical construction informs the message.

Pragmatic Considerations

Another pragmatic argument can be offered in favor of a specifically aesthetic interest in popular music. The social relevance thesis underestimates the degree to which communication exploits aesthetic value in order to circumvent existing ideological conflicts.

One of the most interesting features of popular music and commercial popular culture is that it is always directed at what is at least partially an anonymous audience. Almost every songwriter surrenders control over who'll sing a particular song, and few professional musicians control who, specifically, will hear whatever is performed. So popular music is intentionally designed for at least some accessibility across community and subcultural boundaries. When the Beach Boys joined the Grateful Dead on stage at the Fillmore East on April 27, 1971, they needed common musical ground.

They needed material that straddled the differences between two radically different rock bands, and they had to take account of the audience before them.

Their weakest collaboration that night is probably their sluggish, sloppy rendition of a Beach Boys song, "Help Me Rhonda." The strongest, oddly, is Merle Haggard's "Okie from Muskogee." A hit record in 1970, it is one in a string of Haggard's caustic attacks on the counterculture. So it might seem that Haggard's brand of country music spoke from, and to, one group of Americans (e.g., the so-called silent majority who supported Richard Nixon), while in 1971 the Beach Boys and the Grateful Dead spoke from, and to, another group (e.g., the counterculture and young Americans who loathed Nixon).

Or perhaps there is nothing odd about the Beach Boys joining the Grateful Dead to sing this song. Because it was popular, both groups knew it, and they could expect their audience to know it, too—the common thread among their collaborations that night. Furthermore, the Dead regularly performed Merle Haggard songs. (By themselves, the Dead performed two other Haggard songs that evening.) The group presented themselves as exponents of *American* music or, as country-rock avatar Gram Parsons called it, "cosmic American music." From that perspective, there is very little distance between Haggard's "I'm a Lonesome Fugitive" and the Dead's own "Friend of the Devil." Neither satire nor irony permeate the Dead's frequent performances of Haggard's songs, and "Okie from Muskogee" fit seamlessly into their stew of jug band music, 1930s blues, and psychedelia by providing another opportunity to adopt a fresh persona from within a broad range of American types. Recognizing that the musicians were having fun with their odd choice, the Fillmore audience cheers when "Okie from Muskogee" insults hippies in San Francisco—the members of the Dead were, of course, archetypal San Francisco hippies. But there is nothing slapdash about the performance. The Grateful Dead and the Beach Boys inhabit the song. Its straightforward performance contrasts sharply with the exaggerated, campy vocals they'd just supplied to "Riot in Cell Block #9."

By highlighting their common ground with Haggard, the Grateful Dead regularly invited "their" audience to attend to a representation of American values that originated "outside" that community. Presenting "Okie from Muskogee," they went one step further, asking the audience to value a performance of a voice rebuking them.

Such cases demonstrate that shared aesthetic values do not have to be universal, transhistorical, and transcendent. Local aesthetic values can accompany multiple ideologies, even conflicting ones. However, the Beach Boys and the Grateful Dead could not have expected their audience to accept a straightforward rendition of Haggard's "Okie From Muskogee" if the audience for popular music never distinguishes aesthetic rewards from "pleasures associated with the objects represented."[73]

For too long, aesthetic value and sociopolitical relevance have either been conflated or opposed. Either the aesthetic realm is treated as an autonomous world of intrinsic value, in which case there can be no political evaluation of whatever is aesthetically good, or all values are socially and historically contingent, in which case there is no aesthetic evaluation that is not thoroughly political. Austin Harrington recommends a third approach: "Questions of social power are relevant to questions of aesthetic value; but questions of aesthetic value are not reducible to questions of social power."[74] I've pointed to uses of "Bohemian Rhapsody" and "Okie From Muskogee" that illustrate this possibility. Moving beyond examples, can we formulate a general argument favoring this third position? Harrington offers several arguments. Winfried Fluck and John Guillory advance similar ideas.

The crux of the central argument is that a failure to distinguish between aesthetic and sociopolitical values deprives us of an intersubjective basis to respect or value the aesthetic practices and appraisals of communities besides our own. So we deprive ourselves of a potent tool for political criticism and political change, for we reject a valuable bridge between distinct subcultures and cultures. Bridging these divides requires some shared access that does not depend on prior endorsement of the message being communicated. An obvious access point would be aesthetic values, accessible in advance of the sociopolitical message.[75]

The next step in the argument highlights the fact that music is a performing art. Performing musicians are performers in two different ways. One is obvious. Musicians perform music. In popular music, that generally involves the performance of songs, which introduce a second kind of performing. Most popular songs are imaginative constructs that *represent* reality. In common with other popular media, songs demand a certain degree of imaginative engagement. (In chapter 1, I offered the example of John Prine's "Angel from Montgomery.") Although recent work in cultural studies emphasizes that audiences are active consumers, not passive dupes, the social relevance thesis downplays the importance of listeners' imaginative engagement. It downplays the element of make-believe.

Harrington and Guillory warn of the dangers of surrendering "the special communicative possibilities" of performance traditions that require and reward an imaginative interest. For centuries, imaginative play has been the cornerstone of aesthetic engagement. Springsteen performs "Born in the U.S.A." The Grateful Dead performs "Okie From Muskogee." One invites us to imagine that we are being addressed by a veteran who fought in Vietnam, while the other invites us to imagine a conservative redneck from small town in Oklahoma. In the more complicated case, the pastiche of "Bohemian Rhapsody" invites an imaginative search for a unifying perspective. When we engage in the "free play" of imagination and understanding that traditional aesthetic theory assigns to aesthetic response, we have an incentive to attend to imaginary identities with whom we may have no preexisting affinity.

Some will disagree and respond that an aesthetic interest is merely a political response by another name. However, if that is true, then imaginative engagement does not play any special role in the communicative process. One consequence, Guillory cautions, is that listeners and cultural critics "need no analysis of the relation between subjects other than a determination of whether they are *like* or *unlike*."[76] As a result, the presentation of ideas associated with subordinate or marginalized groups has *no* claim on the approval of anyone who does not already endorse those values and perspective. Recognition of value will almost always be limited to communication *within* a relatively homogenous community. So if there are no distinguishable aesthetic values, or if there are but we discourage attention to them, we remove a useful "bridge" across the ideological gulfs separating communities. This point reiterates an important theme in John Dewey's pragmatic theory of art as aesthetic experience: "The moral function of art itself is to remove prejudice, do away with the scales that keep the eye from seeing, tear away the veils due to wont and custom, perfect the power to perceive."[77]

In light of this result, let's examine at a fresh example. Consider Tricia Rose's claims about women performers within the male-dominated world of hip-hop. "Black women rappers affirm black female popular pleasure and public presence," she explains, "by privileging black female subjectivity and black female experiences in the public sphere."[78] These women are attacking "the racially coded aesthetic hierarchies in American popular culture."[79] But if we cannot distinguish the aesthetic from the ideological, then once the ideological content is enumerated, there is nothing more to engage— there is nothing additional about the *experience of the music* that could provoke interest or approval in the musical performance. If the music's value is the political "work" it does, then Rose's analysis provides "no basis for agreement about aesthetic value, nor even disagreement about aesthetic value in the light of questions of politics."[80] But if there is no aesthetic appeal separate from approval of the message of a gendered performance that dismantles existing hierarchies, her claims for women in hip-hop provide overwhelming reasons for sexist males *not* to listen. How, then, can Rose suppose that these musical performances "encourage dialogue between young black men and women," challenging sexist male behavior among urban, working-class African-Americans? There's no dialogue if sexist men won't listen. Although she never makes this point, this dilemma might explain Rose's interest in the aesthetic dimension of hip-hop. Aesthetic values can ground a public dialogue by encouraging attention to musical settings and performance skills, thereby encouraging engagement with ideas that would otherwise be rejected as an unwelcome message.

An additional danger arises if we deny that aesthetical value plays a special role in political discourse. What happens when we downplay the distinction between two modes of speech—Bruce Springsteen talking about Reagan in an interview, as opposed to Springsteen implicitly criticizing Reagan by singing songs that portray the consequences of electing Reagan to office? The problem is not, as before, that the role-playing of song performance loses its capacity to forge new communities. The concern is that we change our attitude toward political speech if there are no relevant differences in the attitudes that listeners should adopt toward Springsteen singing "Born in the U.S.A." and toward President Reagan giving a speech about Bruce Springsteen. We should not confuse the speech acts taking place when Neil Young releases a song called "Let's Impeach the President" (2006) and when a Republican member of the House Judiciary Committee votes in 1998 to forward four articles of impeachment to the United States Senate. If a song performance and a congressional vote are merely politics by different means, Fluck cautions, "the aesthetic dimension also extends into the sphere of the political and transforms it into cultural performance, that is, into an aesthetic object." If we downplay traditional differences between cultural performance and political activity, engagement with politicians and political messages becomes just another mode of "imaginary [role-playing] of self-empowerment."[81]

We should respond by reclaiming the distinction between aesthetic and political value. We want to distinguish between governmental actions, such as reducing access to public education and abridging civil liberties, and *staged* political behavior (political theater), such as television commercials and "town meetings" restricted to party loyalists. If we cannot distinguish between the political and aesthetic dimensions of human behavior, Fluck warns, we abandon an important tool for cultural analysis. We relinquish a time-tested tool for identifying and objecting to the shallow cynicism that drives "the growing aestheticization of politics."

In conclusion, there are both explanatory and pragmatic reasons to distinguish between popular music's ideological and aesthetic dimensions. Aesthetic appeal can encourage both an initial and a continued engagement with ideas that would otherwise confuse or repel many listeners. Although he scorns most popular music, I am in full agreement with Roger Scruton that the experience of music is always an engagement with a larger human community. In deciding whether to pursue aesthetic engagement, "we are conducting an imaginative experiment: what kind of a person must I be, I ask myself, in order to sympathize, or identify, with *this*?"[82] A listener who responds favorably to the amazing rush of the guitar solo of "Bohemian Rhapsody" has already joined imaginatively into community with Freddie Mercury. Wayne and Garth are conducting this imaginative experiment each time that Wayne plays "Bohemian Rhapsody." So are we, each time we watch the film and endorse their response to that song. But if Wayne and Garth are appreciated in a game of make-believe, so is the dramatic monologue of "Bohemian Rhapsody." The same applies to Springsteen singing "Born in the U.S.A." and "Dancing in the Dark." In this respect, popular music calls for a mode of evaluation that distinguishes musical performance from many other situations in which we attend to questions of social and political power.

3. Aesthetic Principles and Aesthetic Properties

Music is what a given culture, or some part of that culture, understands as such, not what it should be according to some grand scheme. And if musical systems, or musical values, can change over time, then more than one set of values may coexist at a given time.

—Robert Hatten, *Musical Meaning in Beethoven*

Unprincipled Evaluations

A decade after the publication of Simon Frith's *Performing Rites: On the Value of Popular Music,* it remains unchallenged as the best introduction to evaluative discourses concerning popular music. However, Frith's desire to balance aesthetics with sociology leads him to cram multiple assumptions into one pivotal moment in his analysis.

> I believe that we should begin from the principle that there is no difference between high and low culture, and then see how, nevertheless, such a difference has become a social fact (the result of specific historical and social and institutional practices). . . . I would argue, as a starting premise, that in responding to high and low art forms, in assessing them, finding them beautiful or moving or repulsive, people are employing the same evaluative principles. The differences lie in the objects at issue (what is culturally interesting to us is socially structured), in the discourses in which judgments are cast, and in the circumstances in which they are made.[1]

The phrase "I would argue" suggests that Frith knows he should pause to pursue these points. But he does not take the time to do so. He wants us to grant him his premises on the presumption that he's got a good argument in reserve. However, I do not think that we should grant all of these assumptions.

The first assumption involves a distinction between ultimate and derived differences. I have already endorsed this assumption. The distinction between high and low is a social construction that obscures our common human practice of aesthetically assessing cultural and natural objects and environments. The second assumption is that we all employ the same evaluative principles. The third assumption is that our assessments always reflect a specific discourse.[2]

Whatever one thinks of the other two, I will argue that we should reject the second one. We can endorse common human capacities without tying them to universal evaluative principles. The first task is to clarify what principles are and what they do.

In chapter 1, I cited the universal human impulse to aesthetically evaluate experiences. I also proposed that we use language that refers to aesthetic properties when we explain why we value certain experiences. Monroe Beardsley looks at the latter fact and concludes that these references to aesthetic properties constitute *reasons* for favorable and unfavorable aesthetic judgments. When we offer reasons, we rely on principles:

> If one proposition is a reason for another, in the sense of actually supporting it, then there must be a logical connection of some sort between them. And, being a logical connection, it must relate general concepts in an abstract way. Thus, for example, if a certain degree of sharpness is a merit in knives . . . then to say that a knife has that degree of sharpness must always be a reason to support the conclusion that it is good, and it must apply to all knives of the relevant sort.[3]

On this model, if expressive power counts in favor of appreciating any piece of music, then we must have a principle according to which all expressively powerful music is aesthetically good. The third movement of Beethoven's *Hammerklavier* piano sonata (Op. 106) is good by virtue of its expressive power. Because Captain Beefheart's "Dachau Blues" performance on *Trout Mask Replica* has considerable expressive power, it must also be good. So aesthetic principles offer a straightforward way to defend the aesthetic merit of a lot of popular music. However, I will argue that this defense of aesthetic merit is a dead end. The remainder of this section outlines my basic reasons.

For starters, there is a considerable difference between saying that expressive power is a merit in music and saying that anything possessing it is aesthetically good. "Dachau Blues" starts abruptly, but it sounds like a traditional blues. The initial line ("Dachau blues those poor Jews") is sung twice, setting up a contrasting third line. What initially seems like a horrible lapse in taste gains power through the juxtaposition of gruesome images ("War Two rained death n' showers n' skeletons"), culminating in a plea for sanity before the onslaught of another world war. Beefheart's caustic vocal is excessively loud compared to the backing instruments, which grow increasingly random and unhinged from the sung tune. Now suppose that we evaluate "Dachau Blues" by reference to the evaluative principle that endorses the Beethoven piano sonata. Both are expressively powerful. If principles guide our aesthetic evaluations, then someone who recognizes Beefheart's considerable expressive power would be *irrational* to claim that the harsh loudness of the voice and the cacophonous supporting music constitute serious flaws. But it is not at all clear that someone who recognizes the merit of expressive power is *irrational* for not appreciating Captain Beefheart. So individual principles—such as a principle grounding value in expressive power—fail to offer sufficient conditions for an evaluation.

Second, individual principles do not seem to identify necessary conditions for a positive evaluation. Frith invokes aesthetic principles to explain why we find music "beautiful or moving or repulsive." Presumably, each of these three aesthetic properties will have a separate principle. Let's consider beauty. Ever since I first heard it more than thirty years ago, I have regarded "Corrina, Corrina" on *The Freewheelin' Bob Dylan* as a thing of beauty. But I do not find it as moving I do "Girl from the North Country" on the same album (a performance that I find both expressively moving and beautiful). Given these two cases, does it follow that I am operating with the principles that all expressive music is beautiful, yet some beautiful music is not expressive? Not at all. Despite its expressive power, I find Captain Beefheart's "Dachau Blues" too caustic and jarring to be beautiful. Music can be aesthetically good without being beautiful. If there are evaluative principles, we will need a vast number of them, each one capturing a different reason why a piece of music can be aesthetically good. However, the proposal that we need so many different principles casts doubt on both their universality and utility.[4]

Third, what is the normative force of saying that "Dachau Blues" is aesthetically good? If references to aesthetic properties are reasons that music is good, then what, exactly, are we supporting with those reasons? There is a huge, complicated literature on this topic. To cut through it, let us set aside the issue of comparative evaluations—whether, say, Beefheart's "Dachau

Blues" is as good as Robert Johnson's "Me and the Devil Blues"—until the next chapter. Beardsley clearly intends "This knife is good" to mean that it is instrumentally good, as a tool for cutting. It will become clear in the next section that I interpret the straightforward "This music is good" as a claim about its instrumental value in providing aesthetically valuable experiences to an informed listener. Discussions of the ideal critic or judge in this chapter and the next will furnish reasons not to grant it any additional prescriptive force.

The fourth issue is a very general one. Must all norms take the form of principles? Is it even the case that *most* of them do? As we saw in the example of the sharp knife, principles are understood to be rules that carry us inferentially from facts about a situation to an evaluation of that situation. The idea that we routinely employ such principles is probably a spillover from ethical evaluation. Many ethical norms guide public behavior, so they invite verbal articulation and circulation and find expression in formulaic principles or rules, such as "Do not commit adultery." (Thomas Aquinas goes so far as to argue that a law lacks moral validity if it is not publicly advertised; thus every morally binding law must be articulated as a principle.) Prior to their formulaic articulation, however, it is strange to treat them as shared principles. Furthermore, aesthetic and ethical judgments do not function in a strictly parallel fashion. Therefore aesthetic norms do not necessarily point to aesthetic principles.

So are there really any principles of beauty? While many people assume that aesthetics involves a search for such principles, many (perhaps most!) of the canonical writers on aesthetic theory deny that there are such principles. Consider Immanuel Kant's famous formulation of this point, "There can be no objective rule of taste by which what is beautiful may be defined by means of concepts."[5] The subjective conditions for perceiving beauty can be identified, yet beauty cannot be defined by describing any features that all beautiful things share. Hence there are no principles of beauty. Although I won't defend Kant's reasoning, I will defend his conclusion. Aesthetic evaluations are reasonably defended by appeal to the presence of aesthetic properties, such as beauty and ugliness, without recourse to principles.[6]

The most promising alternative account to using principles is particularism. It says that we can evaluate "Dachau Blues" without reference to general evaluative principles.[7] Particularism acknowledges that after-the-fact generalizations provide useful guidance about what someone will or won't appreciate. But the only way to find out is for the person to experience it.

I favor a particularism that assigns a special role to a listener's developed sensitivities to aesthetic properties. The importance of aesthetic properties is seldom discussed in cultural studies or popular music studies.[8] In chapter 1, I defined aesthetic properties indirectly, as ones picked out by aesthetic terms. In turn, aesthetic terms are defined as terms used to support an aesthetic evaluation, requiring an appreciative stance toward an experience. On this approach, aesthetic terms support evaluations without recourse to principles.

In saying that aesthetic terms pick out aesthetic properties, I resist reducing evaluation to a verbal facility with evaluative language. Evaluating music requires learned habits of listening. So I want to supplement the three sources of difference that Frith mentioned—differing objects, discourses, and circumstances—with a fourth, the acquired musical schemata that individuals learn and apply to music. These schemata are similar to the socially conditioned schemes of perception that Pierre Bourdieu calls habitus. But where Bourdieu assumes that each person acquires one general scheme, it is far more likely that most people develop multiple schemata—one for each distinct style of music they learn to enjoy. At the same time, these acquired habits are barriers to hearing and evaluating unfamiliar styles of music.

To be more precise, minimally competent aesthetic evaluation requires two sets of habits. Following Robert Hatten, we need both stylistic and strategic competencies.[9] *Stylistic competencies* involve a grasp of the basic features of a distinct category of music. *Strategic competencies* position us to grasp what is salient about a particular song or piece of music. Both competencies are necessary to determine, for example, that both Johnson's "Me and the Devil Blues" and Beefheart's "Dachau Blues" are expressively powerful and therefore aesthetically good. However, even if it turns out that stylistic competency for blues music can be captured in general principles, those principles must ignore the rich particularity that strategic competence unlocks. So if there are principles for evaluating blues, they inform stylistic but not strategic competencies. Evaluative principles will fail just when we need them most.[10]

Listening to the Blues

W. C. Handy's decision to perform and then publish blues music was a turning point for twentieth-century popular music. Born in 1873 and raised in rural Alabama, the self-proclaimed "father of the blues" was in his midthirties when he first heard a blues musician.

Living in the heart of the Mississippi delta, Handy led a nine-piece orchestra of African-American musicians. Dances provided most of their income. Here is his description of what happened one night as he waited for a delayed train to take him home:

> A lean, loose-jointed Negro had commenced plunking a guitar beside me as I slept. . . . As he played, he pressed a knife on the strings of the guitar in a manner popularized by Hawaiian guitarists who used steel bars. The effect was unforgettable. His song, too, struck me instantly.
>
> Goin' where the Southern cross' the Dog.
>
> The singer repeated the line three times, accompanying himself on guitar with the weirdest music I had ever heard. The tune stayed in my mind.[11]

Handy was no stranger to African-American work songs and other "low folk forms." But this "earth-born" music sounded weird.

The crucial step in Handy's conversion to the merits of blues music was another chance encounter, this time in a commercial setting. Handy's band was playing a dance in Cleveland, Mississippi. Someone passed Handy a note, requesting "our" music. When he responded with a "Southern melody," he was asked to take a break in order to give some time to a local string band. Delighted to take an unscheduled break, he made way for a trio of guitar, mandolin, and bass.

> They struck up one of those over-and-over strains that seem to have no very clear beginning and certainly no ending at all. The strumming attained a disturbing monotony, but on and on it went, a kind of stuff that has long been associated with cane rows and levee camps. Thump-thump-thump went their feet on the floor. . . . It was not really annoying or unpleasant. Perhaps "haunting" is a better word, but I commenced to wonder if anybody besides small town rounders and their running mates would go for it. . . . A rain of silver dollars began to fall around the outlandish, stomping feet. . . . Then I saw the beauty of primitive music. They had the stuff the people wanted. . . . Folks would pay money for it. . . . My idea of what constitutes music was changed by the sight of that silver money.[12]

As before, Handy experienced a mixture of positive and negative aesthetic properties. He found the music monotonous and poorly structured, yet haunting. This time, however, he saw its instrumental value, giving him a reason to begin performing it.

Ideologically invested in the superiority of European music, Handy was surprised that the audience preferred the blues. As a commercial musician, he decided to cater to the tastes of paying customers by providing a more "highbrow" version of the same music. Returning to Clarksdale, Handy set to work on band arrangements of African-American songs, among them "Make Me a Pallet on Your Floor." Although he found the music monotonous, he was able and willing to perform it. In a short time, his band was in high demand from both black and white audiences.

Once he had a reason to take the music seriously, Handy found that he already possessed stylistic competencies for making sense of what he heard. A former college music teacher, Handy identified four basic elements of the blues.[13] Each verse consisted of the same line, repeated three times. The melody employed a variation of a pentatonic (five-note) scale, with flattened thirds and sevenths. A steady pulse set the stage for rhythmic syncopation. Finally, musicians provided musical ornamentation to fill the rests and gaps between the regular segments of sung melody. Although these same features remain central to textbook accounts of the blues, blues fans can attain stylistic competence without becoming consciously aware of them. Most acquire tacit knowledge of them. Because Handy could articulate them, he was able to develop his strategic competencies relatively quickly, arranging and playing blues in a manner that satisfied paying audiences. We might think that these basic traits point the way to "blues principles." But if they are, they are nonevaluative criteria for deciding if something counts as a blues. They are classificatory, not evaluative.

A few years later, relocated to Memphis, Handy wrote a tune that evolved into the song "Memphis Blues." Although only portions of it feature a twelve-bar blues with blue notes, its 1912 publication and subsequent popularity was an important step in spreading the blues. In figuring out how to present blues music to a broad popular audience, Handy developed his strategic competencies.

Contrast Handy's descriptions of the blues with those offered by two other listeners, one with less stylistic competence than Handy and one with similar stylistic and strategic competencies. The first is Dorothy Scarborough, a best-selling novelist, Texan, and sometime folklorist. In 1925, she published one of the first scholarly books to include a chapter on the blues.

Blues fans will be both offended and surprised by her description of blues melodies and progressions.

> For the last several years the most popular type of Negro song has been that peculiar, barbaric sort of melody called "blues," with its irregular rhythm, its lagging briskness, its mournful liveliness of tone. It has a jerky tempo, as of a cripple dancing because of some irresistible impulse. A "blues" . . . likes to end its stanza abruptly, leaving the listener expectant for more—though, of course, there is no fixed law about it. One could scarcely imagine a convention of any kind in connection with this Negroid free music. It is partial to the three-line stanza instead of the customary one of four or more, though not insisting on it, and it ends with a high note that has the effect of incompleteness. The close of a stanza comes with a shock like the whip-crack surprise at the end of an O. Henry story, for instance—a cheap trick, but effective as a novelty.[14]

Although she obviously dislikes the blues, Scarborough writes about the style in order to endorse it as an authentic expression of nonreligious African-American concerns.

By 1925, the blues had become a vaudeville staple. Although it was not the first recorded blues, Mamie Smith's "Crazy Blues" (1920) encouraged record companies to release numerous recordings of African-American women. Bessie Smith's 1923 recording of Alberta Hunter's "Downhearted Blues" popularized a slower, vocally rougher style, spurring record companies to seek "Southern" singers.[15] Given this background, Scarborough wonders whether the blues is a commercial invention of sheet music publishers and record labels. But she suspects that this style of popular music is "more or less connected with Negro folk-song," a suspicion she confirms in her book's lengthy and genuinely informative interview with W. C. Handy.

Set aside Scarborough's claim that the music is barbaric. This remark might strike us as racist, but it should be read in the context of a long book about the great value of African-American folk music. It should also be read in the context of understanding that the next generation of folklorists would *celebrate* the blues for being an unrefined expression of what Scarborough calls an "irresistible impulse."[16] As with Handy, Scarborough's evaluation demonstrates that a familiarity with other black music did not immediately translate into appreciation of the blues. Unlike Handy, she writes about the blues without having attained stylistic competence. This deficiency creates aesthetic obstacles.

Coming upon blues music late in adult life, Scarborough heard it very differently than I do. Together with its descendent, rhythm and blues, blues music has been a staple of American musical culture from the time of my earliest memories. Listening to a standard twelve-bar blues, I hear the third line of the sung lyric as moving toward closure and completion. There is nothing abrupt about it. Why did Scarborough hear blues stanza as incomplete and ending abruptly?

Early country blues feature a variety of line lengths. The opening stanza of Blind Lemon Jefferson's "Long Lonesome Blues" is, surprisingly, sixteen-and-a-half bars long. Thanks to Handy and other early popularizers, the twelve-bar form became relatively standard. Although there are many exceptions, the harmonic structure of each stanza is relatively predictable, moving from the tonic chord to the subdominant, back to the tonic, then to the dominant seventh before returning to the tonic.[17] The sung melody of a standard twelve-bar blues will generally conclude in the tenth bar, leaving two bars of instrumental music. Those two bars are, of course, the two bars in which the music returns to the tonic chord. Because this return is independent of the vocal melody, undue attention to the vocal melody leaves Scarborough feeling that the music cuts off abruptly. (Notice how the experience of music has an important imaginative component, as the listener anticipates what is not yet heard.)

Another obstacle is that standard European harmonies would not position a tonic chord between the subdominant and the dominant.[18] For Scarborough, a blues was always incoherent.

Furthermore, Scarborough hears the song as she hears other songs, as supplying a musical background to a sung melody. Based on standard song forms of the time (including other African-American songs, most of which had been standardized according to European song patterns), she cannot help but anticipate a fourth line. She does not perceive the thoroughly antiphonal nature of the blues, as a call and response between voice and instrumentation, with instruments functioning "as antiphonal answers to the voice in those measures in which they are featured."[19] Scarborough writes intelligently about the antiphonal character of African-American work songs. But there, one human voice answers another: "the leader would give out a line of song, which [the workers] would take up as a refrain."[20] Few blues feature two distinct vocal parts. Unable to grasp that the songs are duets between voices and instruments, Scarborough hears them incorrectly, with expectations that distort her sense of location in the musical pattern. So she perceives an aesthetic quality of incompleteness that a more experienced and competent listener simply does not hear. Not comprehending the antiphonal structure, she falsely believes that the blues lack any unifying conventions.

In summary, Scarborough misperceives the music because she has not heard enough of it to listen with appropriate expectations. She mistakenly guesses that a blues is a melody that, like an O. Henry story, surprises us by intentionally defying conventions. She listens with expectations appropriate to other types of African-American music, the work songs and church music about which she is knowledgeable. However, she does not grasp the underlying conventions that Handy points to as distinguishing features of the blues. Her book includes an account of standard blues features only because Handy explains them to her. She may know what they are, but she has not integrated them into her musical thinking in a way that generates the requisite perceptual sensitivity.

Finally, consider a third listener, generally familiar with the blues and then exposed to a "new" blues musician. In the first volume of his autobiography, Bob Dylan describes hearing the music of Robert Johnson for the first time. On the day talent scout and music producer John Hammond signed Dylan to his first recording contract, in 1961, Hammond gave Dylan advance copies of two long-playing records. One of the pair was the first compilation ever assembled of recordings by Robert Johnson. Dylan's performing repertoire already included several blues (he would soon record Blind Lemon Jefferson's "See That My Grave is Kept Clean"). But Hammond knew that Dylan would have had little or no opportunity to hear any of Johnson's scarce recordings. Dylan was so impressed by the album, *King of the Delta Blues Singers,* that four years later its album jacket appears dead center in the photograph on the cover of Dylan's *Bringing It All Back Home.*

Dylan had both stylistic and strategic competencies in place when he first heard *King of the Delta Blues Singers.* What did Dylan hear when he first heard Robert Johnson?

> When Johnson started singing, he seemed like a guy who could have sprung from the head of Zeus in full armor. I immediately differentiated between him and everyone else I had ever heard. The songs weren't customary blues songs. They were perfected pieces—each song contained four or five verses, every couplet intertwined with the next but in no

obvious way. They were utterly fluid. . . . [They had] short punchy verses.[21]

Dylan hears perfection. He reports that his friend and mentor, Dave Van Ronk, was less impressed and took the time to demonstrate that Johnson's songs were musically customary—most of them are quite derivative. But even after Dylan grasped this, Johnson's music captivated him. He credits Johnson's "startling economy of lines" as a direct inspiration for his own songwriting.[22]

Secure in his knowledge of how a country blues is musically constructed, Dylan immediately noticed how thoroughly *composed* Johnson's lyrics are. These are not the improvisations about local trains that Handy heard in the train station. Many other listeners have singled out the same quality.[23] However, because twelve alternate takes of the songs did not appear until 1990, Dylan could not know that Johnson introduced slight lyrical variations each time he performed a song. "Cross Road Blues" takes on a rather different meaning in the version that repeatedly asks a woman, rather than the Lord, to "save poor Bob."[24]

Confronted with the same kind of music, listeners with different learned expectations hear different elements as the most important or salient features. Handy listens and hears a monotonous yet haunting song. Scarborough hears jerky rhythms and unstructured music that ends abruptly, without completion. Dylan hears a mastery of form and sophisticated, disciplined songwriting. At the end of chapter 1, I identified aesthetic properties with perceptual features that we cite as contributing to—or detracting from—the aesthetic value of an experience. Aesthetic properties of monotony, incompleteness, and originality are assigned to the blues according to expectations formed by previous listening. Handy knows the African-American source music for the blues. But as a professional musician, he evaluates the blues in light of "a fair training in the music of the modern world."[25] Handy's contemporary, Scarborough, is a commercial author, not a musician. She values the music for its "folk" element, as an oral repository of tradition. But she has limited access to noncommercial African-American music. Most of it is of the sort thought proper for a genteel Southern white woman. (In one anecdote, she reveals that "Swing Low Sweet Chariot" is her favorite.) Consequently, she has great difficulty in grasping the basic musical structure of a blues. She knows that what she hears deviates sharply from what is "customary" for songs, but this knowledge does not help her when she actually listens. Dylan represents a mixture of their two perspectives. When he first hears Robert Johnson, he is already a professional musician with a strong interest in American traditional music. He lacks formal musical training. Already familiar with several styles of blues, Dylan all but ignores the standard and derivative musical features and concentrates on the superiority of Johnson's lyrics.

As Hatten predicts of listeners with adequate stylistic and strategic competencies, Dylan concentrates on the "strategic markedness" of Johnson's songs, on what is expressively *salient* because of deviation from the norm.[26] Sensitivity to salience requires knowing what is standard and unremarkable. Lacking stylistic competence, Scarborough feels that blues songs are dominated by a "cheap trick," one that *would* be salient in the context of a four-line stanza. Thinking that harmonic change is standard for good music, Handy regards the endless repetition of the same progression as salient, rendering the music monotonous. The important point is that these aesthetic properties—expressive power, formal ugliness, and monotony—are contextually relative to what the listener finds salient, which depends on a disposition to regard specific features as standard. If Kant is correct, and beauty involves approximation of an experience-based formal ideal, then the aesthetic properties of beauty and ugliness are perceived through stylistic competence. Even so, many other aesthetic properties seem to be perceived relative to strategic competence.[27] This would make sense of Scarborough's emphasis on ugliness. More at home with the music's form, Dylan emphasizes expressive merit.

If we account for overall aesthetic response by reference to universal or "deep" aesthetic principles, we will have to explain this pattern of response. It will not help to suppose that the responses vary for nonaesthetic reasons, such as according to their ideological commitments. Handy and Scarborough approach the blues with opposite ideologies about folk music. Scarborough wants to approve of the blues (as folk music), but she finds the music incoherent and unpleasant. Handy is a musically astute listener struggling with a prejudice against such music. He initially looks down on the music for what are clearly ideological reasons. Nonetheless, he recognizes its expressive power. Dylan is initially more pleased to receive a bluegrass album from Hammond than a blues album by an unknown name, but hearing the music reverses his ranking.[28] In his or her own way, each listener has an unpredictable response. Their responses focus on unexpected aesthetic properties.

However, we want more than an explanation of why the three listeners perceive and respond to the music as they do. We also want to *evaluate* their responses.

If aesthetic principles exist, Scarborough and Dylan share the same ones, while Handy and Dylan do not. Yet Dylan demonstrates more strategic competence than Scarborough. We do not arrive at this conclusion by identifying Scarborough's evaluative principles. Instead, we look to see whether she "knows" the music. The relevant knowledge is practical knowledge (what philosophers call "knowing how") rather than intellectual understanding (what philosophers call "knowing that"). Scarborough's description reveals that she cannot hear the gestalt organization of a blues progression or a blues tune, so her aesthetic characterization of the blues is relatively worthless. Comparing our three listeners, the most interesting variable is each listener's accumulated knowledge about music.[29] We are not surprised to find that Scarborough lacks the acquired perceptual and imaginative habits required to appreciate the music.

Even if Scarborough employs her principle that authentic folk music is good, and Handy convinces her that the blues fit the bill, we do not want to say that her principles have brought her to the right conclusion. If they are to be worth citing, principles should link the right information to the right evaluation in the right way. For aesthetic judgment, the perception of aesthetic properties should play some role. This does not happen in Scarborough's case. Her ultimate endorsement of the expressive power of the blues occurs despite her personal failure to experience any desirable aesthetic properties. While her endorsement displays rational consistency, we also want to say that Scarborough is an incompetent judge of the blues.

On what basis do we evaluate Scarborough's response? Examining her habituated knowledge of stylistic norms, we questioned her competence to hear the antiphonal organization of blues songs. But we only know this because she describes her experience of what she hears. Her account reveals that she fails to attend to what is salient about the blues. She should listen again while imagining that the blues is a call and response between two voices. So perhaps we have one principle: competent listening attends to whatever is salient. But this is a principle for evaluating listeners, not music.

This proposal might seem like stale news, especially to anyone who has taught and evaluated music appreciation. However, the point of working up to it by contrasting the three listeners is that it does not say that every competent listener has the same response every time.

Stylistic and strategic competencies permit a certain degree of freedom in listening. Recall that Handy and Dylan both grasp the blues structure and recognize the music's expressive power. Although Handy and Dylan do not focus on all the same features, both offer defensible aesthetic evaluations. Handy notices their monotony and lack of harmonic sophistication. Yet he gives a qualified endorsement (for expressive reasons). Dylan praises Johnson's music (for both expressive and formal reasons) even after he recognizes that it is musically derivative. Although their evaluations are not identical, both listeners display listening competency.

Handy and Dylan cite different reasons. If reasons imply evaluative principles, then they must be citing different principles.[30] Because they reflect their listening histories, let's call them local principles. To deal with them, we either construct a theoretical superstructure of rules for coordinating distinct sets of principles that evaluate the same thing according to different sets of salient features, or we identify a single set of shared principles by eliminating the incorrect ones adopted by Handy, Dylan, or both. On the first option, where neither listener has adopted incorrect local principles, the universal principles must remain vague enough to accommodate the local ones. As a result, universal principles cannot *themselves* generate defensible evaluations. They must be supplemented with practical know-how for applying them. Once again, principles offer no more explanatory insight than does saying that Handy and Dylan exhibit some correspondence in their dispositions.

Pulling together the argument so far, we can say that if everyone employs the same universal principles, then Scarborough applies the same ones as Handy and Dylan. Furthermore, she applies the same ones to the blues that she applies to "Swing Low Sweet Chariot." Yet Scarborough's aesthetic response to the blues is flawed. So what is the explanatory value of aesthetic principles if it is so easy to misapply them? Scarborough's problem is that she improperly *perceives* the blues when she listens.

I have not yet offered my primary arguments against universal aesthetic principles. However, I have made the case that we can reject evaluative principles without endorsing the equality of all musical tastes. Scarborough's response illustrates that not every aesthetic evaluation is equally defensible.

Her ability to articulate reasons does not establish that the blues are aesthetically deficient in the ways she suggests. In aesthetic matters as in so many other matters, an ignorant response is an untrustworthy response. Finally, Handy and Dylan suggest that an experience can be aesthetically rewarding despite aesthetic flaws. Monotonous music is not necessarily bad. Nor is derivative music. Competent listening weighs positive aesthetic properties against negative ones. This complication furnishes additional reasons to ignore principles and to endorse particularism.

Four Challenges to Aesthetic Principles

The basic problem with appeals to principles is that evaluation becomes a two-step procedure: we plug salient information into a principle, then the principle leads us to our verdict about the object of evaluation. Someone hears the music and notices various features, then "weighs" the overall value.[31] Furnished with Handy's certification of the blues as an authentic expression of African-American concerns, Scarborough endorses greater attention to them. It is just not clear that she endorses them for aesthetic reasons.

One model for principled evaluation is a jury verdict. A jury arrives at a verdict by establishing the presence of the right features, as laid out in relevant statutes. These stipulate what counts as an acceptable reason for a guilty verdict. Nothing else is to be taken into account. The jury is certainly not supposed to assign guilt or innocence based on the degree to which they feel moved by the defendant's plight. Epistemologically, a verdict does not require the jury to have any perceptual interaction with the person judged.[32] A good verdict is determined by the facts, not the jurists' personal responses. This method of remote validation appears to be what Scarborough seeks when she interviews Handy about the blues.

So the most obvious problem with principles is that the resulting evaluation is not necessarily an *aesthetic* one. Evaluation can be separated from the experience of what is being evaluated. One person could gather the information, write it down, and hand it to someone else. The second person could use the principles to produce the evaluation: "Reading a description stating that [a] blues piece cries and whispers, groans and moans, might be enough to come to appreciate its aesthetic quality."[33] As long as we trust the information that someone else supplies, we can calculate the value of a musical genre, such as the blues, without ever hearing a blues. Generalizing, no one will have had to actually appreciate any music, by listening to it, before determining its value. One might cynically observe that, were there principles of this sort, the entertainment industry would consult them more frequently in order to release more hits and fewer duds.

Fresh challenges to evaluative principles emerge when we scrutinize what counts as a reason for an evaluation. To count as an aesthetic evaluation, the supporting reasons will cite aesthetic properties, or at the very least will introduce an aesthetic use of some term. Although both aesthetic and nonaesthetic predicates can direct attention to experiential features, aesthetic terms refer to properties with "an inherent polarity or spin, either positive or negative."[34] To take the most obvious examples, beauty has positive polarity and ugliness has negative polarity. Tom Leddy points out that because meaning is a function of use, "there are aesthetic meanings for almost all terms."[35] Without further clarification, *fast* is nonaesthetic, for it does not signal either positive or negative evaluation. But it becomes an aesthetic predicate when it indicates the negative polarity of a musical property, as it does in the context of Chuck Berry's great line, "Unless they try to play it too darn fast / And change the beauty of the melody." To support an aesthetic evaluation, each reason supporting it must involve either an aesthetic predicate or an aesthetic use of an otherwise neutral term.

To illustrate this point, recall Scarborough's description of the blues. She says that the three-stanza verse is not customary. This fact lacks evaluative polarity, for being uncustomary can be either a merit or a flaw. It can contribute to originality, which is normally meritorious. Or it can be a flaw, for many situations are less desirable when our expectations seem pointlessly frustrated—it takes much longer to bake a cake, for instance, if one cannot locate the sugar and flour because someone has not put them back in their customary place. Scarborough provides at least one reason that is explicitly evaluative. She says that a blues stanza normally "ends with a high note that has the effect of incompleteness." Here, she offers an aesthetic reason why many blues songs are musically poor stuff. She explicitly cites a relation between two features, the high note and the incompleteness. Like being uncustomary, ending on a high note is neither a flaw nor a merit. But "incompleteness" has negative polarity—it weighs against a positive evaluation. So Scarborough uses *incomplete* as an aesthetic term: it refers to a negative feature that makes the experience less valuable.

Scarborough's description of the "incomplete" music illustrates another important feature of aesthetic properties. Aesthetic properties are only present by virtue of their emergence from nonevaluative features.[36] For example, the graceful curve of a drawn line emerges from its width, smoothness, and curvature. The width, smoothness, and curvature are not aesthetic properties, for these features do not themselves carry evaluative polarity. Because the gracefulness results from their presence, they constitute the *resultance base* for that particular aesthetic property.[37] In the Scarborough example, ending the melody on a high note in the third line is the resultance base for the incompleteness. If we could identify all of the nonevaluative properties that she finds salient to her negative verdict, we would have her total resultance base. From it, we could identify her evaluative principles—assuming there are any.

Now we can launch three arguments that particularism makes better sense than principled aesthetic evaluation. First, there are no good candidates for principles that will take us from the resultance base to the overall aesthetic evaluation. Second, even if we concentrate on principles that generate inferences from aesthetic properties to overall verdicts, we will find that these are only plausible when they operate in complete isolation from one another.[38] They will merely report the positive or negative polarity of isolated aesthetic properties. But aesthetic evaluations seldom rely on a lone reason. Third, even if we treat the isolated reasons as contributory and not decisive, we face the problem that many situations will reverse the polarity identified by the principles. Consequently, the principles encourage us to make the wrong evaluations.

The first problem rests with the limited usefulness of the principles that carry us from a nonevaluative resultance base to an overall verdict. The obvious difficulty is that we cannot infer an overall verdict from a partial resultance base. "Is *The Big Lebowski* a good movie?" you ask, and I assure you that it is, because it contains many very funny lines. However, we have not yet identified the resultance base, for *funny* is being used as an aesthetic term with positive polarity. The base will be every nonaesthetic property that immediately grounds any aesthetic ones. A large part of the resultance base will have to be the actual words spoken, such as, "Man, it really tied the room together." Identifying all lines of dialogue that are salient to a positive evaluation will generate the total resultance base.

But we certainly don't want to set up a principle saying that any movie will be a good one simply because it has just that resultance base. I observed in chapter 1 that the line about the rug is funny just because it interacts as it does with the visual information (the messy room) and the character's personality. Positive aesthetic value depends on perceiving that a resultance base is set in a particular context. Set the scene in a different room, where it is clear that a particular rug really does tie the room together, and it's no longer funny. Or change other elements of the script (rearrange all the lines into a random order) and the movie becomes incomprehensible and tedious. Simply having the right resultance base does not generate aesthetic value. It's a matter of *this* resultance base in *this* context.

The application to music and aesthetic value is straightforward. Someone who does not understand why Muddy Waters is an emotionally gripping blues singer will be directed to his sense of timing and to his ability to introduce microtonal variations into his singing and guitar playing. As a bandleader, he assembled groups that accentuated these features of his music. Recommending *The Best of Muddy Waters*, Robert Santelli explains Water's achievement: "With Waters leading the way, a blues band could create new levels of musical tension and release them at will, making for a heightened listening experience. It could start and stop beats in ways that gave the blues a new rhythmic edge."[39] For his time, his early bands also played louder and "harder" than anyone else. When Santelli praises Muddy Waters's 1950s recordings, he directs us to salient nonaesthetic features that ground the relevant aesthetic properties.

Taken at face value, these references to tension and release, a rhythmic edge, and hardness do nothing to recommend the music as good. Hardness and loudness, for example, can detract from music—jazz bandleader Fletcher Henderson reprimanded trumpet virtuoso Louie Armstrong for playing too loud and hard, destroying the dynamics of the band arrangements. And it is easy to find cases where an enhanced rhythmic edge would spoil music—the Grateful Dead would not achieve better performances of the blues tune "Don't Ease Me In" if Jerry Garcia's lead guitar lines were staccato instead of fluid. Finally, we often downgrade blues playing that emphasizes the loud and hard parts of the music without providing the tension and release. The results are amateurish, not powerful. (For evidence, listen to the Grateful Dead's earliest blues recordings.)

Aesthetic evaluation is a matter of holistic perception, not inferential necessity. Santelli is directing us to a resultance base as a step toward a holistic perception of everything we hear. So we might construct a principle that links the *total* resultance base to the positive evaluation. This expanded principle still fails to get us the right results. If you own a turntable and vinyl copy of *The Best of Muddy Waters,* you can play it at 45 rpm instead of the customary 33.[40] Doing so will not change the resultance base, but it will ruin the music and drain the authority from Waters's voice. (Once again, recall Chuck Berry's line, "Unless they try to play it too darn fast / And change the beauty of the melody.") Although changing the speed and pitch preserves all the features Santelli identified in the resultance base, it changes the overall aesthetic value. But we have no principles that tell us, in advance, when faster and higher-pitched music will be ruined.

What options remain? Perhaps a successful evaluation rests on identifying middle-level properties, so called because they arise from a resultance base and then serve as the base for the overall evaluation. So the most plausible candidates for evaluative principles do not describe the resultance base. Instead, they link various middle-level aesthetic properties to an overall verdict, carrying us from evaluations of *parts* to an evaluation of the *whole.* Beardsley offers a theory of this type, proposing that at least three middle-level aesthetic properties are always desirable in an aesthetic experience.[41] The three aesthetic properties of unity, complexity, and intensity are identified as universal criteria for aesthetic value.

But, again, playing *The Best of Muddy Waters* at 45 rpm preserves unity, complexity, and intensity. However, it changes the character of that intensity. The mood of suffering and moral seriousness gives way to an intense silliness. We can retain Beardsley's middle-level properties while ruining the music.

We can also preserve the middle-level properties by taking recorded songs with minimal accompaniment and overdubbing continuous counterpoint using a kazoo or theremin. Suppose we did this with Joni Mitchell's *Blue* album or Nick Drake's *Pink Moon* album. While the counterpoint would make each set of songs more complex, we would expect the sound of the kazoo or theremin to be extremely distracting. We might propose that the result is less intense, but again it is more plausible to say that the music is now intense in a very different way. We might then propose that we have reduced the unity of the music, because the new intensity is inconsistent with the lyrics. Again, that is not necessarily true, as anyone knows who's familiar with the presence of kazoo in 1930s jug band renditions of blues. The real objection to kazoo or theremin will be the shattering of stylistic expectations. Singer-songwriters of the 1970s don't use kazoos and theremins for counterpoint. (Although, as a matter of fact, some occasionally do.) The real objection will be stylistic authenticity, which presumes appropriateness in terms of even broader contextual considerations. While there might be no problem with cello counterpoint for Nick Drake or early Joni Mitchell, this judgment rests on habituated familiarity with their other music and standards of propriety based on learned expectations about proper combinations of instruments for specific styles of music.

Generalizing, evaluative principles face a huge problem. Adherence to the principles does not always produce a positive aesthetic experience for competent listeners when the principle endorses one. But the examples suggest an even more radical problem. Aesthetic properties that generally have either a positive or negative polarity do not have that polarity in all cases. Some interactions among aesthetic properties can reverse the polarity of one or more of those properties.[42] Intensity and complexity are normally merits, but sometimes there is no merit in being *too* intense or *too* complex.

In the example just cited, kazoo counterpoint would give Joni Mitchell's *Blue* album a pervasive intensity of tone color. But it would also ruin it. Similarly, occasional flashes of humor add a complexity that sharpens the melancholy that pervades *Blue.* Yet polarities can reverse when we add more complexity by adding more humor. On the live album *Miles of Aisles,* Mitchell parodies a lower-class voice where the song "The Last Time I Saw Richard" has a waitress say, "Drink up now it's gettin' on time to close." (This mimicry does not occur on *Blue.*) The audience laughs, but the cheap joke is so out of place that it destroys the dramatic tension of the narrative. Here, greater complexity reduces the overall value of this performance of the song.

Reversed polarity also occurs in the other direction, from negative to positive. Scarborough cites incompleteness as a defect. Here, we can meet Beardsley halfway by saying that it is a defect when it creates a lack of unity. Never mind that Scarborough misperceives the blues. If we ignore other aspects of an experience and find ourselves confronted with incompleteness, that property contributes an aesthetic defect. However, interaction with *other* aesthetic properties can make incompleteness a merit, not a flaw. Let's examine a case where incompleteness interacts with emotional expression.

By themselves, expressive properties are not aesthetic. A song can express happiness or sadness without making the experience better or worse because of it. But an expressive property becomes valuable when it is intense. Intense exemplification of any property tends to be desirable, which is why very simple objects can nonetheless be very beautiful.[43] Insipid, trite, and predictable displays of expressive properties are aesthetic defects. Furthermore, expressive properties interact with other properties, helping us to make sense of what happens in the music. In these cases, expressive properties contribute to higher-order aesthetic qualities of balance, coherence, and narrative order. As an example of the latter, consider Van Morrison's recording of "Slim Slow Slider," a relatively standard blues. After four stately verses, it suddenly collapses into a cacophony of sounds. Percussive slapping, arrested motion from the guitar, and short bleats of saxophone cut off the song's gentle forward movement. The disruption continues for a few seconds as the sound fades without closure.

So the ending of "Slim Slow Slider" has the aesthetic property that Scarborough attributes to most blues, "the effect of incompleteness." The obvious interpretation is that these sounds represent the narrator's emotional turmoil, for they arise just as he concludes the line, "I just don't know what to do." Heard as an "illustration" of the lyric, the song's *musically* incoherent ending provides a heart-wrenching conclusion to both the song and to the album it concludes, Morrison's *Astral Weeks*. Although incompleteness might be a defect when considered in isolation, its strategic interaction with intense emotional expression is a positive property of *Astral Weeks*.

As with so many of the other examples, "Slim Slow Slider" suggests that many aesthetic properties are only apparent when the experience is directed by extramusical knowledge. The ending of "Slim Slow Slider" would not be sudden, disturbing, and emotionally wrenching if it were the standard way to end every blues songs. I explore this point in the next section.

If there are plausible aesthetic principles, they merely tell us that certain *isolated* aesthetic properties have positive or negative polarity. However, we do not experience music by isolating such properties. Furthermore, isolated principles aren't very useful to guide reasoning—imagine trying to decide if eighty-seven divides evenly by two if you know that even numbers divide evenly, but you lack the principle that a number ending with seven is odd, not even. Then compound the problem by knowing that there are situations where seven is even, not odd, but we lack a principle for saying when. Reversible polarities create just such a problem.

Principles have little or no practical application unless they tell us how to derive an overall evaluation from any given combination of positive and negative properties. Evaluative principles about isolated properties are atomistic, but aesthetic evaluation is holistic.

We are now positioned to combine several important ideas. Aesthetic properties are cited as reasons in aesthetic evaluations. Considered in isolation from one another, aesthetic properties have distinctive polarities. Recognition that something is beautiful or graceful or expressively powerful occurs as a result of evaluating it aesthetically, not before. Music's aesthetic properties emerge when we engage in an evaluative exploration of the experience it offers.[44] We don't *conclude* that something is aesthetically good or bad by identifying the correct resultance base. Instead, our most reliable decision procedure is to *experience* properties that emerge from a resultance base, and to experience their mutual interactions.

The overall lesson is that when we cite aesthetic properties as reasons for our evaluations, we are not offering value-neutral descriptions of whatever is so described. Because good reasons cite salient properties in a way that presupposes stylistic and strategic competencies, some appreciative responses are unjustified. Finally, there will be few (if any) cases where an aesthetic property is "isolated" in any interesting sense. So it is unclear what evaluative work is ever done by evaluative principles—they do not help anyone to decide *which* music is beautiful or otherwise good. Aesthetic principles are useless unless one has the appropriate skills, at which point the principles have little or no utility.

Musical Categories and Ideal Critics

At the beginning of the chapter I highlighted three assumptions. The third was that what is culturally interesting to us is socially structured. I want to explore the parallel claim that *how* something is interesting to us is socially structured. Competent aesthetic evaluation requires perceptual habits that appropriately reflect the sociohistorical location of whatever is evaluated. But how widespread are these habits for music?

Kant thought that a denial of aesthetic principles ensures that aesthetic judgment is free to evaluate each thing as a completely unique individual. Kant calls such assessment a free aesthetic judgment. He offers the example of determining that a rose is beautiful without any concern for what kind of thing a rose is.[45] But even Kant denied that we make free judgments about things that are obvious products of human action.[46] Listening to music, we are confronted by human agency. We do not make sense of human actions by treating them as completely unique. We *interpret* human actions, and part of doing so is the identification of ends intended by the person or persons responsible for the action. Thus W. C. Handy saw "the beauty of primitive music" when he reconsidered the music's monotony in light of its commercial possibilities. A popular audience was willing to pay for it, demonstrating that they valued the experience it offered. Suddenly, Handy had a reason to perform such music, and a reason to put aside his aesthetic principle that "polished," less repetitive music is superior to simpler, highly repetitive music.[47]

Aesthetic evaluations of music do not have to isolate music from awareness of human agency. Given their symbolic functions, Kant observes that what we value in the appearance of a church is going to be very different from what we expect of a restaurant or summer home. We can push the example another step, and say that the religious differences between Roman Catholics and Protestants should encourage an informed appreciation of the aesthetic differences between Gothic cathedrals and Quaker meeting houses, respectively. Dance rhythms inform both a third movement minuet in a Haydn symphony and the 1930s protest song "Sales Tax," a "hokum" blues by the Mississippi Sheiks. Informed listening expects something very different in each case. Rather than principles, aesthetic responses to music are guided by a listener's recognition that each piece of music belongs to one or more families or genres of related pieces. Even highly original music betrays stylistic influence. The music of guitarist James Blood Ulmer is relatively avant-garde for popular music, but it's still recognizably rooted in the blues. On this basis, Allan Moore equates the aesthetics of popular music with the stylistic parameters constraining musicians.[48] Style, however, may be too narrow a concept.

In a well-known essay, Kendall Walton explains why listeners who remain ignorant about the music's origins fail to experience some of its aesthetic qualities. One important fact is the identity of the instrument(s) used to produce the music.[49] Another is the historical context of its creation. Listeners must understand what is standard and what is not standard for music in a "perceptually distinguishable category." At the very least, listeners must know how the music sounds both similar to and different from other music made in the same sociocultural context.[50] So although a three-line stanza is standard for both twelve-bar blues and the classical Korean song form of *sijo*, their distinct histories make them distinct musical categories. For our purposes, we do not have to worry about the precise boundaries between categories. Categories develop over time, and music frequently draws on multiple categories. The more categories that we can perceive an instance in, the more information that we can bring to it in judging its aesthetic character.

Walton's proposal is more than a recommendation to learn about musical instruments and musical styles because it is useful to do so. It is *necessary* to do so in order to experience any aesthetic properties that are made salient by extramusical facts about the materials or circumstances of production: "certain facts about the origins of works of art have an *essential* role in criticism [because] aesthetic judgments rest on them in an absolutely fundamental way."[51] Much as one learns to balance on a bicycle by actually balancing on a bicycle, appropriate listening arises from listening. Experienced listeners develop an "implicit grasp" of various musical categories, and when listening to any music, relate it "to a background repertoire of other pieces that have been heard."[52]

For example, Handy initially heard the blues as weird. This property vanished when he became strategically more competent. Everything that struck Handy as weird about the song in the train station seems to have been a standard feature of a blues song. *Any* blues would have sounded weird to him, as violating standard song forms of the beginning of the twentieth century. Weirdness only belongs to a specific blues if it has perceptual characteristics that are significantly contra-standard for that musical category. But to be contra-standard, a feature has to be more than unusual. It has to be one that would normally disqualify the music from belonging to that musical category.

On "Dachau Blues," Captain Beefheart's singing employs standard elements of a blues vocal. His lyrics open with a standard three-line stanza. The range of instruments is standard (slide guitar, saxophone, bass, and drums). But another standard feature of the musical category is that the instruments follow a predictable chord sequence and engage in call and response with the singer. However, with "Dachau Blues," the instruments don't work this way. The musical arrangement that supports Captain Beefheart's voice is notably contra-standard.

Variable features are ones that do not influence our classification of the music into one musical category rather than another. Use of a kazoo is a variable feature of 1930s blues music, but it probably counts as a contra-standard feature of 1950s Chicago blues, which is a perceptually distinguish-able musical category. Without going into greater detail, we can safely say that much of Captain Beefheart's music falls within Charles Keil's category of the urban blues.[53] Beefheart's voice is unusual for a professional singer, but it falls within the variable range for urban blues. The sung melody also falls within the variable range. To the extent that "Dachau Blues" is a kind of social protest song, his subject matter is merely an extreme case of what is variable within that tradition.

These considerations provide a reasonably knowledgeable listener with a sort of salience map. A listener who finds all blues music weird or incoher-ent will not perceive what is aesthetically interesting about "Dachau Blues." A listener who hears it in terms of the urban blues will focus on the specifics of the lyrics and the shifting background music. Now imagine a world in which there has never been a genre of urban blues. Suppose earlier blues somehow led to a genre of extreme blues, all of which have lyrics about the Holocaust and all of which display this level of independence for the back-ing instruments. However, suppose that almost all other extreme blues fea-ture the interplay of ten or more musical instruments at a time. If this were the right historical context for hearing music that is perceptually indistin-guishable from Beefheart's "Dachau Blues," it would, in Walton's descrip-tion of a parallel case, strike us as "cold, stark, lifeless, or serene and restful . . . but in any case *not* violent [or] dynamic."[54] Therefore our understand-ing of the musical category for "Dachau Blues" accounts for the aesthetic properties that emerge from its resultance base.

The point of this thought experiment is that relevant historical facts are partial determinants of the aesthetic properties of human artifacts, including all kinds of music. Recall my example of finding Dylan's recording of "Cor-rina, Corrina" to be beautiful. As Dylan jokes on his debut album, the recent commercialization of folk music made him sound like a hillbilly, not a folksinger. If Dylan normally sounded like Frank Sinatra, "Corrina, Cor-rina" would have an unpleasantly rough and nasal quality. Coming from Dylan, it sounds lyrical.

To slightly complicate the matter, some listeners will recognize that Cap-tain Beefheart's music overlaps with the musical categories of free jazz and the poetic tradition of the beats (especially as filtered through Dylan's blues lyrics of 1965 and 1966). This gives use more variables to consider, and increases the range of aesthetic properties that can emerge when listening. And we might then imagine a similar set of overlapping categories for the extreme blues, in which case something perceptually indistinguishable from "Dachau Blues" might be extraordinarily tranquil.

Nick Zangwill challenges this line of thought. He doubts that acquired perceptual dispositions are important here. Perhaps we see or hear various aesthetic properties, and then think of them as enhanced or diminished when we compare them with other, similar things. After all, "we *do* ascribe properties such as lyrical and fast to music even when we do not know" the proper facts about origins.[55]

Although correct about what people *do,* this objection misses the point. One implication of my earlier discussion of different responses to the blues is that people do not restrain themselves from aesthetically evaluating music. As a consequence, initial responses to a new musical category generate "reasons" that more knowledgeable listeners do not confirm (Scarborough's "effect of incompleteness") or learn to ignore as too standard to be salient (Handy's concern about structural monotony). The issue is not what people do, but whether those who know more about the correct category are better qualified to identify aesthetic properties that emerge during experiences of it. When there are disagreements about aesthetic values, they usually hinge on disagreements about which aesthetic properties are present. In this matter, some responses are better than others.

Having concluded that not every response and evaluation is on the same footing, we might be tempted to embrace a theory of ideal critics. If Scarborough is an inexperienced and untrustworthy blues critic, and if we get more accurate descriptions and evaluations from more experienced listeners (e.g., Charles Kiel or Peter Guralnick), then the upper limit must be best. In short, whoever has experienced all music will be the best judge of any particular case. This listener is the ideal critic. When we want to know which of two pieces is better, or which of two styles is more deserving of our time, we should shape our tastes in the direction of agreeing with the judgment of the ideal judge. From the perspective of the ideal critic, Western classical music is superior to popular music. So Handy was correct to look askance at the repetitive, simple music of rural Mississippi and Scarborough was better off never learning to like the blues.

This is a thorny issue, and I will defer the bulk of my response until the next chapter. But there are serious problems with postulating an ideal listener. For now, I will simply note one of them. It is not obvious that, for any given category of music, someone who has experienced *all* music will perceive notably different aesthetic properties and arrive at different evaluations than someone who has merely "become familiar with a considerable variety of works similar sorts."[56] I would guess that Joel Rudinow, a professional philosopher and blues pianist, is about as familiar with blues music as someone can be. But I also venture to guess that his evaluations of *The Best of Muddy Waters* and Waters's *Electric Mud* are the same today as they were ten years ago. And they will probably be the same ten years from now. Why should we agree that experiencing *all* blues music (the factor that differentiates the ideal critic from mere mortals) would change well-founded, established evaluations? Aesthetic evaluation depends on *perception* of emergent properties. Up to a certain point, more experience transforms and improves perception. After a certain point, it is unlikely that more information will introduce additional refinements or insight. In other words, once the *perceptual* system is fine-tuned to a musical category, more experience is unlikely to result in noticeable changes to future experiences within the same category.

Decades ago, E. H. Gombrich argued that there is no such thing as an "innocent eye" for looking at paintings.[57] When it comes to music, there is no innocent ear. The experience of music is shaped by previous experiences with music. Better listeners respond to standard features the way that good drivers pay attention to stop signs. Good drivers stop without consciously thinking about the shape or color of the sign. The experienced driver is more alert to the many variables of the road. Like good drivers, better listeners know how to sort through the variables and attend to what is salient. But if relevant historical facts provide the background for correctly deciding what is salient, so might any number of additional relevant contexts. Rather than endorse the one best response (whichever conforms to evaluative principles, or the response of the ideal critic), we should explore ways that different musical categories serve different nonmusical functions. Because a single musical performance or musical work can belong to many different musical categories, different aesthetic properties will emerge in different functional contexts. There can be multiple plausible evaluations of the same music, as well as many different evaluations that are off the mark.

Part Two

The Aesthetic Value of the Popular

4. Appreciating, Valuing, and Evaluating Music

The value, which all men put upon any particular pleasure, depends on comparison and experience; nor is a porter less greedy of money, which he spends on bacon and brandy, than a courtier, who purchases champagne and ortolans.
  —David Hume, "Of Refinement in the Arts"

Functional differentiation is aesthetically more relevant than material differentiation.
  —Carl Dahlhaus, *Analysis and Value Judgment*

Distinguishing among Objects of Evaluation

To this point, I have avoided the perennial question of standards of taste. To what extent does the aesthetic value of certain *experiences* support a distinction between aesthetically better and worse *music*? Furthermore, is there any sense in which a taste for one sort of music might be aesthetically superior to others? To the extent that we can control it, do we want to live in a culture in which people assign a great deal of value to popular music?

Exploration of these topics will remain hopelessly muddled unless we distinguish among three focal points or objects of evaluation. First, there is the evaluative process by which we become aware of aesthetic properties. This evaluative activity is appreciation. It is directed at an experience shaped by the music. But it is a very short step from appreciating music (evaluating the experience) to evaluating the music. In the latter case, some level of instrumental value is assigned to the music. These two evaluative procedures are frequently confused, for it is difficult to resist equating the music with the experience of the music. In T. S. Eliot's frequently quoted line, "You are the music while the music lasts." Yet there are cases where an evaluation of a particular experience of the music diverges from the evaluation of the music that is experienced. A third focal point emerges whenever it becomes apparent that others do not respond as we do. These discrepancies invite us to evaluate individuals or groups on the basis of their musical activities and preferences. Here, the evaluation falls on the evaluating, as when we find the musical tastes of others admirable, incomprehensible, or threatening.

Although these three objects of evaluation are distinct, it is often difficult to tell which one someone is talking about. Furthermore, we've seen that some theories deny that we can distinguish between an evaluation of the music and of its audience.

My first step in disentangling them will employ the well-known contrast between valuing something instrumentally and valuing it for its own sake. This distinction underwrites the claim that there is an important difference between evaluating an experience and evaluating the object that informs the experience. The distinction between evaluating the music and its audience is based on something else altogether, namely the difference between internal and external judgments of value.

Because they have intended functions, virtually every product of human activity can be evaluated instrumentally, in terms of results. For most people, a first-class postage stamp has limited instrumental value, as a means of getting a letter delivered. But philatelists (stamp collectors) value postage stamps for multiple reasons. One is economic. Some stamps are rare and worth a great deal of money. Another is aesthetic. Many philatelists enjoy looking at their stamps, even common ones worth only pennies, because many of them are quite lovely. The small squares, rectangles, and triangles of paper are assigned economic or aesthetic value according to their ability to perform economic and aesthetic functions. As such, the *stamps* have various instrumental values.

Notice that we can assign instrumental value to things without having any personal use for them. We simply have to understand what they are and how they are used. Medieval battle swords in a history museum retain their instrumental value as weapons even if they are never again used in battle. A parallel case holds for aesthetic value.[1] If competent observers aesthetically value certain postage stamps, then anyone who knows this fact should admit that those stamps are, instrumentally, aesthetically valuable. Similarly, by knowing that critic Greil Marcus is very familiar with three decades of rock music and that he assigns aesthetic value to music that he is competent to judge, we know that some rock music is aesthetically valuable. For example, his most recent book, *Like a Rolling Stone: Bob Dylan at the Crossroads,* is evidence that Dylan's music has some aesthetic value.[2] But this establishes nothing about the music's overall aesthetic value. Virtually everything we see and hear has *some* aesthetic value.

A few pages into Marcus's book, it is perfectly clear that he is making the case that Dylan's music is politically, and thus instrumentally, important: "he raised the stakes of life all around himself."[3] But Marcus resists reducing Dylan to politics. The music also has considerable aesthetic value. In fact, Marcus spends almost no time explaining how Dylan "raised the stakes." Ultimately, Marcus values "Like a Rolling Stone" because it provides experiences that are holistically appreciated for their own sake. Again, this is relatively uninformative until we discover that Marcus is using this one song in order to emphasize how much "the" experience of it varies from one occasion to the next. "Like a Rolling Stone" can sound weird and startling to a listener who is not familiar with Dylan. It can sound weird and startling in a different way to someone who is. In chapter 3 I argued that much depends on what else the listener has experienced. But it also depends on how recently and how often the same or similar music has been experienced, and what is happening while experiencing it.

Consider this passage, in which Marcus tries to capture the experience of listening to Dylan's 1965 recording of "Like a Rolling Stone."

> The sound is so rich the song never plays the same way twice. You can know that, for you, a certain word, a certain partial sound deep within the whole sound, is what you want; you can steel yourself to push everything else in the song away in anticipation of that part. . . . It never works. You lie in wait, to ambush the moment; you find that as you do another moment has sneaked up behind you and ambushed you instead. . . . Though one instrument may catch you up, and you may decide to follow it, . . . every instrument shoots out a line that leads to another instrument, the organ to the guitar, the guitar to the voice, the voice to the drums, until nothing is discrete and each instrument is a passageway. You cannot make anything hold still.[4]

If anything is being valued here, it is the experience of interacting with the music.[5] That experience is valued for its own sake, not instrumentally.

To avoid misunderstandings, I must clarify one point. Throughout this chapter, I follow Marcus's lead by concentrating on recorded music. Doing so has two advantages. First, it is true to the way that most popular music circulates and is experienced. Second, it stabilizes the "object" that we are evaluating. Assigning value to the *song* "Like a Rolling Stone" either treats it as an abstract object or a free-standing text, which is to assign it a generalized instrumental value that is one step further removed from interaction with a specific recording. As performance vehicles, songs vary greatly according to whichever version happens to come to mind.[6] Many people dislike Dylan, and "Like a Rolling Stone" is seldom played on the radio. So Jimi Hendrix fans are likely to think of Hendrix's ramble through it during his live performance at the 1967 Monterey Pop Festival—"a thing by Bob Dylan," Hendrix announces, "[and] that's his grandma over there." David Bowie fans might only know his 1994 recording of it. Rolling Stones fans might think of their 1995 live recording of it. Each version is very different, and an evaluation of one version is a poor indicator of what is good and bad in each of the others.

Marcus expects *and looks forward to* a mixture of similarity and difference each time he experiences the standard 1965 recording of "Like a Rolling Stone." (If it routinely delivered the same undifferentiated experience, we would expect him to dismiss it as boring.) If Marcus additionally believes that his own response is not idiosyncratic, and that other competent listeners should have similarly valuable experiences, then he can justifiably endorse the recording as instrumentally good.[7] He must believe, in short, that the *music* contributes to the experience in a significant way, and that it will do so for others, as well.[8] We say that a song, or performance, or recording has aesthetic value when we believe that it predictably provides aesthetic experiences, that is, experiences that we can value for their own sake.

So "aesthetic value" can refer to either of two things. It can refer to instrumental value that adheres to public objects, or to noninstrumental value that adheres to the experiences offered by those public objects. Furthermore, one and the same thing can have both aesthetic and nonaesthetic instrumental value. There is no difficulty, therefore, in saying that Dylan's music is both aesthetically and politically interesting, and that the two values might be relatively independent of each other.[9]

An additional evaluation is possible, bringing us to the central issue of this part of the book. We can assign aesthetic value to postage stamps and "Like a Rolling Stone" and still wonder whether there are cultural reasons to want more philatelists or more Bob Dylan fans. Should people develop musical tastes that are aesthetically satisfied by popular music, or specific styles of it? But this question introduces a radical shift of perspective.

Aesthetically evaluating a specific musical work or performance is a different project than evaluating popular music as an institution of contemporary life. The former requires an internal perspective. The latter requires an external one. This epistemological distinction is explained by legal philosopher H. L. A. Hart: "When a social group has certain rules of conduct . . . it is possible to be concerned with the rules, either merely as an observer who does not himself accept them, or as a member of the group which accepts and uses them as guides to conduct."[10] This distinction is employed in philosophy, sociology, and anthropology under a variety of names.

Some evaluations only make sense from an internal perspective, by participating in practices that are taken for granted as the basis for evaluating a range of things or activities. An internal perspective is an "insider's" view. *Appreciating* "Like a Rolling Stone" requires an internal perspective.

An internal perspective on a musical category also encourages comparative rankings of individual pieces of music. Reading Marcus's *Like a Rolling Stone,* one can find it hard to ignore his litany of unsupported internal evaluations. As a reviewer complains,

> Out of nowhere, [Marcus] pronounces that the Beatles' *Rubber Soul* is "the best album they would ever make." (Why? Marcus never explains.) The Rolling Stones' *Let It Bleed* and Dylan's *Highway 61 Revisited,* which leads off with The Greatest Song of All Time, share the title of "the best rock 'n' roll album ever made." Dylan's 1966 Manchester concert with the Band (then known as the Hawks), released as *Live 1966,* was "likely the greatest rock 'n' roll show ever played." Such hyperbolic assessments are the stuff of consumer guides, of course, but do they have a place in serious cultural criticism? Is *Hamlet* the Greatest Play Ever Written?[11]

Because it is obviously self-defeating to assign the same ranking of "best" to two different albums, Marcus seems to have included these evaluations solely to provoke arguments. After all, Marcus can safely assume that anyone who'll read a book devoted to one hit song from 1965 will have an opinion about these rankings. He expects his readers to respond from an internal perspective.

It can be difficult to determine which perspective—internal or external—informs an evaluation. Learning about Marcus's book, some will wonder whether it is a good thing to spend so much time on a single rock song and its recording sessions. Asking whether "Like a Rolling Stone" is worth the time might be internal. We might answer in favor of "Like a Rolling Stone" while doubting that a similar effort is justified for Al Martino's 1952 hit "Here in My Heart" or Culture Club's 1983 hit "Karma Chameleon." In contrast, if the question about a book devoted to "Like a Rolling Stone" is rooted in a suspicion that rock music just isn't worth this much attention, then we have an external evaluation, one directed at a broad category of music and its attendant musical culture. For reasons that will become clear, justifying an external evaluation is dauntingly complex.

Whereas internal evaluation is an "insider's" determination of value, external evaluation assesses the evaluating. So even in cases where internal and external evaluations seem to be directed at the same music, there is a radical difference in their focal points. Aesthetic properties ground Marcus's internal judgment that the fourth take (the version released in 1965) of "Like a Rolling Stone" is better than the eleventh (the only other complete performance of the song during the recording session).[12] I have argued that Marcus's competence to make this comparison rests on acquired understanding of relevant musical categories, which in turn requires participation in a musical culture with various institutional structures.

The internal/external distinction becomes important to my argument because it reminds us that there are two different ways to evaluate participation in a musical culture. We saw an example of this in the last chapter, with Scarborough's qualified endorsement of the blues despite her lack of an "internal" ability to appreciate the music.[13] Yet external judgment should not ignore the *range* of internal judgments that are made—Bob Dylan and W. C. Handy emphasized different aspects of the blues. Turning to parallel cases in contemporary music culture, we see that criticisms of heavy metal and hip-hop music arise from their subcultural affiliations. These challenges are generally from an external perspective. But they can also arise as internal evaluations, as when champions of one style of hip-hop music disparage and sometimes physically attack fans of a rival style.[14]

However great "Like a Rolling Stone" is, an external perspective might remain skeptical about the value of acquiring the skills to appreciate it. Because aesthetic instrumental value is entangled with other instrumental values, the consequences of developing a specific musical taste cannot be confined to the experience of the music. So there is far more to the value of a *kind* of music than the aesthetic achievement of its best exemplars. We should agree with John Frow that "there is no escape from the consequences of possession of cultural capital," and we will want to face the question of what nonaesthetic consequences arise if our aesthetic sensibilities are satisfied by popular music.[15]

Before I say more about the external perspective, I will use the next section to explore the distinction between appreciation and evaluation. I make two claims. First, aesthetic properties emerge in the context of appreciation, which becomes the basis for aesthetic evaluation. Second, while aesthetic properties play a central role in *appreciating* the music, additional nonaesthetic values are relevant to *evaluations* of it. Because this concession introduces a plurality of incommensurable standards into such evaluations, I am skeptical about our ability to defend most comparative evaluations of particular cases—there is little chance of producing convincing reasons why *Rubber Soul* is the best Beatles album. The *experience* of music has too many permeable boundaries.[16] At this point my major claims are not very clear, so I will elaborate them with a fresh example.

Appreciating and Evaluating

I vividly remember the day that I purchased Elvis Costello's third album, *Armed Forces* (1979). It had appeared in the stores only a day or so before, and although I was an avid reader of the popular music press, I was not aware that the album was due for release. But there it sat in the front rack of Rasputin's Records on Telegraph Avenue in Berkeley, and because *My Aim Is True* (1977) and *This Year's Model* (1978) were among of my favorite recent records, I bought *Armed Forces* without waiting for the critical word on it. My wife and I were on our way to dinner at a friend's apartment, and when we arrived I asked if I might play the new Elvis Costello after we'd heard the Bob Marley album that was on the stereo. I can no longer recall the conversation that evening, but I do recall my response to *Armed Forces,* which struck me as surprisingly complex and melodic. My first hearing thrilled me—the record *grabbed* my ears and pulled me into the music. It was not the sort of music that I expected from Costello.

Upon repeated hearings, I formulated an evaluation of *Armed Forces:* it is a superb and daring piece of post-punk, and I concur with Dave Marsh's assessment that it is Costello's very best record.[17] But as with many books, films, and records, when I play it now, decades later, I do not experience the thrill of the many hearings I gave it over the first few days. This loss of pleasure is not due to any change in my sense of its worth. I certainly don't suppose that my loss in pleasure correlates with a reappraisal. In many respects I find it more *interesting* now, hearing details in the music and lyrics that escaped me in 1979. By itself, pleasure is a feeble measure of aesthetic value. We expect different experiences upon repeated listening, but these differences are consistent with a single, relatively stable evaluation. Rather than suppose that *Armed Forces* is of value simply for its capacity to *cause* pleasure, articulate fans are likely to report that they take pleasure *in* its achievement. But I am less interested in the quality of the reward than in its source, which is the listener's stance of exploratory appreciation.[18]

To make sense of this experience with *Armed Forces,* I will distinguish more sharply between appreciation and evaluation.[19] My comparative claims—that is a daring piece of post-punk, and that it is the best of Costello's releases—render *evaluative* rather than *appreciative* judgments. As I noted in chapter 3, both evaluation and appreciation presuppose patterns of standard and variable features of a musical category. Unlike appreciation, which is an evaluative appraisal of a specific experience, evaluation abstracts from any particular experience. Evaluating is fundamentally comparative and it assigns instrumental value to the object responsible for the experience. (Where it is appropriate to differentially attend to a "musical work" and its performance in the same listening process, different instrumental values may be assigned to each.) Although appreciation is also informed by past experience, it is not fundamentally comparative and it does not always lead to an assignment of instrumental value.

An evaluation assigns instrumental value to the music by concentrating on features that should be salient to any competent listener. An experience can be aesthetically valuable even if it cannot be repeated—in some ways, we value them more highly for their uniqueness. In the case of appreciation, such knowledge usually remains tacit, manifesting itself only as an acquired skill. Evaluation requires an articulation of some general criteria that contribute to repeatable elements of the experience. When we evaluate, we arrive at conclusions by reference to criteria that can be specified in advance of our experience with any particular instance of the kind of thing we are evaluating. Carl Dahlhaus emphasizes this point, arguing that an assignment of instrumental value to a "musical work" always "presupposes a cogent theory with firm norms concerning types of musical composition."[20]

In principle if not in practice, we can formulate reasons to praise or condemn music without experiencing it firsthand. J. O. Urmson offers the example of grading apples. Apples less than 2.5 inches in diameter never make the supergrade category.[21] If I want supergrade apples to sell in my market, and if I have a sorting machine or some other way to sort apples by size without additional inspection, I can arrive at negative evaluations of a lot of fruit without directly examining each apple. This approach was applied to Hollywood movies for three decades under the auspices of the Motion Picture Production Code of 1930 (the Hays Code). The code prohibited a range of situations and visual images, stipulating that "sex perversion" is always a breach of "the dictates of good taste." In a parallel manner, most people try to avoid music in certain styles, and they do so in advance of learning enough to appreciate those styles.

Although the term *appreciation* suggests a positive experience, the appreciative stance is not always positive. The point of choosing this label is to suggest openness to every aspect of the experience. One might decide that the experience is not worth having. In this passage from a review of a Johnny Winter album, an appreciative listener cannot find much that is worthwhile:

> Now, it's an interesting idea to have parallel guitar parts playing contrapuntally, but the end result here is just so much busyness. The two parts tend to cancel each other out because instead of being complimentary, interlocking parts that work together as contrapuntal voices, they pretty much attempt the same thing, with only the minor variations . . . If we assume that the slide part was the basic accompaniment, then the other just muddies up the texture [and] merely duplicates, with an excess of decoration.[22]

These lines illustrate the difficulty of verbalizing and sharing appreciation: it is easy to miss the fact that the reviewer recognizes that the aesthetic properties of muddiness and busyness are the "result" of base properties in the musical arrangement. These aesthetic properties may or may not appear in your or my listening experience of this recording.

It is telling that when Jon Landau wants to insult the Grateful Dead, he does so by calling attention to the audience, who "applauds about the same for every song. To me, that kind of lack of discrimination is indicative of an insensitivity to the Dead's music in particular, and music in general."[23] Landau expects applause to indicate performance "quality." He ignores the possibility that the Dead's audience is more appreciative than evaluative in declining to judge one song better than another. Landau may have witnessed a case of heightened sensitivity to the musical experience.

In contrast to evaluation, appreciation is directly concerned with experiencing a specific work or performance or recording. Appreciation attends to *this* experience in its particularity.[24] Appreciation is open to discovery, for there is no prior decision to stay within boundaries that can specified in advance of experiencing the music. Our guiding principles cease to function as principles. At best, they call attention to standard features that frame expectations for the relevant musical categories. Instead of "checking off" qualities we anticipate, appreciation aims at discovering whatever is to be found in experiencing a particular work—standard and nonstandard, good and bad.[25] With evaluation, the absence of a standard feature yields a negative evaluation. With appreciation, the absence of a standard feature can be a positive base property.

So two main factors distinguish appreciating from evaluating. First, they have different goals: they aim at different results. Appreciation explores whatever is there.[26] The listener's goal "is to savor it at the same time," investigating its experiential possibilities.[27] With evaluation, the goal is to assign the music a ranking. Second, appreciation is open to consideration of any and all properties that the music might possess. Evaluation focuses on a preferred set of properties. With appreciative experience, we sometimes discover value in aspects of a work that were previously dismissed on principle. Although on principle I formerly disapproved of the Grateful Dead, I occasionally found their music interesting when I encountered it on the radio, leading me, eventually, to more listening and then to an appreciative stance.

Finally, appreciative listening is never simply an endorsement of content. If that is what we want from music, we need not listen. It will often be more efficient to extract the message from a synopsis, as so many literature students have discovered with Cliffs Notes. Yet, as Stephen Davies emphasizes, appreciative interest in the individuality of a specific piece of music does not rule out interest in it "as an individual *something*." It does not rule out "bringing to one's experience of that thing a knowledge of the traditions and conventions within, and against which, it is intended to be understood and appreciated."[28] Much of my response to *Armed Forces* stems from its subversion of my expectations, expectations dependent on listening to it in relation to its place in British rock in the wake of punk. It is difficult to imagine a teenager who would hear it this way today.

To summarize, appreciation does not inspect an object in light of its ability to satisfy fixed criteria or some standard that can be formulated in defending one's evaluation to another person. In contrast, evaluation places a work into a specific category and rates it as an exemplar of that category. The important "discovery" is the degree to which the work exemplifies relevant features.

In the case of *Armed Forces*, I have been presuming that the relevant long-playing recording is the American configuration. The British release features the track "Sunday's Best," deleted in order to make room for "(What's So Funny 'Bout) Peace, Love and Understanding." (Cataloguing the minutiae of British life as reflected in Sunday tabloids, "Sunday's Best" was deemed too "English" for Americans.) To say which configuration is better is to evaluate. This ranking requires a limited framework of distinct criteria.

For example, many rock fans (as opposed to "pop" fans) apply a criterion drawn from the aesthetics of romanticism: the best music draws from "the deep place where new and unexpected feelings burst through."[29] Music critics Paul Williams and Clinton Heylin treat this criterion as the primary basis for judging Bob Dylan's work. Consequently, Heylin evaluates the unreleased first version of *Blood on the Tracks* as superior to the released album. In rerecording six tracks, Dylan made the songs "less personal . . . compromising his art to tone down his previously naked pain."[30] Heylin even claims that the remake of "Tangled Up in Blue" succeeds because it "clearly retained its emotional connection" to Dylan's personal life—as if it had nothing to do with Kevin Odegard's advice to move the song from the key of E to A.[31] Forcing Dylan to reach for the notes, Odegard's *musical* advice contributes a great deal to Dylan's sense of emotional urgency. Bill Berg's drumming and Billy Peterson's bass line also contribute to the heightened expressive character of the performance. Like the decision to play it in the key of A, neither of these changes from the earlier sessions has anything to do with Dylan's personal life, yet Heylin posits that the new arrangement remains "connected" to Dylan's personal life. If one dogmatically insists that self-expression is central to artistry, one might agree with Heylin that the more polished version of *Blood on the Tracks* is an artistic travesty. However, fans who've heard the "original" album usually regard the reworked, less personal version as the superior one. Highly personal work is not always the aesthetically richest and most interesting.

Even if I endorsed it as a guiding principle, I am not sure how the Romantic notion of personal self-disclosure helps in many cases. It does not help me to choose between the two versions of *Armed Forces*. Seeking a different evaluative principle, we might highlight the fact that Costello is a British musician. So the British release of *Armed Forces* might take the prize, since that configuration better reflects its British origins and obeys the principle of fidelity to the author's original wishes. Yet I prefer to *listen* to the American version, as the stronger set of songs. Depending on which criteria we prioritize, we generally reach different evaluative conclusions.

Cognitive Value and Appreciation

Appreciating *Armed Forces* involves an interest in the music's aesthetic properties, and appreciative listeners discern considerable aesthetic value in the experience of it. But perhaps *Armed Forces*, like *Pet Sounds*, falls at the "arty" end of the popular spectrum. What if aesthetic properties make a negligible contribution for most listeners of most popular music? If evaluation depends on knowing what experienced listeners typically attend to, an aesthetic evaluation of *Armed Forces* will be pointless if most listening is indifferent to its aesthetic dimension.

An emphasis on communication might undercut the appreciative stance. The primacy of content is endorsed by aesthetic cognitivism, which claims that aesthetic properties are instrumentally valuable for how they guide our thinking. They enhance the cognitive experience. Thus aesthetic value is subordinate to another function. However, we cannot paraphrase aesthetically rich symbols because their "aesthetic" dimension creates unusually dense and multireferential symbols.[32]

But what nonmusical knowledge do we gain by filling our lives with music? If the claim is the weak thesis that such value is *one* of music's values, then I have no quarrel with it. After all, most children learn the alphabet by learning to *sing* it. Other music offers us practical knowledge about our emotional lives, or instructs us in the emotions appropriate to various ideas. But art's cognitive value is generally an imaginative *exploring* of various symbols. We need not *endorse* art's messages.[33] Few people confuse imagining with believing, so exploration of symbols can be interesting without generating beliefs. My admiration of the Velvet Underground's "Heroin" and of Jimi Hendrix's version of "Hey Joe" does not, I hope, indicate my unconscious endorsement of drug addiction and the murder of unfaithful women. Their value is the way they direct an interested, imaginative response.

Aesthetic cognitivism is distinguished by the claim that music's symbolic function always takes evaluative precedence. Cognitivism runs into trouble when we remind ourselves that music is genuinely multifunctional. The debate cannot be reduced to a choice between the relative value of attending to aesthetic properties for the sake of the experience and doing so for the sake of enhanced thinking about some nonmusical content. In the same way that different aesthetic properties become salient according to one's interpretation of any given song, different ones emerge in experiences that put the same music to different uses—rhythms that enhance a dance floor can feel hideously oppressive when you're sitting in a dental chair.

Aside from any meanings that songs have, popular music often serves the basic function of providing a rhythm or pulse for extramusical activity, or perhaps even for a common mode of life.[34] Consider the enormous body of music that is "popular" without being *consciously* sought out. Contemporary life offers "musics that are always there, beyond our control, slipping under our thresholds of consciousness."[35] Consider the many varieties of "mood music" and "elevator music," the background music played in virtually every retail space and in most professional environments.[36] The "musics heard most by the most people every day" generally regulate emotional tone or the pace of activity, aside from any function they may serve in communicating status or serving another cognitively useful function.[37]

Another important function of music is providing dance rhythms. "Oliver's Army," the single from *Armed Forces,* qualifies neatly. It is the best-selling single in Costello's career, yet it is unlikely that most of those who danced to it in the clubs or sang along on the radio knew that the title refers to Oliver Cromwell and the song as a whole explores the lingering effects of British military imperialism in the postcolonial period. Functionally, "Oliver's Army" works as a dance tune, and its melody and arrangement attract casual listeners who have no idea about Costello's intentions. For those who grasp the words, the result is an ironic tension. Cognitivism can now respond, of course, that dancing is a symbolic activity, so listeners who failed to grasp the irony got less value from it than it offers, for they oversimplified what it communicates.

A different argument against this version of aesthetic cognitivism emphasizes that we can appreciate aesthetic properties of the natural environment without taking them to be symbolic. Many people adopt a parallel stance toward instrumental music that lacks a guiding text or program. This perspective is often directed at classical music, but there is no shortage of such music in the popular realm—a great deal of it, if we count jazz as a species of popular music, including two very accessible and influential jazz recordings, Miles Davis's *Kind of Blue* and Keith Jarrett's *The Köln Concert.*

But unless we are engaging in a strange imaginative exercise that ignores the human presence in *Armed Forces,* we hear it as a communicative artifact, rich in symbolism. Perhaps it is possible to interpret every one of its aesthetic properties as relevant or irrelevant in terms of symbolic function. However, this idea runs up against the fact that popular music is extraordinarily repetitive.[38] If a song is a symbol, it seems to repeat the same message again and again and again. This redundancy is intolerable when we are primarily interested in meanings. Yet our heightened interest in relatively small variations—and, with improvised blues, cover versions, and most jazz, more complex ones—suggests an interest in communicative *means* as much as in whatever is being communicated. So when listeners attend to music in categories they understand, attention seems to fall in the wrong place for cognitive value to be the primary value.[39] Subsuming all aesthetic value under cognitive value strikes me as incorrect, therefore, for neglecting the rewards of the experience valued simply as an experience, apart from any cognitive benefits that might accrue.

A more plausible version of aesthetic cognitivism emphasizes the *general* cognitive benefits of listening to music. But this external perspective is indifferent to the particularity that interests appreciative listeners. To find out if aesthetic properties are important in a particular case, we need to know what listeners with a taste for such music attend to when they listen to it. Are aesthetic properties important to the experience? Returning to Elvis Costello, I defer to Greil Marcus. Appreciation of *Armed Forces* involves perceiving its overall sound as "suppressed, claustrophobic, twitching." Although many of the melodies are catchy and hummable, "it's soon clear that just below the messy, nervous surface of the music is a very stark and specific vision."[40] His description of the record makes it clear that he does not recommend it as entertainment. Its power is related to its serious treatment of complex issues, its major theme being the insidious effects of "secret, unspeakable realities of political life" upon our most personal relationships. But its impact is largely a matter of Costello's aural choices in expressing his lyrical themes. An interest in representational content does not necessarily compete with an aesthetic interest. In the song "Green Shirt," his voice "bites out a defense," then becomes "a sensitive, rushed lover's plaint," culminating a cry of "hysteria."[41] Marcus is not a critic who dwells on the musical constructions generating these effects, but *Armed Forces* is Costello's leap forward in exploiting harmonic devices to achieve communicative ends. The musical details of "Hand in Hand," another writer observes, are crucial to the song's ironic tone, "most notably in the one-dimensional, almost mock-triumphant repetition of I-V-I harmonies (particularly the final martial anticipation of I) and the long subdominant (chord IV) pedal, ensuring that the final coda is overprepared."[42]

Marcus primarily values *Armed Forces* as an opportunity to reflect on the issues that gradually emerge as one comes to understand it. In short, he recommends it for its cognitive import. But he also regards it as an object of aesthetic interest: *talking* about *Armed Forces* is no substitute for *experiencing* it. I take it that Marcus wants us, as readers of his analysis, to listen to the recording, hearing it anew in light of his suggested interpretation. Yet there is no invitation to reflect on the music's conformity to any general standards for such music. (Earlier in the chapter we saw that Marcus adopts the same stance with Dylan's "Like a Rolling Stone.")

It will be objected that this appreciative reception is a cognitive experience—the pleasure of the music depends on its communicating certain themes and its expressively commenting on those themes. In short, it will be argued that the "aesthetic" appreciation of *Armed Forces* is really a "reading" of its very complex cognitive import.

My response is brief. In chapter 1, I offered reasons to reject the two most common approaches to distinguishing aesthetic value from cognitive value. First, I do not believe that we should treat *Armed Forces* like forty minutes of absolute music. Second, I do not agree with the proposal that an aesthetic appreciation of *Armed Forces* necessarily incorporates an appeal to its *artistic* value, that is, an explicit or even implicit understanding of it as a work of art.[43]

So I have staked out a narrow ground for saying that the value of *Armed Forces* is not equivalent to the cognitive purposes it serves. Appreciation is not in conflict with an interest in a message. It is not a detached interest in pure structures. It is not an interest in the exemplification of specific artistic values. It is not an interest in a purely sensuous kaleidoscope of sound (as such, a great deal of rock music is harsh, ugly, and distinctly unpleasant). So where do I locate its aesthetic value? Although cognitive content is a timeless morsel that I can extract from the experience, each of my experiences of *Armed Forces* occupies a particular stretch of time in my life. What I primarily value about it is the transitory experiences I can have of it, not some fixed content that I take away from it. The album has aesthetic instrumental value because it provides the opportunity for aesthetic value that arises from (and is restricted to) an internal perspective on particular experiences of it.

When music has a cognitive value, however minimal, appreciation is enriched by an exploration of how well suited the aural object is for conveying its cognitive element. To borrow Nelson Goodman's formulation, our "primary purpose is cognition in and for itself," and we relish the "apprehension and formulation of what is to be communicated" in the use of symbols.[44] Attending to the formulation as well as the message, appreciation discovers value in the way that particular aesthetic properties support various cognitive purposes. With *Armed Forces,* that includes admiration for the clarity and force with which the sounds embody the cognitive content. (Clarity and force are *perceived* in the listening experience.) An appreciative audience attends to the *sensuous* display of any content that might be found there, cognitive or otherwise.[45] With *Armed Forces,* we feel the tension in the interplay of the chipper melodies, the staccato punctuation of the percussion, and the dark, ugly mood of the stories Costello narrates: Kafka by way of Abba.

Finally, the American configuration offers the climactic release of the final song, "(What's So Funny 'Bout) Peace Love and Understanding." In the album's one burst of unmitigated joy, Costello eschews the irony of Brinsley Schwarz's original version of the song. Its surging pulse and exuberant vocal are a burst of sunlight following the dark bile that has come before. Within the context of albums or compact disc sequencing, combinations or groupings of songs take on a complexity that cannot be predicted from their qualities when taken as individual songs. On its own, Costello's cover of "What's So Funny" is a blast of uncomplicated, feel-good rock and roll. In the context of *Armed Forces,* its roaring rejection of easy cynicism is deeply moving, largely through its sharp contrast with the bitterness of the self-described "emotional fascism" leading up to it. To endorse the aesthetic value of this sequence is to recommend the experience it facilitates.

Functionality and Value

My second general point about evaluation and appreciation is that the aesthetic dimension of any given piece of popular music does not exhaust everything relevant in *evaluating* it. I have suggested that the transition from appreciation to instrumental evaluation requires a decision about which criteria are most important for comparing one case to another.[46] These criteria operate as general standards that should prevent us from valuing music improperly by regarding it too highly ("Janis Joplin's performance of 'Ball and Chain' is the greatest blues singing ever!") or dismissing it too quickly ("All rap music is just a load of noise").

At this point, I might be expected to say that comparisons can only be made between two things in the same category, sharing a common function, and that the primary function of *Armed Forces* is to be an object of appreciation. So, generalizing from that case, we should evaluate popular music in terms of that function. Unfortunately, that sounds suspiciously like an endorsement of the traditional criterion employed to endorse music *as art,* which is just what I do not want to assume.[47]

Instead, suppose that we return to the core idea of "everyday" aesthetics. Every experience is a candidate for aesthetic value. Music does not become aesthetic by moving it from functional situations to art settings—that merely changes the parameters of the experience that might be aesthetically valued. Suppose I sit still in a chair for twelve minutes while I listen intently to Sinéad O'Connor's 2002 recording of the ballad "Lord Baker." Attending closely to the subtleties of her singing as she relates the redemptive story of love lost and regained, I am deeply moved. I appreciate the intense experience it offers. Suppose that I leave the compact disc in the changer and play it again while preparing dinner with my wife, who likes to sing along to this album. On nights when making dinner feels like a chore, the right music lightens the task. Although this second experience of O'Connor's music is not *as* focused on the music, the music interacts with other elements of the experience, infusing the environment with rhythms and expressive textures that it would otherwise lack.[48] Circumstances might come together in a way that, when I reflect on the experience, I find that the confluence of music, chore, and my wife's company is, experientially, the highlight of my day and of value for its own sake.

Once we give up the old idea that aesthetic value cannot be combined with other sorts of value, many social situations can be recognized as aesthetically valuable. Music frequently contributes to such value. Our aesthetic manipulations of our lived environments don't end with our visual decorating.[49] Either way, as foreground or background, music is often chosen for its expected contribution to an environment. If that experience is aesthetically valued, then the music has instrumental value for that context.

When Marcus claims that *Rubber Soul* is the best Beatles album, his comparison presupposes that Beatles albums share commensurable values, that is, each can be judged according to the degree that it possesses the same specifiable features. But we settle nothing by observing that two pieces of music are instrumentally good for furnishing aesthetic value. Beatles albums are valued for diverse reasons, and it is a mistake to suppose that they are all valuable in the same way (as, say, serious and complex aural constructs) or used in the same ways by everyone. We value different performers, songs, and recordings for different reasons, and the same ones for different reasons on different occasions. Some of these occasions encourage more attention to aesthetic values than do others. Dahlhaus proposes that a similar multifunctionality was the norm for art music until "the romantic period," at which point composers increasingly deprived their music of functionality for naive listeners.[50] Unless one is engaging in the extreme case of treating a piece of popular music as a self-contained world, music's multiple functions require consideration of various merits and demerits in relation to human activities.[51]

It is doubtful that there is either a distinctive or a unifying function for recent popular music. As Peter Wicke notes, "Rock'n'roll also broke the conventional functional pattern of popular music forms. Before, popular music had mainly been based on dance and entertainment. Rock had a nonspecific accompanying and background function for all possible activities."[52] The music has multiple functions, many of them unknown to the musicians in advance of the music's use. In other words, the criterion "It has a good beat and you can dance to it" is only part of the story; Jimi Hendrix's "Purple Haze" was poorly received on *American Bandstand* in 1967 by a review panel of teenagers, yet it is one of rock's most sublime achievements. No one could have predicted in 1977 that Fleetwood Mac's "Don't Stop (Thinking About Tomorrow)" would become a theme song of President Clinton's 1992 campaign. And who would have guessed, in the early years of MTV, that Cyndi Lauper's "Girls Just Wanna Have Fun" (1984) would accompany a 1997 television commercial for communications giant AT&T in order to sell teleconferencing services to career women with children? Who, in the early 1970s, would have predicted that Led Zeppelin's recording of "Rock and Roll" would supply the music for television advertisements for luxury cars in the twenty-first century?

Even within a functional category, such as dance, there is no privileged set of features that will fulfill that function, for dance is itself a range of quite different things. Chuck Willis was the "King of the Stroll" in the 1950s, but his signature tunes were not functional if one wanted to dance the hand jive or, in subsequent decades, do the twist or the hustle or break-dance.

Many popular music functions are far less obvious than providing background music or a certain sort of dance beat. Although it may appear that the adulation and hysteria of the Beatles' female fans reflected prevailing gender expectations at the height of Beatlemania, in hindsight some of these fans have come to see their adolescent behavior as resistive rather than submissive. Behaviors such as declaring allegiance to a "favorite Beatle" may appear to echo traditional gender expectations of paring with one male; in reality, the young women were actually *identifying with* the strength and independence of pop stars, in a way that they could not identify with their male peers. And the screaming, crying, and fainting that female fans displayed in response to concert and television appearances were at odds with the decorum and passivity expected of young ladies; by responding to males who were safely out of reach, they found a way to act on sexual feelings that they were otherwise expected to deny. In short, the Beatles' music served multiple nonaesthetic functions for their female fans, some of them distinct from the functions served for male fans.[53]

This is not to say that *all* popular music is equally multifunctional. Greil Marcus relates being in a bar in Hawaii in 1981: when Bob Dylan's "Like a Rolling Stone" came over the FM radio station carried by the sound system, "feet began moving, conversations died. Everyone *listened,* and everyone looked a bit more alive when the last notes faded. It was a stunning moment: irrefutable proof that 'Like a Rolling Stone' cannot be used as Muzak."[54] It is not particularly good for dancing, either. What "Like a Rolling Stone" is mostly good for is attentive listening. Marcus's anecdote is an important reminder that the appreciation of popular music is, at least some of the time, strikingly of a piece with the listening posture thought to be most appropriate for serious music. Popular music is *not always* a background to other activities. Gordon Graham offers this description of music's special character: "music is the 'foregrounding' of sound, the bringing to primary attention sound itself . . . and aural experience becomes the focus of interest in its own right."[55] However, Graham is discussing music that is art. Popular music is only *sometimes* the focus of aural interest in its own right.

In observing that "Like a Rolling Stone" is better for attentive listening than as background music, Marcus undermines his own claim that Dylan's *Highway 61 Revisited* is "the best rock 'n' roll album ever made." Because popular music is multifunctional, there are multiple standards for assigning instrumental value to any given piece of popular music. Each use requires its own evaluation. For example, I carry a pocketknife that has one blade that is both a screwdriver and a bottle opener. Is it good? It is a good bottle opener but a poorly designed screwdriver. Similarly, music that is very good relative to one use might be very bad relative to another. Because appreciation attends to the fit between design and use, different contexts of use will change assignments of aesthetic value, too.[56]

In chapter 3, I argued that different categories of music establish overlapping frameworks that inform listening. A piece of music normally belongs to multiple musical categories. When a piece of music has multiple functions, each function locates the music in a category with perceptually similar music that performs that same function. Music that is impressive as an instance of one category can be woeful as an instance of another. So we should expect a single piece of music to have multiple aesthetic values. Describing the merits of Captain Beefheart's *Trout Mask Replica,* Langdon Winner remarks, "If the purpose of a phonograph record is to soothe us, to provide a beat for dancing, a pulse for making love, a set of themes to reassure us in the joys and troubles of life's daily commerce, then *Trout Mask* fails utterly."[57] In other ways, he thinks it is marvelous.

Extending this idea, there is no question that Madonna's early albums are complex expressions of third-wave feminism. They are also dance music.[58] Depending on the function, different properties emerge as more salient. But as Winner observes about *Trout Mask Replica,* an aesthetically rich political gesture may be relatively weak dance music. Conversely, what is very good as dance music may or may not be aesthetically interesting as political theater. Madonna's first three singles, "Everybody," "Physical Attraction," and "Holiday," are prime examples. If we add a third function, such as working as the auditory portion of a music video, music that is less suitable for a dance floor—Madonna's "Like a Prayer" is a good candidate—contributes forcefully to the impact of a music video. So the same music often requires multiple aesthetic evaluations, one for each anticipated function.

Suppose we simplify the problem by adopting Simon Frith's proposal that three social functions are central to the value of popular music: "in the creation of identity, in the management of feelings, in the organization of time."[59] Again, each function might call different features into play. A sin-

gle piece of popular music can readily yield multiple instrumental evaluations, each of which also yields a distinct aesthetic evaluation. But when
multiple functions generate multiple aesthetic evaluations of a single thing,
we have no basis for placing all of them in the same overarching category
for purposes of aesthetic evaluation. There is no single function for the category of "rock and roll album," so there is no ultimate or privileged category in which Dylan's *Highway 61 Revisited* (or any other album) is best.
Since we cannot pretend that it has only one function, we oversimplify
Rubber Soul in calling it the best Beatles album. Such claims may be fun to
argue about, but the arguments have no hope of clear resolution.

To sum up: some listeners value rock music as an opportunity for aesthetic appreciation. But even when they do, there is more than one standard
for aesthetically evaluating the same music. Popular music is intended to
have diverse functions. Different standard criteria apply to the same music as
it serves different functions in different contexts. As a consequence, the
same music is instrumentally valuable for facilitating multiple experiences
that have different levels of aesthetic value. The question is whether these
multiple standards are reasonable when considered from an impartial perspective. My intuition is that they generally are. Recognizing this diversity,
we should refrain from evaluating popular music by appeal to a uniform set
of evaluative principles.

To complicate matters yet again, none of this yet speaks to ongoing
debates about the relative values of broad categories of music.

The Value of a Taste for a Musical Style

Popular music is still widely regarded as inferior to classical music. Some
attacks on popular music are launched by critics who cannot be bothered to
make comparative evaluations of individual instances. Their sweeping dis-
missals are external evaluations. One can know the value in developing a
sense of humor while feeling sorry for someone who only laughs at slap-
stick. Similarly, one might contend that it is good to learn to appreciate
music but unfortunate if one wastes one's time on popular music. Furthermore, there can be internal parallels, as when we regard our actual tastes as
sources of "guilty" pleasures. There is no inconsistency in saying that popular music is trash while granting that Costello's *Armed Forces* is better than
his *Goodbye Cruel World*.

I will focus on Alan H. Goldman's version of the position that "some tastes (and correlatively some genres of art) are better than others."[60] He argues that rock music is the clear loser in comparison with classical music. Goldman evaluates broad categories of music by postulating the sorts of responses they would elicit for the *ideal* listener. A genre or musical form's value is to be measured by evaluating the experiences it offers ideal listeners. Generalizing from the value of experiences with individual instances when we consider "the total experience of the works," Goldman contends that those who appreciate Mozart have "better taste" than those who prefer rock music. A better taste is a more mature, more discriminating taste. It favors rich, challenging works whose significance is "durable."[61] So much the worse for the Ramones and their rallying cry, "Gabba Gabba Hey!"

This analysis incorporates a central premise of my own view, which is the idea that developing a taste for rock (as one's preferred type of music listening) interferes with developing a taste for classical music. This is distinct from saying that a taste for rock as *incompatible* with a taste for classical. Violin prodigy Leila Josefowicz has recorded Bartók's Sonata for Solo Violin, yet she has a passion for the music of U2. Most people develop a taste for some kinds of music at the expense of all others, for we do not live long enough or gain enough experience to attain the status of ideal listeners. I don't know if Josefowicz is equally passionate about Tejano music and Balinese gamelan, but there comes a point in every life where one is merely dabbling.

A comparison can be made with the rewards of friendship. Friendship presupposes partiality—another person is not your friend if she means no more to you than a stranger who lives on the other side of the world. Musical tastes also presuppose partiality. Josefowicz could not be said to have musical *tastes* if she eliminated all partiality. Yet that is what we expect of the ideal listener.

By definition, the ideal listener possesses the background knowledge needed to grasp any music.[62] The odd thing is that this listener is positioned to compare and evaluate any two pieces of music, but it is not clear that an ideal listener would ever find any music *interesting*. Unlike ordinary listeners, no additional background knowledge is ever acquired by listening to music. Presumably, the ideal listener knows this about herself. But then an ideal listener cannot *appreciate* music, for she has no need to experience the music. She will always have the same response. Musical taste is important in human life precisely because we are not ideal listeners. "If everything was black and white and written in stone," the Grateful Dead's Jerry Garcia once noted about music, "it wouldn't be that interesting to me."[63] Because we live in time, we individually and collectively discover new categories of music and new uses for existing music. Ideal listeners are "above" the lived experiences that ground the exploratory response that characterizes the process of appreciation.

Finally, appeals to an ideal listener do not really do the job that they set out to do. The ideal listener is supposed to support the judgment that one musical genre is better than another, or one performer is better than another. However, we have no access to ideal listeners. We only have access to real ones, all of whom have a partial experience of music. Some of these listeners are understood to be nearer to the ideal than other, depending on their approximation to the breadth and depth of experience required of the ideal listener. But if they regard one thing as better than another—*Rubber Soul* as better than *Revolver* and Memphis soul music as superior to Motown—then they can aptly be described as having a preference for one over the other. Recognizing this, the appeal to the ideal listener asks the less qualified among us to set aside our own partiality in favor of the ideal listener's preferences. However, the ideal listeners are not expected to set aside their own partiality! So appealing to an ideal listener employs a double standard.[64]

Rejecting the ideal listener is neither an embrace of ignorance nor the equality of all tastes. Education influences taste—but we must be careful not to equate "education" with formal education. Samuel Lipman blames multiple factors for the "current weakened condition" of the audience for classical music. Chief among them is "the destruction of classical-music education in elementary and secondary schools . . . [and] the calamitously large availability of meretricious pop music."[65] The mean age of the classical music audience is inching upward because children come of age in a world saturated with popular music. Individuals who might have been supporters of the classical repertoire are instead paying huge sums to see Madonna and the Rolling Stones in concert, while the next generation of listeners downloads a hodgepodge of music from the Internet. That is to say, popular music is a cultural *rival* to traditional high culture, replicating within itself a full hierarchy of tastes, from lowbrow to highbrow. Increasing exposure to classical music in the schools is unlikely to alter most people's leisure activity. Literature remains a staple subject in every high school in America, but the voluntary reading of literature continues its sharp decline.

So is it better to have a taste for classical music? One can recognize the cultural competition for the hearts and minds of listeners without belittling popular music. Two crucial steps are required to move us from the recognition of this competition to the normative conclusion that popular music's ascendance is an unfortunate victory. First, we must think that the two fields of music fulfill at least some of the same functions (i.e., that they exemplify some commensurable values). Second, that it makes better sense to support classical music as our means to fulfilling those functions, *all things considered*. My earlier discussion grants the first, at least insofar as both kinds of music are instrumentally valuable objects of appreciation. I will challenge the second.

Even if popular and classical music are similar enough to serve parallel functions, particularly in providing objects for appreciation, the very fact of their rivalry suggests that they constitute relatively independent musical cultures. All of my discussion about internal evaluation presumes that I have been talking about music's value to appreciative listeners for whom it sounds like a "natural" musical language. To listen from within a culture is to adjust one's listening to the kind of music heard, to understand it with historically appropriate listening habits, and to listen imaginatively, with the expectations or imaginative projections appropriate to the style of music in question.[66] It is, in short, to belong to a specific musical culture demanding distinct cultural capital.[67]

Evaluating popular music with understanding normally demands less cultural capital than listening to Bach's *Goldberg Variations* with understanding. Yet even a relatively superficial piece of pop music fluff demands considerably more cultural capital than an hour playing jump rope or Go Fish. The situation is *not* that classical music yields its rewards only to those who acquire the right cultural capital, with no cultural capital needed to enjoy what's popular. No music is of aesthetic value except in light of appropriate cultural capital. The phrasing, intonation, instrumentation, and aesthetic properties of a musical performance are meaningful only to those for whom such features *matter*. As Patricia Herzog puts it, musical meaning "exists in an intentional space created by the critical or evaluative interests of the listener."[68] Like musical meaning, music's aesthetic value is a function of its use by appropriately knowledgeable and engaged listeners.

The issue of any musical category's general value therefore turns on the question of which cultural capital to acquire. Even an ideal listener must possess cultural capital. But since there are no standard principles underlying all evaluation and since aesthetic properties are response-dependent, the ideal listener must be quite indifferent concerning *which* cultural capital to possess and what sort of taste to develop. Provided that two musical traditions offer varying degrees of challenge and richness "of the perceptual, affective, and cognitive experience they afford,"[69] there is no clear difference in their general value as objects for such activity. Provided one does not load the theoretical dice by assuming that only harmonically complex music can offer such experiences, popular music appears to satisfy the aesthetic needs of the ideal listener. I explore this topic at greater length in the next two chapters.

Debates about the general value of a musical culture are not carried out among ideal listeners. The aesthetic and cognitive rewards of comprehending a particular piece of music are only two elements in the broad decision frame needed to determine the comparative value of two musical cultures. We must consider factors that have no direct relevance for comparative evaluations within a tradition.

Value as Choice and as Importance

Measuring value by appeal to an ideal listener ignores the broader sociocultural context in which choices are made. I have no quarrel with the position that everyone should listen to rich, challenging music whose significance is durable. Yet nothing at all follows about "Like a Rolling Stone" or *Armed Forces* or about people who value them, or at least nothing follows until we know a good deal more about the people in question.

The final stage of my analysis relates these points to the distinction between something's value and its importance to specific persons.[70] Value can be assigned impersonally, from an external perspective, by determining how well a thing meets standards for the sort of thing that it is. When guided by appropriate principles, an evaluation can be granted by anyone who learns to apply the appropriate standards. Computer programs impersonally evaluate and rank applicants for bank loans by crunching numbers. Humans can learn to grade apples apart from liking apples. Not liking apples, I might recognize and yet be indifferent to the fact that the apples on sale at the market are top quality fruit. Similarly, I know music students who learn to analyze and evaluate the scores of Beethoven's piano sonatas while quite indifferent to such music. Evaluation ignores questions of *who* is going to want the things being evaluated (whether apples or music), what they will do with them, and what specific situation those persons will occupy when using them.

So we have already set the stage for a distinction between value and importance, reflecting the disparity between an impersonal sense of value (in which anyone can agree that a certain thing is of high value under specified criteria) and a personal sense (in which only some people find such things important). For example, when Dave Marsh ranks *Armed Forces* as better than *This Year's Model,* he is doing more than expressing his personal preference. He offers reasons for his recommendations. He's engaging in internal instrumental evaluation that presupposes a very limited scope of comparison. But Marsh also advises readers that the progressive rock band Emerson Lake and Palmer is "hapless," and that "you're better off listening to classical (or 'serious') music" instead of progressive rock. At this point, he's changed the subject.[71]

Notice Marsh's shift from an internal to an external perspective, from evaluating *things* to examining the *activity of valuing those things.* No one else can find *my* experience of *Armed Forces* valuable for its own sake, but others in my neighborhood certainly find my activity of painting my house to be either more or less desirable, depending on the color I choose. Similarly, others might have any number of reasons to think my activity of listening to Elvis Costello is a good or bad activity.

Saying "you're better off listening to classical" than progressive rock is a prescriptive judgment that one ought to like a certain style or genre of music. But this judgment seems completely empty unless it also prescribes changing one's tastes if one does not currently appreciate that music.[72] What are the grounds for this proposal? Notice also that the shift in evaluative focus can be repeated for any music. Marsh and I value *Armed Forces.* Ought we to engage in the activity of listening to it? Would we both be better off listening to classical music? It is not *the music* that needs justification. What requires justification is a general pattern of listening.

Marsh sees that he has to ground his evaluation in something more than his personal response to progressive rock. Although Marsh "hates" such music, he sees that he needs some additional grounds to support his shift to an external evaluation that denigrates its audience. Employing a version of the social relevance thesis, he posits a nonaesthetic appeal for progressive rock. Its attraction depends on the mistaken "presumption that art and culture move in a ladder-like process of 'progress' in the first place."[73] Progressive rock encourages a false belief about art and culture, and we're better off without it. But why does that make classical music the alternative to progressive rock? If the point is to avoid the ideology of progress, perhaps listeners of progressive rock should listen to ancient musical traditions that do not lend themselves to ideas of musical progress—the traditional "classical" music of India might be just the thing. But then there would be no reason to give up progressive rock for classical music, for one could learn one's lesson in another way. Unless, of course, Marsh is assuming that Emerson Lake and Palmer's classical sources, such as Mussorgsky's *Pictures at an Exhibition,* are just *better* than anything in progressive rock.

Not every valuable cultural product can be equally important to everyone. Nor *should* it be. We must avoid the hasty inference from a work's being instrumentally valuable to the conclusion that anyone who listens to music ought to value that music. But aesthetic value does not exhaust the value of great music. The splendors of Mozart's *Jupiter* symphony (No. 41 in C major) might be *a* reason to want to listen to Mozart, but symphonic richness is merely one of several factors to consider. Because different musics involve distinct cultural capital, the best music of the classical tradition need not be important to (or valued by) listeners immersed in another tradition.

So what standard shall we adopt for evaluating an individual's activity of valuing? I have nothing original to offer here. What we need is another impartial standard, additional to the standards for internal evaluations of specific works. It cannot be "loaded" with assumptions that will automatically favor what the evaluator favors. To adopt a recent criterion of impartiality, something is justified when it meets "a test of interpersonal reflective endorsability from a suitably impartial point of view."[74] It is not enough to have standards or principles securing the interpersonal dimension of evaluation. If two people are in a position to agree on the range of aesthetic properties present in *Armed Forces,* they have obtained the interpersonal dimension. We must also reflectively determine whether it makes sense for the individual to internalize those standards and to value the things valued.

Elizabeth Anderson emphasizes that because individuals have "different talents, temperaments, interests, opportunities, and relations to others," different persons should "adopt or uphold different ideals" out of all those that make sense for various persons to adopt.[75] Let us grant the value of professional sports. Given the demands of professional basketball, it can be shown that a particular athlete, such as Michael Jordan, is a superb basketball player. Jordan has skills that demand the admiration of those who see how he contributes to the sport. However, given the concrete situation of her life, it makes little or no sense for a child growing up within a traditional Mayan family in rural Guatemala *to take a personal interest* in either professional basketball or in Michael Jordan. Nobody supposes that she should find these things important, despite their very genuine value in accordance with reasonable standards, for she is not suitably situated to make any choices relating to such evaluations.

Similarly, standards for evaluating popular music will only have importance for those who have a personal investment in the continuation of that musical culture. Many people possess the cultural capital to have rich musical experiences with rock, country, or hip-hop, and insufficient cultural capital to discuss the relative merits of Bach's *Goldberg Variations* and Mozart's *Jupiter* symphony. Defenders of classical music fail to evaluate the popular audience from a suitably external, impartial point of view. Perhaps they confuse their own (quite reasonable) indifference to the music's value with something else, namely its relative lack of value. But once we allow that a type of music can be an object of appreciation, there is nothing irrational or unreasonable about its importance to persons suitably situated to take a personal interest in it. The same holds for its lack of appeal to others (e.g., lovers of classical music and Guatemalan peasants). But is this a *justification* of popular taste? Not in itself.

The remaining step is to block attempts to justify a taste culture *in general*. A standard is only justified to the degree that it makes sense for specific persons to care about it, relative to the actual circumstances in which their decisions are situated. What remains is to decide what justifies a personal investment in a specific musical culture.

Any such justification must consider the circumstances framing the decision to listen regularly to a type of music. My sympathies are with Will Kymlicka's observation: "it's only through having a rich and secure cultural structure that people can become aware . . . of the options available to them, and intelligently examine their value."[76] But how often are individuals in a position to choose their musical tastes? Cultural choices always arise against an existing context of choice, and one's cultural heritage is the most basic such context. Options concerning taste generally arise *after* one has acquired considerable cultural capital. While we may criticize a culture and wish for its improvement, and may criticize an individual's choices *within* a culture, there are seldom reasons that would persuade an impartial judge to endorse a wholesale rejection of an individual's "home" culture. Like it or not, increasing numbers of people occupy a cultural space dominated by mass media and interactions between previously segregated cultures and subcultures. Their tastes are effortlessly informed by mass art, and they are well situated to hear, use, and appreciate popular music. It is the nearly ubiquitous soundtrack to contemporary consumer culture. A polyglot product of that very situation, popular music "naturally" meets the aesthetic and communicative needs of people who want music suitable for multiple, everyday uses in a consumer culture. As such, popular music has a stronger claim on contemporary taste than classical.

Nonetheless, some people contend that everyone should internalize the values of classical music. Peter Kivy observes that what is most significant about the classical tradition is the flowering of *absolute music*.[77] Many champions of classical music want people to transcend their ordinary expectations about music and its role in everyday life in order to reap the unique rewards of absolute music. That is, they think it best for everyone to endorse the ideals of autonomous music and to join them in preferring music whose appeal is "timeless," transcultural, purely musical, and independent of the social situation of the audience. But it is not clear that everyone currently rewarded by the very real merits of popular music will reap an equivalent reward from absolute music. The process of acquiring a taste for such music (involving personal investment in a new and complex set of evaluative standards) flies in the face of contemporary culture. So it is hardly obvious that impartial judges would routinely recommend acquisition of a taste for classical music on that basis. (Appealing to nonunique rewards does not help, for they are duplicated by much other music.)

The acquisition of a taste for the absolute music of the classical tradition remains an option for many people, but more often as an auxiliary than as a primary source of aesthetic reward. Impartial judges would hardly take the literary merits of William Shakespeare, Alexander Pope, and John Milton as a reason for every college student to major in English literature. At best, a case could be made that everyone in the English-speaking world should have some acquaintance with those authors, if only to be aware of an important element of their cultural heritage. Likewise, we might urge some exposure to the instrumental music of Mozart and Beethoven on educated Europeans and, to a lesser extent, Americans. But this is a far stretch from concluding that everyone should invest in the cultural capital that would lead them to *prefer* those authors to current authors or classical music to contemporary popular music.

Actually, I have been too generous in my argument. Thinking about the thousands of students I have taught, I doubt that it matters that they are exposed to Shakespeare, Pope, and Milton. A superficial exposure convinces most students that it's not to their "taste" even when they are in no position to appreciate it. Students do not need exposure to specific writers. They need experiential validation of the claim that literature, *any* literature, offers an aesthetically valuable experience. But like classical music, leisure reading is losing favor as a vehicle for such experience. Regarding music, I am likewise pessimistic about putting more resources into music teaching aimed at getting everyone ready for Beethoven's late string quartets.

So I will end with Mary Mothersill, who observes that "someone who had the opportunity to become acquainted with [Beethoven's first Rasumovsky quartet] and who deemed it valueless would be making a mistake. Such error is not culpable but sad: it is a pity (life being what it is) to miss what can be an inexhaustible source of joy."[78] But it is not a life without *that quartet* that would be pitiable. We certainly do not pity Bach and Mozart, who never heard it.

Consider any three people. I'll choose three. Patti Smith, poet and rock musician, loves the poetry of Arthur Rimbaud and the music of Jimi Hendrix. The producer of her first album, John Cale, loves the paintings of René Magritte and the poetry of Dylan Thomas. Mary Mothersill, author of *Beauty Restored,* loves Beethoven quartets and the novel *Madame Bovary.* There is no reason to look for any one work common to their lists of prized works. Agreement does not matter, Mothersill suggests, as long as "for everyone there is something . . . which he takes to be unequivocally beautiful and worthy of love and admiration."[79] I will go the next step. A human life devoid of beauty is pitiable. But I hope we all find aesthetic properties in addition to beauty. It does not matter which they are, or even if they are experienced through music, as long as for everyone there is something.

In sum, an individual's social, practical and personal concerns are not relevant to evaluating individual musical works, but they are quite relevant to evaluating an individual's musical tastes. Music's aesthetic value emerges when experiencing it. Its aesthetic rewards are generally limited to persons possessing appropriate cultural capital and to whom such music personally matters. Music's value is therefore a function of joining in a musical culture. On this matter I defer to Roger Scruton: "Our aesthetic preferences become values just as soon as . . . they become part of the attempt to create a place for ourselves in the world, and to situate ourselves among our fellows."[80] I part company with Scruton on the question of whether a taste for classical music is somehow obligatory for anyone in the twenty-first century. The classical tradition that reigned from the eighteenth century until the dawn of the twentieth is no longer our "natural" musical language.[81] The *ease* with which some music is enjoyed (reflecting ample opportunities to do so as well as the relative simplicity of the basic forms that must be understood) must not be misread as its triviality.

Arguments that champion classical music at the expense of popular music are ultimately criticisms of popular taste. But there is quite a leap from the real value of great music to the conclusion that everyone in our culture should value it. Such arguments downplay the degree to which the formation of taste is a function of the situation in which it is to be exercised. Elitist critics worry that popular music redirects cultural energy away from classical music. Unhappy that many of the musical achievements of the past do not matter to large numbers of people, their condescension is tinged with resentment. Because our choice of music involves knowledgeable participation in a particular form of life, because popular music provides a vibrant musical culture that speaks to the lived needs of its participants, and because an impartial judge would not advise most people to reorder their lives to acquire the cultural capital that would make classical music significant to their lives, we have good reason to think that, for many people, a taste for popular music is perfectly justified. Yet because we can distinguish better from worse instances of popular music, an aesthetic of popular listening does not imply that all such music is equally good.

5. The Ideas of Hearing and Listening

What is unaesthetic about popular art is its formlessness. It does not invite or even permit the sustained effort necessary to the creation of an artistic form. But it provides us with an illusion of achievement while in fact we remain passive.
—Abraham Kaplan, "The Aesthetics of the Popular Arts"

Hearing is the reception of a program heard by chance, admitted, sometimes even endured . . . Listening, on the contrary, involves a search for a program, a choice and maintained attention.
—Georges Friedmann, "Rôle et place de la musique dans une société industrielle"

A serious objection confronts the proposal that popular music has substantial aesthetic value. It is the lingering belief that popular music's aesthetic merit evaporates when we engage in genuinely appreciative listening.[1] Because this issue relates so directly to the notion of "listening," I will answer this objection in considerable detail over the course of this chapter.

This objection is frequently presented in order to ground a distinction between popular and serious music. If there are no aesthetic properties that distinguish popular music from serious music, there is nonetheless a widely endorsed account of the different listening strategies employed by their respective audiences. The key idea is that there are two distinct ways to respond to music, and the mode generally adopted for Mozart and Stravinsky differs from the mode employed in response to Chuck Berry, Shania Twain, and U2.

The doctrine does not require locating any distinctive features of two sets of cultural objects in order to divide them into two groups. Instead, they can be grouped according to their distinct modes of consumption. This is highly analogous to saying that there is a difference between spicy food and bland food, but there is no one thing that all spicy food has in common. Some spicy food is spicy because of one set of ingredients. Some is spicy because of another set. Although response-dependent, the distinction between spicy and bland is genuine—a fact that is familiar to anyone preparing food for strangers and wondering how spicy it should be. The difference lies in physiological and phenomenal responses that people have to food's ingredients. The distinction between popular and serious music has a long history of being handled in a similar manner, by positing a difference between active and passive consumption that corresponds to attending to different elements of the music. Historically, it has been presented as the difference between listening and hearing.

A Short History of the Distinction

Listening is usually characterized as a specifically aesthetic—disinterested yet imaginative—contemplation of selected portions of what is heard. It is characterized as demanding informed concentration on the structural qualities of the music. Furthermore, active listening is generally regarded as an exclusive activity. Basic texts on Western music often make pronouncements of this sort:

> We have to learn to *listen,* in the literal sense: to hear accurately and acutely, to differentiate between the various pitch levels, to recognize various rhythmic patterns, melodic ideas, and so on. This is difficult and requires the greatest concentration on the part of the listener. It cannot be emphasized too strongly that it is *impossible to listen to music while doing something else.*[2]

Jazz great Charles Mingus endorsed the exclusivity thesis: "If you listen to music, you can't be jackin' off, playin' with a girl or gettin' high. You have to concentrate on the music to say you heard it fully. Just because you can jump and dance don't mean you listen to the music."[3] In contrast, the paradigm of passive hearing is the instinctive and emotionally charged response of an infant or animal. Supposedly, their responses are to the sounds rather than to the sound structures.

I do not know when or where the distinction between active listening and passive hearing originated. Nor does it matter given my purposes, which are less historical than metacritical. It is enough to note that the distinction plays a central part in Eduard Hanslick's classic monograph, *On the Musically Beautiful* (1854), and in Edmund Gurney's mammoth *The Power of Sound* (1880). Refashioned in new jargon, succeeding generations have defended variations on Hanslick and Gurney. Let us begin with their work and then explore modifications of the doctrine in David Prall and Monroe C. Beardsley. The goal of this selective summary is to show that the distinction between hearing and listening has been employed to devalue various audience responses to music as irrelevant and even antithetical to listening, the mode allegedly required by better music. The "hearing but not listening" response is usually linked with music's capacity to express or manipulate emotion.

Hanslick quips that one "cannot help hearing the most deplorable street organ in front of our house, but not even a Mendelssohn symphony can compel us to listen."[4] He does not write like someone introducing a new distinction. He contrasts the pathological (passive) reaction of the average music enthusiast with the more valuable response of the informed, aesthetic (active) listener. For those who engage in the former, a symphony is no more significant than a good cigar or a warm bath. It lacks the *musical* significance that can only be had by attending to musical form. For the fortunate minority who are capable of listening, music provides an intense aesthetic enjoyment that can only be derived from anticipations and confirmations of the music's pattern as it unfolds in performance. In order for this process to take place in one's imagination while listening to a performance or reading a score, one must know the conventions of the relevant musical tradition.

Hanslick proposes that most people perceive all music as background, even in the concert hall when it is offered as the focus of attention and not as a mere element of their environment. In the concert hall, the pathological or passive listener slips "into a fuzzy state of supersensuously sensuous agitation determined only by the general character of the piece . . . while what is special in every composition, namely, its artistic individuality, escapes him."[5] Hanslick complains that the most "appreciative" members of the concert audience ignore musical form. If we play several similar but unfamiliar pieces, most people have precisely the same reception for each, with no discrimination as to better or worse. Behavior at concerts might be another source of evidence. At concerts of popular music, we might point to the number of people who arrive late in order to avoid the opening act, those who leave their seats to purchase more beer when the headlining act plays an unfamiliar song, and those who stop their conversations with friends only during the "greatest hits." The bulk of the audience wants to hear what they already know, suggesting that they don't want to listen too actively to the music. They respond to the presence of the musician and the familiarity of the sounds more than to the specifics of the performance as a unique performance of the music.

Gurney's *The Power of Sound* devotes an entire chapter to the two "ways of hearing," describing them as the definite and indefinite. Although he recasts the distinction by allowing that an emotional response implies that some understanding is taking place, Gurney continues to defend a limited mode of structural apprehension as the goal of focused listening.[6]

Gurney contends that while "the definite character of Music involv[es] the perception of individual melodic and harmonic combinations, the indefinite character involv[es] merely the perception of successions of agreeably-toned and harmonious sound."[7] With indefinite hearing, auditors neither notice nor remember what is distinctive about the music that is heard. Gurney postulates that each kind of listening rewards us with a distinct sort of pleasure. The basic distinction is then reformulated as a distinction between two types of listeners: the "naive" or instinctive is opposed to the educated, cultivated, or trained. Yet Gurney acknowledges that most listeners can engage in both types of response and most prefer the pleasure of the "definite effect" of active listening. Since almost no one counts exclusively as an "instinctive" hearer of music, what looks like two types of listeners is really a distinction between levels of education, corresponding modes of attention, and corresponding objects of concentration.

Although he is not discussed much anymore, Prall's work in aesthetics was influential through much of the twentieth century.[8] His work remains of interest for making explicit what is implicit in Hanslick and Gurney. Prall agrees that aesthetic response is more than mere sense perception. Successful composition exploits formal structure and offers more than an "elementary" aesthetic experience.[9] Yet artistic composition exploits the brute fact that some sensory qualities are intrinsically differentiated according to structuring relationships. Unlike tastes and smells, visuals and sound have "principles of ordered variation" that permit deliberate and comprehensible composition.[10] When intrinsically ordered elements combine, fresh properties are generated, namely structural relationships and designs. When we grasp a combination of sounds as an organized sequence in time (the horizontal axis of musical organization) or as a specific harmony (the vertical axis), we grasp melodic, rhythmic, and harmonic qualities that can then be abstracted from the specific elements embodying them. When one identifies this objective element in a combination of sounds, one has engaged in structural listening. Intellect, not sense perception, is rewarded.

The experience of music is firmly rooted in tacit or implicit knowledge of principles of relational structures. One need not acquire a technical vocabulary, but Prall cautions that a listener who cannot "distinguish minor thirds from majors . . . can not possibly discriminate either the melodic or the harmonic patterns that he hears." Consequently, "he does not in fact hear the actual music at all." Prall fully endorses the tradition of active listening with one's "full and active powers of attention."[11] He regards any pleasure or displeasure derived from the elements themselves as a subjective response, mere "hearing." On the surface, nothing in Prall's theory is hostile to popular music. By the time most people reach adolescence, they (and thus most popular music fans) possess all of the audiation skills listed by Prall, and will experience structural and corresponding emotional change in the music they enjoy.[12]

Acknowledging the influence of Hanslick, Gurney, and Prall, Beardsley seeks the "phenomenally objective features" that underlie genuine aesthetic value. Like the previous three, Beardsley proposes that only structural qualities can account for music's semantic dimension, including the "pervasive human qualities" that we read into a work's kinetic qualities.[13] Beardsley reasons that a musical work is an auditory design arising from "intrinsic relations" among the four basic qualities of sound. The four qualities of each sound are, of course, duration, intensity (volume), pitch, and timbre. Intrinsic relationships among them "make it possible to combine musical tones into the larger structures that we are familiar with in music."[14] Because the essential quality that differentiates music from the other arts is the presence of "auditory movement," pitch and duration are more fundamental than timbre and intensity. Having fastened on structural relationships as the essential characteristics of musical works, Beardsley treats all expressive qualities that are objectively present in a musical work as gestalt qualities arising from musical structure. Individuals who focus on these properties listen to the phenomenally objective features of a musical work. Listeners who fail to grasp the objective patterns and kinetic qualities have not yet "really heard all that it is."[15] Beardsley's account is similar to that of Leonard B. Meyer, who explicitly concludes that a poorly educated listener is a passive listener who must have a much cruder and more emotionally impoverished experience of music.[16]

Denigrating the Popular

While none of these four authors expresses overt scorn for popular music, the practical result of the hearing/listening distinction is to denigrate popular taste and to dismiss much of what is interesting about a lot of popular music, particularly rock music.[17] While I am not proposing that either result was ever a goal of the distinction, they emerge in at least three ways.

First, the distinction denigrates popular music fans, who fail both to achieve a level of conscious knowledge about music and to practice the disciplined listening that this knowledge enables.[18] But it is doubtful that the ability to note "artistic individuality" (to quote Hanslick) always requires *conscious* exercise of critical categories concerning musical form. If the fundamental criterion for listening is noticing and remembering what is distinctive about individual works, then rock fans do listen. They recognize the appearance of familiar riffs and melodies when these appear in new contexts. Led Zeppelin fans will immediately recognize that Robert Plant has sampled Zeppelin's "Black Dog" and "Dazed and Confused" for the song "Tall Cool One." Almost any fan of the Rolling Stones will recognize that Neil Young directly copies the melody of their "Lady Jane" for his own "Borrowed Tune." A Beatles fan will hear the plaintive quality of the blue notes in the melody of "Another Girl," and will find no such quality in the Beatles' version of the Broadway standard "Till There Was You." This awareness does not require conscious awareness of the particular blue notes in "Another Girl," yet the perceived difference demands awareness of real differences in the tonal materials. Although the popular audience responds to more than just genre clichés and general effects, many aesthetic properties do not demand attentive "listening" in the prescribed sense of an exclusive focus.[19]

Second, "listening" is treated as an activity directed at a limited object within the total aural experience. The understanding listener is expected "to ignore the overwhelming majority of it."[20] The goal is to extract a pure sound structure or musical work from the concrete performance: "The form (as tonal structure) . . . is the music itself."[21] So listening requires ignoring its full particularity. But if we discount lyrics and musical embellishments, each Hindustani raga is equivalent to many others. One twelve-bar blues is remarkably like another. By this standard, Bob Dylan's "Leopard-Skin Pill-Box Hat" (1966) and "High Water (for Charley Patton)"

(2001) are musically (but not lyrically) the same song as Charley Patton's "High Water Everywhere" (1929)—despite the fact that only one of the two Dylan songs is directly descended from Patton's song. As Robert Cantrick points out on the basis of such examples, "musical composition is not the only form that music takes."[22] Any perspective that tells us that "Leopard-Skin Pill-Box Hat" is just "High Water Everywhere" is too parsimonious concerning what music is and what counts as musical activity.

Third, in directing audiences to tonal structures within the aural experience, the traditional doctrine of listening robs popular music of much of its expressive force. Hanslick defended a strict formalism: only structural properties matter, and they matter only for themselves. The other three authors endorse a modified formalism in which objective expressive features can be sources of genuine aesthetic satisfaction, provided those expressive features arise from formal relations of the sound structure. Generalizing from these authors, the doctrine of "listening" asks us to ignore expressive qualities that are present for nonstructural reasons. To note a few examples in the music of the Rolling Stones, "listening" tells us to ignore the sense of anger conveyed by the fuzz tone of Keith Richards's guitar on "(I Can't Get No) Satisfaction," the forward movement that comes from the rhythm guitar and drums rather than from tonal movement in the opening seconds of "Street Fighting Man," and the extraordinarily plaintive "everyman" quality that arises from the appearance of Richards as vocalist (instead of Mick Jagger, the usual vocalist) at the beginning of "Salt of the Earth."

Expressive qualities seem equally objective when they arise from engineering and production decisions in the recording process. Think here of selective use of echo (on Elvis Presley's voice on "Mystery Train," 1955), general ambiance (Bruce Springsteen's *Nebraska* album, 1982), and instrumental texture (the effect of two to four of the same instruments playing identical parts on Phil Spector's production of "River Deep, Mountain High," 1966).[23] The four theorists that I have outlined regard listeners who respond to these nonstructural qualities as naive, insufficiently educated, and not really listening to the music. But if fans of the music agree on the presence of these qualities and agree that these qualities are important to the music, then why aren't they relevant? Is it simply because they are not properly structural? We are dealing with aesthetic qualities, so the test of relevance must be whether the properties are available to listeners familiar with that kind of music. Hanslick and Gurney formulated their views before the appearance of recorded music. The same is not the case with Prall and Beardsley, who simply ignore the implications that arise for music made, distributed, and consumed *as* recorded sound. The most important implication is that we no longer *need* to abstract from the particulars of presentation to find the music: we live in a world where the recording—in all its idiosyncratic particularity—is the musical work.

I do not mean to suggest that elitist distaste for popular music fully accounts for the continued defense of a traditional position about listening to structural properties. Those who cannot allow that the ambiance of a Phil Spector recording is as important as the song it presents may have a deeper reason than cultural bias. Their reasoning may reflect a generic argument that Noël Carroll calls "the specificity thesis." The specificity thesis makes two questionable assumptions. One is that each artistic medium has some feature in which it alone excels. The other is that each art should emphasize whatever differentiates it from other arts. As such, what begins as a description of the essential qualities of the medium turns into a recommendation that we attend to those qualities alone.[24]

As an example of an appeal to the specificity thesis for music, consider the transitions in this argument by Edward Cone: "No musical form, no music. That is as true of improvisation as of symphonic composition, of primitive folk-songs as of Lieder, of hard rock as of dodecaphony. To be music is to have form. To hear music is to hear musical form."[25] The argument moves from the insight that auditory structure is the differentiating property of music to the conclusion that music is of value for this alone.

But rather than attempt to derive appropriate uses of an artistic medium from considerations of the character of the medium, we might look to the different uses of the medium in the hands of different musicians. Many of the "potentials" of a medium await discovery, and "interest in art forms is to a large measure interest in how artists learn or discover new ways of using their medium."[26] Those who deny that popular music demands listening are unable to recognize the diverse ways that popular musicians use the medium of sound.

The argument in favor of exclusive, structural "listening" also rests on the principle that an activity requiring specialized or refined knowledge is superior to one that employs only basic knowledge. But this principle is without basis in fact. Specialized knowledge is required to read the *Journal of Abnormal Psychology,* but it hardly follows that I will gain greater insight into human nature by reading that journal in place of the novels of Charles Dickens and Henry James. John Fisher voices similar reservations:

> It is plausible . . . that the value difference implied by the high/low art distinction has been influenced in part by our tendency to grade the types of cognition and character involved in appreciating various genres of artifacts. As such, it appears to presuppose unexamined, traditional ideas about the value of various mental states and attitudes.[27]

It is equally questionable to assume that different grades of cognition correlate neatly with different genres, so that I employ a different and lower grade of cognition when I attend to a Charlie Christian guitar solo than to Chopin's *Minute Waltz* (Op. 64 No. 1).[28]

Sadly, it may be that our mental effort has a point of diminishing returns, after which the energy expended to acquire greater insight is unlikely to reward that investment with any clear gain. I speculate that, with music, most people reach this point in young adulthood, after which they receive no more music lessons or musical training. Musical tastes become less flexible, even fixed.[29] Yet if an individual's life is enriched by music, even if it is only popular music as a recreational pleasure, I cannot see any clear benefit from adopting analytical listening.[30] Granted, analytical listening will alter the experience of music. In some cases, those who do not employ such listening will never appreciate certain music (e.g., many of the fugues of Bach's *Well-Tempered Clavier*) as the music that it is. But applying the skills of analytical listening to a simple popular song can result in sheer boredom, for some music is just not designed for that mode of listening.

There is an interesting exception to our culture's usual pattern of stifling nonprofessional music making. Music therapy is increasingly provided to individuals with special needs. A number of researchers have explored the positive effects that music performance can have on individuals struggling with the fact that others regard them as abnormal. In the face of physical or mental obstacles to "normal" conversation, music often serves as protoconversation, innately suited to creating and maintaining social bonds.[31] But once again, there is a tendency to equate music with musicianship, and many music therapists dismiss "passive" uses of music. Listening to music is regarded as a recreational activity that provides "opportunities for distraction with an emphasis on pleasure and enjoyment."[32] But this "recreational" use of music is "superficial" and must not be confused with the "difficult" work of music-centered therapy. I hope that this position will be reconsidered in the face of evidence that the "superficial" presence of background music can have its own therapeutic value for persons with many disabilities.[33]

One of the complications of contemporary musical life is that different musics and different listening situations call for distinct levels of concentration on what is taking place in the music. The challenge is to adopt an adequate mode of listening, which involves adjusting one's listening to the demands of the context and type of music.[34] But should this surprise us? Why should music be so different from the literary and visual arts? Knowledgeable readers do not approach a short story as they do a novel. We do not attend to films the way that we attend to stage plays (one reason that good stage plays don't always lead to good movies), nor do we look at impressionist paintings by Claude Monet the way we look at Andy Warhol's pop art canvases. Conversely, when we control the selection of the music we'll hear, what we select is partially a function of how closely we plan to attend to it. Choosing music, we select a style that fits the level and kind of attention that we'll give to the music. The music that I prefer when working in my office is not the music that I prefer while driving across Arizona on a long trip, neither of which is necessarily music that I'll pay money to see performed live. The admission that different musics reward different modes of attention does not prove that one mode is superior to another— unless, perhaps, one independently believes that exclusive attention is a superior activity. But are there any good reasons to suppose that listening should be an exclusive activity? Or that an exclusive activity engages a superior grade of cognition? I will now consider those premises of the doctrine of the superiority of listening.

Is Listening an Exclusive Activity?

Two points interest me about the supposed distinction between hearing and listening. First, I see little to recommend the doctrine that hearing is passive reception (a pathological response) while listening is active engagement that requires conscious, exclusive attention to sound structure. Second, if both are genuinely active, then hearing differs from listening in degree but not in kind—they are points along a continuum rather than distinct activities. The problem with recommending the "active listening" end of the continuum is that it privileges certain *uses* for music, those in which exclusive, active listening takes place. But if "active listening" turns out to be a recommendation of exclusive attention, then there is no clear reason to expect all music lovers to engage in this practice and to work to prefer music that rewards it.

We can start by reconsidering my earlier analogy of spicy and bland food. With bland and spicy, the phenomenal difference is firmly grounded in physiological response.[35] An individual can build up a tolerance and appreciation for spiciness, but that individual is learning to appreciate what is in the first instance independent of memory, learning, or any cognitive process. One favors bland cuisine if one does not learn to handle spiciness through repeated exposure to it. The original appeal of two modes of musical response depended on a similar story. Early theorists stressed that the response to popular music is a direct pathological response. In contrast, appreciation of serious music demands repeated exposure and then application of cognitive judgment to the musical object. Those who fail to acquire and exercise the requisite cognitive skills are left in the position of Nipper, the dog listening to the phonograph in the old RCA Victor logo. We hear sounds and recognize some of them, but we cannot listen to the music in the sounds.

But differences between dogs and human infants should give us a reason to pause. Despite their ability to *hear* sounds that are not heard by humans, dogs can never place themselves in a position to *listen* to music. Dogs lack a human infant's instincts to listen for local musical structures in the sounds. So dogs cannot have the initial experiences necessary for the formation of memories and concepts required for appreciating music.[36] Although non-human primates also engage in musical behavior, no primate has ever been shown to be able to follow or understand any human music. Primates "don't hear" the melodies and so cannot develop the memories and expectations required for grasping music's tonal syntax.[37]

Unlike dogs and primates, human infants hear some of the musical properties of music. The fact that a three-day-old infant "instinctively" moves to the rhythm of music does not demonstrate any talent for music, since the infant is not capable of hearing music at all. It does not yet have the requisite knowledge to "listen."[38] Instinctively preparing for language acquisition, infants listen for musical patterns in every sound in their environment. If anything counts as merely hearing music, this does, for it is not informed judgment about music.[39] Individuals require many years of acculturation with pitch-scale patterns before they "spontaneously" hear pitches in terms of the appropriate tonal frame of reference.[40] Given the right listening environment, children naturally develop an ear for harmony.[41] Dogs and primates never can.

However, if we want to contrast "listening" with the infant's instinctive response, reserving "listening" for *appropriately educated reception,* then there is no obvious reason why listening is restricted to only one such response. The human language instinct leads to the development of many languages, but I hope that no one any longer wants to say that some natural languages are more genuinely language than others! Given the close relationship between our language instinct and music instinct, by parity of reasoning we ought to allow that many musics exist and many learned modes of hearing count as listening.[42] Even Hanslick saw that the difference between hearing and listening is, at best, a matter of degree of cognitive processing, not a real difference in kind between hearing and listening. Even the seemingly "natural" music of peasants is "artistic music through and through."[43] Hanslick goes wrong when he assumes that listening should be tied to pleasure taken in a *type* of music (in a particular way of structuring music), which is identified as the most advanced type of music.[44] Where Hanslick tries to isolate the unique cognitive skills called for by some music, equating listening with an educated response to *that* music, we should resist this conclusion. All acquired knowledge—tacit or conscious—about musical organization contributes to listening, as something distinct from the hearing of infancy.

What puzzles me is why anyone still thinks that cases of "passive" listening are similar to the case of the infant. As with spoken language, the normal course of cognitive development rapidly takes each infant out of this naive state. Listeners do not plunge back into the instinctive state simply because the music is incorporated into other activity. The failure to distinguish between these two cases stems from the claim that active listening is an exclusive activity with special cognitive demands. Lack of experience accounts for the fact that the infant cannot yet follow the music's overall structure. The fact that inexperience prevents sophisticated listening does not support the claim that I cannot listen to the music of Jimi Hendrix (rock) or J. S. Bach (classical) while I wash dishes or fold laundry. Washing the dishes requires practical application of learned knowledge, yet I can wash dishes while carrying on a conversation. Why can't I listen to music while washing the dishes? Or driving a car? Or dancing with my wife? Why should listening to music be so exclusive? Personally, I find that the best way to prepare for an upcoming concert of unfamiliar music is to play similar music as background music during my workday. Nonexclusive listening develops the expectations that I will need when I later engage in exclusive listening in the concert hall.

Perhaps listening is taken to be an exclusive activity because it is thought to require a distinctively aesthetic attitude. Aesthetic value has a long history of being opposed to utilitarian, instrumental value. But if the lack of acquired knowledge explains why infants cannot yet listen to music, it is not for want of an aesthetic attitude or special mode or degree of concentration. Who is engaged in disinterested perceptual satisfaction if not the infant in her crib, transfixed by the dangling musical mobile above her head? Conversely, there is little reason to suppose that the polite audience sitting immobile before an orchestra or ensemble is really listening (Hanslick suspected that few were).[45] When Mingus warns that the ability to dance "don't mean you listen to the music," at least not "fully," he endorses the injunction of exclusive focus. But who displays more attention than a couple dancing to a slow popular song, their bodies moving in time to the music and who, alerted by the harmonic movement that the song is moving to closure, end their dance with the end of the song?[46] If one is dancing with the rhythm of the music, using tonality as a guide to determine when the piece is about to end, surely one grasps the basics of its organization. One is listening to the music in the sounds and not merely hearing sounds that one enjoys.

Listening to David Bowie

Despite my reservations, I am willing to recognize a distinction between hearing and listening. In contrast to the mere "hearing" of infants, listening requires acquired competence to judge the music's particularity as the music that it is. But if this is the right way to cast the distinction, then most people who only listen to popular music really do *listen* to popular music.

Still, there is an almost unavoidable urge to treat popular taste as inferior. It just seems too easy. Where are the dues paid in years of music lessons, appreciation courses, or music theory? But effortless listening is no less active than challenging listening. Unaware of the cognitive processing that shapes each encounter with music, we constantly fall back into the illusion that we simply hear it as it is, without "filtering" and interpreting it through a specific conceptual model: "as they typically function, [our] conceptual models are immediate and transparent."[47] But there is no pure, natural mode of passive hearing. Humans learn to listen. Each listener constructs a conceptual map or model *for* listening.[48] Beginning with our very first encounters with music, each of us begins to construct and actively employ a conceptual model for music. To the extent that "listening" requires a better response, it requires a *competent* response. So the important difference between listening and hearing turns on whether an individual's conceptual model is culturally appropriate to the musical categories.

From a first-person perspective, it is difficult to see that every encounter with music involves *doing* something that can be evaluated as something that is more or less competently done. To avoid the trap of thinking that there is less cognitive engagement with popular music, it is useful to think about cases where our conceptual model fails us. These are cases—far more common when young than in adulthood—where we can see a change in taste that reflects greater listening competence. Apart from the psychological research that shows audiences to be routinely more astute about the music that they normally listen to, I remind myself a specific instance where a shift in my tastes revealed to me that hearing is not always listening.

Sometime in 1973, my brother brought home David Bowie's recently released album *Aladdin Sane*. I'd seen that Bowie's name was increasingly tossed around in the rock press, but I could not recall ever hearing him on the radio. I was curious to hear what he sounded like. The album was sitting on the turntable so I turned it on. My immediate reaction was to recoil in distaste. Song after song struck me as sheer undifferentiated noise. (At the time, my own tastes favored folk-based rock. Remember that this was several years before any of us had heard of punk, or even the New York Dolls.) There was precisely one song that I returned to, to play all the way through: "Drive in Saturday," a ballad with a languid melody.

Several years later I had many hours of rock listening behind me, including more listening to Bowie, who'd started to make hits for American radio. I'd purchased and repeatedly listened to *Young Americans* (1975) and *Station to Station* (1976). I bought a copy of *Aladdin Sane* and now had a very different experience. The opening track, "Watch that Man," was a surreal cry of desperate, paranoid anger. It had a strange dissonance that I now located in Mike Garson's jazz-inflected piano, which darted in and out of the crunch of Mick Ronson's guitar. Although built on an entirely different rhythmic foundation, "Panic in Detroit" was equally desperate and paranoid—it had a Bo Diddley groove and long, arching melody line, punctuated by the syncopated cry of "panic in Detroit!" at the chorus. The title track turned out to retain a fair amount of noise, largely thanks to dissonant bursts of jazz piano instead of guitars. "Time" turned out to be a quasi-cabaret number, something that might have been at home in the decadent nightclubs of the Weimar Republic. The album's ten songs now sounded stylistically and emotionally varied. But of course they had not changed at all. I had. I was now in a position to experience and appreciate more of their aesthetic properties.

One lesson here is that musical arrangements can function as noise, preventing unprepared listeners from grasping the structure of a composition, particularly its melodies. Many who dismiss rock as noise are put off by its abrasive or unfamiliar timbres. Lyrical melodies and clever modulations are often clothed in distorted guitars and nasal shouts. Beatles producer George Martin became aware of this complication when nonrock musicians covered the Beatles. "There were many people who couldn't assimilate their tunes, because they couldn't hear the music for the noise," Martin observes. But when Annunzio Mantovani and others recorded orchestrated versions of their songs "with pleasant, syrupy sounds," the same people who dismissed the Beatles as noise said, "Oh, that's a nice tune . . . They do write good music, don't they?" Orchestration aside, Martin remarks that these were "exactly the same tunes."[49]

However, Martin's comments should not be taken as evidence that rock arrangements are themselves the problem. Rock fans experience a parallel cognitive difficulty when confronted with unfamiliar varieties of rock. Wondering if I could confirm with others what I'd experienced with *Aladdin Sane,* I tried a simple experiment with two groups of students. I played them the Byrds' original recording of "Eight Miles High" (1966) and then the punk rock onslaught of the Hüsker Dü remake (1984). The words are nearly unintelligible on the Hüsker's version. The vocal is a hoarse shout. The tempo is faster and the instrumentation is distorted. Less than half of the students initially recognized it as the same piece of music. But after playing the first minute of each version four times in a row, alternating between the two versions, every student reported that they now heard that it was the same music. If the students had been less familiar with rock, four hearings might not have been sufficient. (In similar comparisons, the majority of my students find it difficult to hear a common melody in two different instrumental jazz arrangements even after four or five hearings.)

What I informally demonstrated to my students is a point well known to researchers in psychology of music. Recognizing music in a stream of sound (hearing the music that it is) requires familiarity with other music in the same style.[50] Within rock music, the Byrds and Hüsker Dü are miles apart (equivalent, perhaps, to the distance between Giacomo Puccini and Béla Bartók). Nonetheless, the Hüsker Dü arrangement of "Eight Miles High" is an instance of "Eight Miles High" and not, say, "Why?" or "Captain Soul" (two other Byrds songs from the same period). The fact that "hard" rock music disguises or obscures harmonic and melodic movement in a flurry of distracting elements helps to explain its limited popular acceptance. It does not make the Hüsker Dü performance less musical, nor is a competent response to it any less a case of acculturated listening than is a competent response to Chopin's Minute Waltz, music that conforms to radically different stylistic rules.

Let's pull things together. The traditional opposition of hearing and listening is usually married to the thesis that when we listen to nondisruptive sounds, the phenomena are distinguishable into two sorts of qualities. Active listening focuses on essential (structural) qualities of musical works, while responses grounded in nonessential (nonstructural) aspects are denigrated as an uneducated mode of hearing. Focused attention to structural properties is the common base of "active" listening, "musicological" listening, Hanslick's "logical" listening, Beardsley's hearing "in the fullest sense," and Gurney's "definite hearing." A psychological thesis about the experience of music is unsoundly derived from the ontological assumption that musical works are sound structures. Music's nonstructural qualities are treated as a necessary evil, as something present only because there is no structure unless there is something to structure.

Musicians who *perform* the musical work are similarly relegated to the lesser role of re-creator. Popular fandom (e.g., Beatlemania), which centers on performances and the identity of the performers, is taken as evidence that the audience is not responding to music.[51]

In the wake of the reification of the independent musical work, critics like Hanslick defended instrumental music as the highest achievements in the art. This aesthetic doctrine reversed centuries of tradition that had put vocal music at the top. Philosophers and critics emphasized a distinction between objective and subjective responses, where listening to musical structure would legitimize pleasure by securing it in something objective. Listening incorrectly might yield pleasure, but only of a contingent and subjective sort. Even composers of program music, otherwise at odds with the formalist defense of absolute music, buttressed their aesthetic ideal by writing detailed programs to guard listeners against "wrong" interpretations of the music.[52] By the twentieth century, density and structural integration and complexity were firmly entrenched as the bases of compositional success. The result? "Our culture may, in fact, be one of the most extreme in the degree to which musical participation is limited."[53] But this way of putting it already assumes that dancing in a nightclub and singing to the radio while driving are not musical participation.

It would be silly to deny that different objective features make different styles more or less suitable for different uses. Punk rock at full volume tends to disrupt conversation during a dinner party, which is why I'm likely to load Alison Krauss or Django Reinhardt into the compact disc player before dinner guests arrive. But there are many uses of music in everyday life, all of which require some application of a listener's musical intelligence if the music is to serve its purpose. My argument has been that exclusive attention to "serious" music is merely one sort of listening—one among several ways that acculturated listeners might incorporate music into life. Popular music is meant to meet the needs of large numbers of people with many different levels of musical education. Nonetheless, popular music makes cognitive demands that can only be met by acquiring suitable background experience to generate tacit knowledge. We must not locate listening at one extreme of what looks to be a continuum of practices. Doing so begs too many important questions about music and its value.

Part Three

Listening as Engagement with Symbols

6. Music's Worldly Uses

There are many mansions in the house of the muses. There is first the great assembly hall of melody—where most of us take our seats at some time in our lives—but a lesser number pass on to inner sanctuaries of harmony, where the melodic sequence, the "tune," as it most frequently is called, has infinitely less interest than the blending of notes into chords, so that the combining wave-lengths will give new aesthetic sensations. This inner court of harmony is where nearly all the truly great music is enjoyed.

In the house there is, however, another apartment, properly speaking, down in the basement, a kind of servants' hall of rhythm. It is there we hear the hum of the Indian dance, the throb of the Oriental tambourines and kettle-drums, the clatter of clogs, the click of Slavic heels, the thumpty-tumpty of the negro banjo, and, in fact, the native dances of a world.

—Editorial, *New Orleans Times-Picayune,* 1918

I have noted, but not explored, the importance of music's symbolic dimensions. Turning to that topic, I should make it clear that I am not pursuing the question of how one piece of music can mean something different from other, very similar pieces. Native English speakers know that *cat* and *cab* mean different things. Similarly, experienced listeners recognize that one blues song addresses racial tensions when a second does not, even though neither explicitly mentions the subject. Those are differences within a musical category, and they are not the sorts of meanings that I will pursue here. What interests me is the belief that a broad category of music represents something different from another category, and that this difference is a reason to value one category over another. Let me emphasize this point with an analogy. Biblical hermeneutics includes an investigation of how the Gospel of Luke has a message different from the Gospel of John. One might be more historically accurate while the other is theologically richer. What I am now investigating about music is a similar but even more sweeping comparison, something akin to looking for the overarching differences in the messages of Christianity and Hinduism.

153

When we make comparisons at this very general level, important differences in musical meaning are often attributed to aesthetic properties that tend to distinguish certain achievements in Western classical music from all other music. If this belief is warranted, it can be used to support a wholesale rejection of popular music, without disputing or even addressing my claim that each category of music has aesthetic properties that merit appreciative listening. This chapter considers and challenges these claims about the inferior status of popular music.

Traditional Elitism

A staggering quantity of music is now available to anyone with a computer and an Internet connection. A rapidly expanding industry provides downloading of digital files of popular music. There is also a new ease of access to less familiar music. Wanting a sample of Bollywood music from India, I went to an Internet retailer and found that I could choose from more than two dozen albums. Later that week, the discs I ordered arrived at my office. One implication of this ease of access is the worry that we will "reduce to functional equivalence music that originates from hundreds of regions of the world and from centuries of human history."[1] This concern is raised because there is a fear that people will come to expect the same ease of interpretative and appreciative access to all music, without concern for genuine differences.

When I choose background music, I have the option of working to the percussive flow of an Indonesian gamelan orchestra, to the bleating trumpets of a Tibetan Tantric Buddhist ritual, or to a choir trilling traditional Chinese folks songs. Although I have recordings of all of them, none of that music really yields a musical experience to me, because I don't know how to listen to it. I have not developed a taste for it, and I am not likely to do so at this stage of my life.[2] Earlier, I allowed that enjoying music does not always indicate that one appreciates the music against the backdrop of the appropriate musical categories. Although I find gamelan music interesting and the Chinese and Tibetan music annoying, I cannot say that I understand gamelan music better. My relationship to gamelan orchestra remains more like my relationship to a hot bath or cold beer than to my listening relationship with the keyboard-rooted songs of Franz Schubert, George Gershwin, and Tori Amos.

Music would not qualify as something that humans understand if it were not also sometimes misunderstood. Music holds limited meaning to listeners outside the continuing culture that gives the music its significance. Nor will it yield its meanings to listeners positioned within its originating culture if those listeners are not yet positioned to engage the music. Conventions by which humans communicate meanings and understand meanings always rely on a context of social practice. At this point, I hope to have demonstrated that music yields little of its aesthetic richness to listeners who have not yet developed appropriate listening habits for that category of music.

My response to a Javanese gamelan orchestra is shallow in two ways, aesthetically and symbolically. I have already discarded the proposal that the problem is my lack of formal training in this music. Much of the time, what I actually listen to is popular music recorded between 1955 and the present. During one recent month, my work was most often accompanied by the music of Led Zeppelin (1970s rock), Yo La Tengo (1990s "indie" rock), Muddy Waters (1950s electric blues), Django Reinhardt (1930s jazz), and some piano music by Erik Satie (late nineteenth century). The next month, Satie was replaced by Chopin's piano Etudes, Reinhardt by Billie Holiday, and Led Zeppelin by the Grateful Dead. I have no formal training of any kind with any of this music, either. But as many theorists have argued, formal training and the skills of musicological analysis are neither necessary nor sufficient for understanding music.[3] What matters is whether a listener *hears* the music in an appropriate way, and doing so requires participation in the appropriate culture of listening.

Traditionally, such ideas have supplied a reason to support liberal arts education—education that aims at something more than producing trained workers. Beyond its vocational dimension, education should enrich lives. This, in turn, is an important reason to support the arts at all levels of schooling.[4] Put aside the appeal to the much heralded but poorly documented "Mozart Effect" (the claim that exposure to classical music improves specific cognitive functions, so the music is desirable because it helps children do better in math class).[5] Because listening requires a knowledge base, it can be developed. But as with reading, one learns to read "See Spot run" before grappling with *Romeo and Juliet*. It makes no sense to develop musical tastes by starting with a Mozart sonata or a Beethoven symphony. Although he defends a traditional hierarchy of musics, Roger Scruton allows that a great deal of popular music employs the tonal language that prepares listeners to grasp the concert tradition of great classical music. Yet it remains unclear how we are to move anyone from the enjoyment of popular music to a musical taste for Mozart. More importantly, it is not at all clear why we should aim for that goal. Education for music appreciation—as opposed to the skill development of musical performance in a specific tradition—has no obvious sequence because, I will argue, it has no clear target.[6]

I endorse some of the central ideas defended in Scruton's massive book, *The Aesthetics of Music*.[7] In two ways, we are both elitists. First, we agree that some listeners are better positioned than others to appreciate certain categories of music. Second, we agree that some pieces of music are aesthetically better than others, and not simply as a means to some nonmusical end. But I reject another type of elitism—let's call it traditional elitism.

Traditional elitism is the view that all styles of music are better or worse relative to one ideal type. All listeners can be graded relative to a single ideal listener: "taste in music matters, and that a search for objective musical values is one part of our search for the right way to live."[8] It is, more or less, the position advanced against "jass" by the *Times-Picayune* in 1918.

Traditional elitism is not a self-evident truth. Its defense requires an extended argument. At the start of the twenty-first century, Scruton is almost alone in his willingness to articulate the case for traditional musical elitism. But where the attack on jazz was little more than a simple analogy, Scruton's case against a broad spectrum of popular music is defended with thoughtful arguments. However, several mysterious leaps are introduced to get him from his central position about the culture of listening to his final conclusion that recent popular music is hardly fit to be granted the status of music.

The major steps of his challenge are as follows. First, we should grant the intrinsic superiority of our harmonic tradition, the tradition of Western art music that reigned supreme from the Renaissance to the early twentieth century. Second, an educated listener's sympathetic response to music has an important feature. It allows us to reach out of ourselves in an experience of feeling that is simultaneously free and disciplined. Third, dancing is identified as the paradigm sympathetic response to music, and even silent listening is "a kind of latent dancing." Expressive aesthetic properties depend on our "sympathetic response" to musical movements and gestures.[9] Because dancing is fundamentally a group or community activity, the appropriate dance response to a piece of music indicates the fundamental character of the social life of those who make and respond to that music. Fourth, as dancing gives way to a distinctively aesthetic response to instrumental music, we arrive at our fullest engagement with music. Listeners seek musical pattern, indifferent to the "actual sound events" (i.e., to the contingent material through which the music is presented in performance). Melody, harmony, and rhythm are to be mentally abstracted from whatever embodies them. At this stage, an ordered social life is symbolically represented by the music, rather than physically enacted.

For traditional elitism, this mental abstraction is significant for the way that it thrusts us into an ideal world. Our sympathetic response is not to musicians and composers but rather to an ideal subject or community. If we attend to the sounds *as* sounds, we remain mired in the physical or material conditions of music production and we are not listening to the tonal dimension that permits one tone to lead to another. Its lack of "worldly uses" invites a sympathetic response with an ideal community that is finer and nobler than any group dynamic that we actually encounter in this world.

Finally, popular music represents a repudiation of musical taste, for it is deficient in the areas of melody, harmony, and rhythm. Most popular music depends on musical clichés. Offering little that demands genuine musical understanding, almost all popular music is a dehumanizing, "impoverished" form of music. Because it is incapable of framing any interesting or sincere expression of emotion, it invites a sympathetic response to a decadent, disordered community.[10] Scruton claims that a taste for the rock music of Nirvana and R.E.M. obliterates aesthetic judgment, "as though a taste in music were on a par with a taste in ice-cream, [which] is precisely not to understand the power of music."[11]

Given the many supporting arguments involved, I cannot subject all of them to scrutiny. Instead, I will point to several holes in the argument that seem to be typical of traditional elitism. At the same time, I hope to show that a philosophy of music must be supplemented by honest descriptions of musical activity and listeners' comprehension before we try to establish evaluative conclusions about the state of music in contemporary culture.

Music as Thought

One important building block in the edifice of traditional elitism is the proposal that music exists in an intentional realm. The intentional realm is the world of thought. Music is not a set of sound structures. Music is *interpreted* sound. Competent listeners are aware of "thought *in* music, or better, *music as thought*."[12] Agreeing about music and the intentional realm, my main argument will be that this fact works against traditional elitism, not in its favor.

The intentional realm is the world of meaning, of intelligible human action. It is not the physical space occupied by the sound waves that reach our ears. Sound waves are events in physical space. Music arises *after* those sound waves reach our ears. Strictly speaking, the presence of *music* depends on the listener's comprehension of those sounds, providing an experience of aesthetic properties and human meanings. The basic point will be clear to anyone who's ever heard a conversation conducted in a language that he or she does not understand. One hears the sounds made by human voices, but there is no comprehension of how one sound relates to any other. Above all, sounds that happen earlier are not heard as establishing the rightness or wrongness of sounds that come later. And just as one can listen to a conversation without hearing it *as speech,* one can listen to music without hearing the relationships that must be heard to hear it *as music.* In this sense, music is often said to exist in a space or realm all its own. But no more so, I think, than does the semantic dimension of the words on this page.

I will say a little more about the idea that music lies in the intentional realm of interpreted sound. If English is your first language and you are less than fifty years old, I wager that if you happen to hear the phrase "The cat in the," your immediate expectation will be that "hat" will be the fifth word in the sequence. But even if you lack background experience with the children's books of Dr. Seuss, you will anticipate that either an adjective or a noun will follow "the," and that if you get an adjective as the fifth word, a noun will soon follow. The phrase "in the" demands it. None of this implies that you're consciously aware of the need for adjectives or nouns, or about the difference between direct and indirect objects. But linguistic competence implies expectations of a certain kind, allowing us to unconsciously anticipate what should and shouldn't happen next. Thanks to these expectations, we can follow the meaning of speech (and writing, where visual shapes substitute for sounds) without fussing about the rules of syntax. This is what we mean by the proposal that language is constituted intentionally by the shared understanding of the participants, emerging in an intentional realm that is not to be equated with the physical stuff that conveys language from one person to another.

In short, we do not hear music simply because we hear sounds which happen to be music. We hear the music when we understand the organization of the sounds and grasp what is conveyed by that organization.[13] It is crucial to note that many aesthetic properties of music fall into this category, not just meanings. As we saw in earlier discussions of aesthetic properties, many of them depend on material and historical circumstances informing the music. As a result, chapter 5 challenged standards of listening that expect us to engage in *too much* abstraction. This issue resurfaces in the traditional elitist's claim that we can read a symbolic failure of community in the alleged aesthetic deficiency of rock bands like Nirvana and R.E.M. But is it possible to make that judgment if we genuinely ignore the material conditions of the music? If I ignore the material evidence that tells me I am looking at an oil painting rather than a fresco, how do I place the visual work in the appropriate category for determining its aesthetic properties?

Traditional elitism holds that Beethoven' music should be heard as a reflection of human life, but not of Beethoven's life. Beethoven's Vienna is a real community. It is not the ideal community that his music conveys. William Echard raises several important points about the interpretation of rock music that bear on this issue. Borrowing from Edward Cone's ideas about "the composer's voice" in classical music, Echard extends Cone's distinction between the composer and the composer's musically constructed persona. For example, I know that Richard Strauss composed *Thus Spake Zarathustra* (best known to many today for its prominent use in the film *2001 A Space Odyssey*). The music is heroic, and we can decide this quite apart from any belief about whether Strauss, the composer, was heroic. In attributing a human quality to the music (its heroic character), Echard notes that appropriate features of the music must be heard anthropomorphically, *as if* a person, "strongly cued by contextual and social factors."[14]

Echard sees that a precisely parallel issue arises with popular music. But the ability to distinguish a musical persona from the person responsible can pull listeners either of two ways: "On the one hand, it is tempting to interpret seemingly agential features of the music as symptoms or intentions of a composer. On the other hand, there is no literal way in which the composer places a piece of himself or herself into the music."[15] Unfortunately, fan identification with favorite performers tends to tip the interpretation toward attributing properties of the music to the performer most identified with it. But the attribution is not direct. It requires "a chain of signs." Echard focuses on Neil Young, whose "noise" mode with the band Crazy Horse is just the sort of music that traditional elitism attacks as inviting a sympathetic response to a decadent, disordered community. Echard writes,

> For example, in the case where a listener hears a jagged quality of movement in a song by Neil Young and concludes that Neil was feeling agitated, we do not assume the listener literally felt as if she was hearing Neil Young move in a jagged manner. Sometimes of course she might, if the jagged acoustic quality is clearly a direct result of Young's performance practice. It is more coherent, however, to suggest that in the first instance the *music* is heard as moving jaggedly. Then, the sign of music-as-jagged is taken up to elaborate the subsequent object, Neil Young *as* someone who for some reason produced jaggedly moving music. . . . The effect of elaborating Neil-Young-as-object through the music-as-object is often to blur the boundary between Neil Young and the music, to see them as extensions of one another.[16]

However, to know whether the jagged quality is the direct result of Young's behavior (and thus a symptom of it) or an expressive property (and thus part of the intentional realm), the listener must make a decision about the material sources of the sounds. We cannot forget them entirely.

To put it another way, we limit our interpretation of the music if we ignore the boundaries that Echard explores. If some of Neil Young's music with Crazy Horse is disordered and decadent, is it that way in its persona, music-as-disorder? Then we might go the next step, and wonder why Young would impart the music with this quality, a question thrown into high relief by familiarity with "Here We Are in the Years" and his other work with orchestration. This music demonstrates that the sound of Young's work with Crazy Horse is part of the music's intentional character, and not because he doesn't know better, as a symptom of decadence and disorder. But again, context becomes crucial. Because the complex sectional structure of the early "Here We Are in the Years" proves that Young *could* make the sort of popular music that brings him closer to the elitist's favored tradition, Young's decision to crank the volume and play "Sedan Delivery" or "Last Dance" should inform our interpretive conclusion.

Another point in Echard's analysis of Neil Young is pertinent to traditional elitism. If music-as-jagged is correctly attributed to a guitar line, it is there as a musical gesture. Gestures should be distinguished from postures. Gestures are local. They happen at specific points in the musical performance—Echard mentions the startling moment in "Motion Pictures" when Young's voice drops to "a fourth below middle-c, far lower than his norm for the period."[17] Postures are more pervasive. In Young's music, ranting songs ("Sedan Delivery") have a different feel from drifting songs ("Helpless"), and both are different from anthemic songs ("Cinnamon Girl"). But talk of "posture" and "gesture" is metaphorical, purposely calling attention to our experience of musical movement and our tendency to anthropomorphically regard music as human movement. Remember the earlier claim about the importance of our interpretative response to musical movements and gestures. How do we perceive these in the music in the first place?

There is no controversy about our tendency to hear musical change as musical movement. But we cannot perceive movement without a corresponding sense of space and energy. The music is fast or slow, it rises and falls, it expands and contracts, and it rants or drags. Echard points out that gesture and posture must be perceived as two interrelated features of a single thing in order to allow us to take the relatively fixed posture as the backdrop for the more dramatic movements that we regard as significant gestures. For example, when Young performs solo at the piano, we take the piano and the voice of "Love in Mind" to be two elements of a single persona, not two voices talking to one another. (In a traditional blues, they might deliver call and response.) However, gesture and posture are not purely structural. Timbre, the signature sound of an instrument or human voice, plays an indispensable role in establishing the posture against which gestures emerge. Consider Young's use of power chords:

> in the introductory riff to "Cinnamon Girl," . . . two beats of power chords in motor eighths are separated by two beats of (relative) silence, followed by a more continuously filled measure. This pattern repeats itself four times. . . . The effect of the blocks of motor eighths is striking. On the one hand, next to the silent beats they feel like a continuous presence, some kind of monolithic block of stone. This effect demonstrates the object-like presence enabled by timbre. . . . In this riff, then, postural and gestural potentials are used in tandem to create at least two composite images.[18]

Echard's point is that the motionless feel of the two beats requires the timbre of the electric guitar, played in just that manner. Supplied by piano, the same chords would lack the motionless, hanging "block" quality that generates the gestural movement of the rest of the riff. Timbre, of course, is one of the things that we will ignore if our attention shifts from "actual sound events" to an ideal world. To the extent that rock, hip-hop, and other categories of popular music employ timbre to ground musical gestures, elitist disdain for the *sounds* guarantees an impoverished interpretation.[19]

With this background in place, we can challenge two more points that support traditional elitism.

First, we grasp the intentional realm only because we are members of a community with a tradition. In my writing and your understanding this piece of written English, you and I participate in a community enterprise with a long history. But we do not simply participate in that community. Our participation shapes us: we think and act in certain ways because we have internalized that tradition. Since this is true of language, it is also plausible that its holds true of music. This point is the mainstay of the idea that music is social practice. But there is another dimension to it, somewhat less acknowledged. As Plato originally recognized, because our interest in music reflects engagement in a certain social life, it reveals something about our character. Echard's argument about timbre does not directly address this point, for he offers no reading of the community and social life that is symbolized by the gestures of Neil Young's "Cinnamon Girl."[20]

Second, suppose it is true that when composers highlight sounds *as* sounds, they remind us of the physical or material conditions of music production. Such compositions redirect listeners' attention away from the tonal dimension that permits one tone to lead to another. In much the same way, Edouard Manet's critics in nineteenth-century Paris faulted him for the unfinished quality of his paintings; artists were expected to blur and obscure the evidence of the artist's brush in finishing a painting. How can the audience look at the painting if the artist insists on calling attention to the paint? From this perspective, abstract expressionists such as Jackson Pollock repudiated the goal of communication when they obsessively explored the *painted* quality of painting.

This conclusion strikes me as rather curious, yet it can be made consistent with the claim that music is always gesture. Sounds can be gestures in either of two ways. There is physical gesture, and then there is gesture in the sense of something that is to be understood as conveyed through that gesture, as when one thrusts out an arm to gesture *toward* something. Someone who focuses on the *arm* has not grasped the communicative act. We should not confuse the physical movement with the intentionality of the action, in this case the meaning of the gesture. If the gesture is unclear, I might recognize *that* it is a gesture without understanding *what* it gestures.

But does this distinction between the physical gesture and its meaning demonstrate that attending to the material conditions of music must distract us from the intentionality of the musical experience? I do not think so. To make my case, I will draw on my own experiences as a fan of popular music.

For two decades I paid no attention to the music of Led Zeppelin, even though I am demographically of just the right age to have been a fan during their creative peak in the 1970s. I owned three Led Zeppelin albums (the second, third, and fourth), but other than side two of *Led Zeppelin III,* I doubt that I ever played them over the course of twenty years. The fact that I kept hearing the same five or six Led Zeppelin tracks constantly on "classic rock" radio during those years reinforced my lack of interest in hearing more. Like many rock fans, I assumed that popular music is best when it's located a bit further from the mainstream. Like the music critic I quoted in chapter 2, I had preconceptions about what it would say about me if I liked Led Zeppelin. The group was the soundtrack of suburban high schools of the 1970s, precisely what I felt I'd left behind when I went to college and then graduate school.

But I had an awakening some years later, when Led Zeppelin's presence in my life had been reduced to the occasional dose of "Stairway to Heaven" or "Whole Lotta Love" on the radio. On my way to the grocery store, I heard the song "D'Yer Mak'Er" on the car radio.[21] It occurred to me that I hadn't heard the track in ten years. Hearing it with fresh ears after so long, I realized how much humor is built into its musical arrangement. I was surprised to find myself chuckling.

Led Zeppelin's recording of "D'Yer Mak'Er" kicks off with a distinctively syncopated drum pattern: bam-bam-bam-BAM, pause, BAM, pause, and drum roll.[22] A rhythm guitar enters on the right and the song unfolds at a much slower tempo than the percussive introduction leads one to expect. The bass guitar provides the true tempo and the busy drums subdivide the beat. The drums lag as they emphasize the offbeat, which is complicated by frequent subdivisions of the beat that are again interrupted by brief pauses. The song's rhythmic arrangement is decidedly that of Jamaican reggae. The reggae feel is reinforced by the way that Jimmy Page's slightly distorted guitar scratches out the song's chords in the right side of the stereo mix. As with most reggae, the guitar often falls silent at moments of heightened percussive action.

When it arrives, Robert Plant's vocal contribution is entirely at odds with the musical setting. The lyrics are a trite plea to a departed lover, sung with an exaggerated swoon and a frequent repetition of simple words ("oh, oh, oh") and syllables ("cry ay ay ay ay ay"). At a time when reggae was regarded as the militant expression of Jamaican nationalism, Plant's vocal line could only come across as trite and therefore politically incorrect. In a word, it was just plain silly.

The moment that really caught my ear and made me laugh comes late in the song. After fifteen seconds of introductory music, the song is constructed out of two simple segments, A and B, arranged AABAABAA. After two verses and one contrasting chorus, then two more verses and the chorus, the song's logic calls for another verse. As the chord progression signals the beginning of that verse (at 2:36), Jimmy Page's guitar steps forward (stereo left) in place of Robert Plant's voice. But two elements of the solo are out of place. First, Page does not improvise upon the established melody or upon the chord changes, as is to be expected in such music. Instead, his lead guitar simply plays the melody that Plant has established in the verse. Second, there is the actual sound quality or tone color of the guitar. It is not the shrieking, heroic, wailing guitar that we expect from Led Zeppelin. This guitar solo has a weak, anemic, and distant quality, as if the guitarist is isolated in another room. One obvious response is to wonder what *this* guitar is doing in this song. The guitar solo is not merely a surprise. It is a surprising letdown. It deflates all expectations about what should appear at this point in "D'Yer Mak'Er." Here, the joke is conditional on the listener's awareness of the sound quality chosen for the arrangement. Far from turning the listener away from the experience of meaning, meaning arises from a worldly awareness of the brute fact of a guitar solo with a specific tone color. But because the guitar solo's melody echoes Plant's vocal line, it also suggests a parody of that line, reinforcing the distance between Plant and the rest of the musical arrangement. As Echard suggested, timbre is important to a meaningful gesture.

Humor arises in the intentional realm. Awkward as this will sound, the music's amusingness is as much a feature of the intentional realm as is the meaning of Plant's sung phrase, "every breath I take."[23] (Think of how common it is for two people to hear the same joke, but for only one to see the humor in it.) Furthermore, "D'Yer Mak'Er" cannot be dismissed as a case where my finding it humorous is to be written off as my personal response. For starters, others find it just as funny, as when Susan Fast observes, "it's funny because they sound incompetent" and "the band's assumed rhythmic ineptitude makes fun of their whiteness."[24] (Here, a posture of ineptitude sets up a social gesture.) In press interviews, the members of Led Zeppelin have confirmed that they intended to convey humor through the arrangement. The song's title, pronounced so that it sounds much like "Jamaica," is part of a rather silly British joke. So I seem to have independently heard in the music something that I was meant to hear in it. I found it funny because it is amusing, and I was finally ready to experience it for what it is. It helped that I'd heard a lot of reggae in the intervening years.

Led Zeppelin is not a band remembered for their sense of humor. To a large extent, that is because it is so much easier for most listeners to grasp verbal humor than musical humor. But Led Zeppelin favored musical over verbal wit. Contrast them with Frank Zappa, who emphasized both. Whether one laughs or takes offense, the satirical edge of many of Frank Zappa's lyrics are impossible to miss, while his equally satirical mash-ups of classical music and 1950s doo-wop strike many listeners as strange or chaotic, not as funny.[25] Led Zeppelin offered a similar playful humor during live performances of "Whole Lotta Love." Wrenching blues songs were intertwined with the silliest of 1950s teenage rock-and-roll.

But Led Zeppelin's musical humor is not restricted to their frequent playful juxtaposition of songs and styles. Sometimes it occurs in an original musical design, as in "Black Dog." The song is memorable for a virtuoso guitar riff, written for Jimmy Page by John Paul Jones. The riff is rapid and metrically complex. When Page and Jones taught the music to drummer John Bonham, he modified the planned 4/4 beat with a 5/4 variation (a "time slip," in Plant's description). Plant remembers, "We were messing around when the other lads suddenly came up with that passage on 'Black Dog.' They just played it, fell about all over the floor for 20 minutes in fits of laughter, played it again, burst into more laughter, then put it down on tape."[26]

The humor is not at all obvious. Bonham's inspiration resulted in a recorded track with constant "metric displacement that takes the listener off guard, destroying expectations."[27] In fact, so much displacement occurs that singer Robert Plant could not coordinate his vocal lines with their playing except afterwards, by overdubbing his vocal. So what did Bonham do that had the band rolling on the floor? Evidently, he showed them how one small change could introduce bewildering rhythmic displacement into an already complicated piece of music. Without disrupting its seemingly spontaneous carnal power, "Black Dog" became fiendishly clever and impossible to perform with a vocalist. In live performance, Bonham eliminated the 5/4 variation so that Plant could perform his *a cappella* vocal interludes and then have the instruments return together, properly synchronized.[28]

The important point is that the humor of "D'Yer Mak'Er" and "Black Dog" display musical intelligence.[29] However, their humor is not confined to the intentionality that arises from expression through expectations centered on the song's tonic. The songs' arrangements are the key to their humor, rather than the movement of tones and of harmony formed through voice-leading. "D'Yer Mak'Er" could be played and sung in a way that strips it of its humor, in which case it would emerge as the 1950s rock-and-roll ballad that is suggested by the lyric sheet's obscure mention of the "girl group" Rosie and the Originals. In fact, the guitar solo in "D'Yer Mak'Er" has a sound remarkably similar to the electric guitar that opens "Angel Baby" by Rosie and the Originals, as if Jimmy Page is consciously reminding listeners of how electric guitars *used* to sound. This example shows that we cannot always divorce musical meaning from an awareness of the material conditions of the music. In addition to the actual sound of Page's guitar solo, part of the joke is that knowledgeable listeners do not expect Jimmy Page to play anything so obvious. Part of the joke involves recognition that Page is a guitar virtuoso—compare the "D'Yer Mak'Er" guitar solo with the one at the end of "Black Dog." But how do we derive musical meaning from these facts if we leave music in an abstract, ideal realm? Aesthetics of music that makes no room for recognition of instrumental virtuosity is hardly a philosophy of *music*.[30]

Finally, Led Zeppelin confirms the expectation that my listening requires sympathetic participation in a rich and fertile musical tradition, one that pulls together multiple musical categories. This is culturally self-conscious music.

Led Zeppelin's music participates in a rich and fertile tradition in just the way that the English language is rich and fertile. Both traditions are firmly *of this world*. Of course, I do not mean that Led Zeppelin is primarily within the tradition of Western art music. I mean the popular music that traditional elitism rejects as decadent and debased. My sympathetic response to "D'Yer Mak'Er" draws upon Caribbean rhythms that originally derive from Africa. It also draws upon the musical and lyrical conventions of popular love songs of the 1950s. (An additional dimension to the humor of "D'Yer Mak'Er" is that Led Zeppelin reminds us that reggae partially derives from Jamaican appropriations of American rock and roll of the 1950s.) My response also requires an ear for European harmony. But instead of aiming at the closure of the music's final tonic, this music subordinates harmony to the role of support for melody, rhythm, and language. The musical joke of the song's instrumental guitar passage assumes familiarity with multiple conventions of these traditions.[31] One cannot grasp the meanings of this music if one is deaf to the voices of the past. Reaching past the crude stereotype that Led Zeppelin's music is all about sex, we can also recognize that some of it was "world music" before the category was recognized.[32] This music is rich in cross-reference and allusion. Its riches have nothing to do with its unworldly character or its harmonic organization and complexity.

So what does a response to this music say about those who prefer it to the European classical tradition? Or about listeners who love both? Such a response involves sympathy with the project of multiculturalism. This music is multiculturalism in action. It reveals a cosmopolitan orientation in which cultural boundaries are continually erased and then redrawn, integrating diverse traditions without erasing differences and without any expectation that any one dimension of one musical culture should rule supreme. It reflects a willingness to tolerate cultural ambiguity. It betrays an orientation to finding our community here, in the empirical realm, through trial and error. It abandons the presumption that there is one musical tradition that is inherently superior to all others, and with it the view that there is only one right way to live. It deflates the utopianism of any insistence on music as a realm of pure abstraction. But the result is not that listeners are thrown back into the self-regarding narcissism of their own private desires. Music really is something into which we *join*, and all response to music is indeed a sympathetic response to a social order.

Unexpected Communities

Let us suppose that listeners simply do not understand a piece of music if they do not grasp its expressive character. At the same time, understanding is not a private matter. It demands a public act that allows individuals to determine whether others have the same response. Music is objectively expressive when informed listeners can respond to it in recognizably parallel ways.[33] The public character of that response (laughing with "D'Yer Mak'Er" or dancing in waltz time to the verses of the Beatles' "I Me Mine" and then moving in common time to the chorus) is a defining element of our relationship to the larger community of listeners.

Two other examples interest me. Both provide a reason to wonder about the superiority of Western art music as a civilizing force. More specifically, they address the ideas that music is always gestural and that corresponding dance gestures reveal the character of the social life of those who make and respond to that music.

There is something very odd about Scruton's invitation to *imagine* what sort of dancing goes with Renaissance music and then the music of the band Nirvana, and then to extrapolate in imagination to the further social relations of people who listen to such music and dance in that (imagined) manner. Why don't we look and see? We really have no idea what sort of dance is represented by a style of music if we know nothing of the lived social practices of real communities. What would we gain by trying to imagine what ethical philosophy is most appropriate to Chinese paintings of the Tang Dynasty? In the absence of a study of Chinese culture, would anyone arrive at the right mix of Daoist and Confucian principles?

As long as we dwell on the question of how any music can ever be expressive, we are in the realm of philosophical theorizing. However, specific associations between a style of music and the gestures associated with that style are contingent facts about the world, not a priori truths. If we want to discuss the mores of an audience, we ought to investigate matters of fact to determine how the audience uses the music. Only then can we say what they understand when they understand it.

My first example in illustrating this point is drawn from a film by writer/director Cameron Crowe, best known for the 1996 movie *Jerry Maguire* (1996). While each of Crowe's film projects have employed popular music with sensitivity rivaled only by Martin Scorsese, only two have been about musicians. They are *Singles* (1992) and *Almost Famous* (2000). The scene that interests me is one of the emotional highlights of *Almost Famous*.

On one level *Almost Famous* is a simple coming-of-age story. Modeled on Crowe's own initiation into journalism at sixteen, it is Crowe's first film project to draw heavily on his own life. A bright teenager loves rock music and becomes a rock critic. Crowe calls his alter ego William Miller (played by Patrick Fugit). William Miller's first major assignment involves an extended road trip across the United State with a rock band that's just on the cusp of becoming major rock stars. On another level, the story of the boy's adventures is an excuse for a series of vignettes that allow Crowe to explore rock music at the point where it emerged from underground status to become the geopolitical force that so irks traditional elitists. Prying into different relationships among musicians, fans, music promoters, and the rock press, Crowe addresses the perennial concern that popular music is both sentimental and idolatrous. But having observed the process first hand, Crowe sees evidence that it can be otherwise, and that it often is. Traditional elitists see an inevitable decline. Crowe sees both a decline and a continuing possibility for a community that finds common public expression in the popular arts.

The sequence from *Almost Famous* that interests me is one that explores the theme of musical experience as active participation in a public arena. The band's guitarist, Russell Hammond (played by Billy Crudup), has emerged as the only member of the group likely to achieve stardom, and as the tour grinds through middle America he is increasingly tempted to follow his muse and his management company and to pursue his own solo career. (Earlier rock fans will be reminded of Peter Frampton's solo career following a stint with Humble Pie or Sting's success after leaving the Police; more recent audiences might think of Beyoncé Knowles's solo success beyond her group, Destiny's Child.) One night Hammond flees the group, rock journalist Miller in tow, and hooks up with a group of teenagers who invite him to a party. Fueled by alcohol and drugs, he ends up on the roof of their house, threatening to dive into the swimming pool. Miller gets him off the roof and into the arms of the tour manager, who hauls Hammond onto the tour bus. His bandmates, the road crew, and assorted hangers-on silently observe his sullen return to their little community. No one talks. They all know that Hammond wants to leave. The radio breaks the awkward silence with a cascading piano melody, which turns out to be Elton John performing his 1971 song "Tiny Dancer." A few voices softly sing along. (It is itself a song about a girl who identifies with and sings along to a song by a pop musician.) Soon Hammond joins the singing, and the tension of the group quickly dissolves. The singing grows stronger. William Miller tells the girl seated beside him that he wants to go home. "You are home," she assures him. The bus continues its journey past the farms of the American Midwest.

It is important that the scene features a community joined in song. Often, they are a community only in being joined in song. Traditional elitism's emphasis on instrumental music received in rapt silence in the concert hall makes it plausible to focus on "latent dancing" as the most relevant audience response. But if we remind ourselves that most people are interested in songs, not absolute music, then it is relevant to ask how people really do respond to songs. (This point is the founding insight of the Kodály system of music education, which then loses sight of it with its own version of elitism.) The public activity of *joining in* is itself an expressive act, one in which we remind ourselves that we belong. In the *Almost Famous* example, the act of singing is a mending of fences, a gesture of reconciliation and mutual forgiveness. More fundamentally, raising voices in common song is a public response that creates rather than expresses community.[34] This use of song is common at sporting events and other public gatherings when the national anthem is used to unite the crowd into a common community before the other activities begin.

It is also important to consider songs because the gesture of dance is primarily a response to rhythm and not a response to tonality and melodic line. Dancing to music does not reveal everything that music can express, and if it did, then tonality would play little role in the experience of musical meaning. If we overemphasize dance as the paradigm of aesthetic response to music, we sell short the idea that informed listeners grasp a complex intentional object that conveys a range of emotions and ideas.

Consider formation dancing as an enactment of social order. Suppose the audience is dancing to a song. Participants do not understand that song unless the response is to the complex whole of music and lyric. But what sort of understanding is necessary to engage in formation dancing? The country-and-western line dance is immensely popular in the beer halls of America and much of the rest of the world. (By some measures, country music is more popular than rock music.) But it does not matter whether the actual song is a cheatin' song, a love song, or an assertion of working-class pride. The pattern of the dance is fitted to the tempo and the rhythm, not to the harmonies and the lyric. One does not have to understand very much about music to engage in communal dance. The audience's ability to synchronize their movements (physical or imagined) with the music's pulse and beat does not demonstrate a significant transition from the physical to the intentional realm. So there is no relationship between the ability to join in a Scottish Highland reel and the supposed superiority of European art music as a vehicle for presenting messages through tones.

We are merely speculating about what is to be found in a certain type of music or in a specific piece of music if we do not know what knowledge-able listeners recognize in it. I once played recordings of traditional songs from Burundi for a group of American university students. According to the liner notes, a song that my students heard as salacious was really the story of a homesick man remembering his youth. Attributing a sexual dimension to the rhythm and then to the whole song, my students demonstrated their verbal *and musical* ignorance. Similarly, a listener's ability to enter into the intentional realm when presented with the music of Beethoven does not rule out the possibility that the same listener will misunderstand hip-hop, the music of Nirvana, and other cases of seemingly simple popular music. My next example illustrates this danger of jumping to conclusions about musical meaning when one does not know what an appreciative audience actually finds in a particular piece.

As recordable compact discs became more common and more affordable at the start of the twenty-first century, the Phillips electronics corporation ran a series of print advertisements and television commercials for the Phillips CD recorder. (This equipment was not yet standard in personal computers.) They faced the challenge of making the personal CD recorder attractive without ever admitting that consumers might want to use the machines to "bootleg" music. So the Phillips advertisements emphasized the technology's use to compile music from different compact discs in one's own music collection on one disc.

One of these television commercials is particularly clever for the way that it plays with the major themes I have been examining. A clean-cut young man sets an elegant dining table: wine glasses, cloth napkins, candles. Large abstract paintings adorn the walls. The young man loads a recordable com-pact disc into his Phillips compact disc player. The doorbell sounds just as he places a single flower into an exquisite vase as the table's centerpiece. An attractive young woman is at the door. She is clearly impressed by his efforts as they sit down to dinner. He picks up a remote control unit, aims it at the CD player, and a crude, grinding, industrial noise erupts over a steady, brutal beat. A deep, growling voice joins the clanging, discordant grind of "industrial" rock. The guttural timbre of the voice is the sort that's used in horror films for characters subject to demonic possession. It rasps, "Let me call you sweetheart / I'm in love with you." Cut to a close up of the young woman. Her eyes widen. She is confused. Then a sly smile appears on her lips. She starts moving to the rhythm of the music, and a moment later they are both swaying to the same rhythm.

The joke, of course, is the moment when her surprise gives way to delight. We are invited to think that she's horrified by his horrible lapse in taste: you can't let *this* music into *this* social exchange! But she isn't horrified. She's touched by his expression of love and by its being an expression that provides her with an opportunity for response. He has correctly provided music that gratifies her tastes, and she conveys her appreciation of the musical gesture by moving joyfully with it. This style of music is just the sort that Scruton attacks as "a dehumanizing of the spirit of song." Yet the young woman is clearly responding to what the music says to her. She understands that this musical gesture is also his gesture. Had he chosen music expressing something contrary to the spirit of the evening, she would not have welcomed the music. At the same time, she might not grasp and accept the gesture if it were rendered in another musical style: a Burundi folk song or the jazz singing of Billie Holiday might convey exactly the same sentiments to a different audience, but not to her. Mere philosophizing cannot tell us whether grunge and industrial rock music are really so different from Franz Schubert and Richard Wagner when it comes to questions of musical expression.

The Politics of Noise

Appealing to broad symbolic meanings, traditional elitism argues that the aesthetic success of one category of music is allied with its "claim to moral superiority."[35] In response, my closing argument is entirely speculative. It is the proposal that an important ideal is expressed by the abrasive eruption of beat and sounds that is characteristic of recent rock music. That ideal is the ideal of music as an expression of ordered living. But where European art music has offered that "spiritual" ideal by sublimating rhythm in favor of tonal adventure, rock music offers a more earthbound metaphor for life. Rather than "reminding" us of utopia, rock offers a continuing metaphor for the struggle to build human community.

The central insight behind this proposal is Jacques Attali's point that musical organization is a species of political organization. There are strong parallels between Attali and the fourth theme we identified in traditional elitism. For instance, there is Attali's thesis that "the code of music simulates the accepted rules of society." The conditions underlying the existence of a musical culture are the condition for the creation and consolidation of every community.[36] Hence, deviations from the communal project are literally noise, and the existence of music requires the suppression of noise and a "silencing" of discordant activity. When an individual develops a taste for the musical organization typical of that individual's culture, Attali proposes that she literally subordinates herself to the body politic.

But what of music that embraces noise, allowing it to coexist with melody and harmony and rhythm? Scruton listens to a recording by Nirvana and complains that it is deficient in melody and its "amplified overtones" drown out its inept harmonies. He concludes that fans of such music cannot possibly be listening *to* the music, and so their interest must be in something else. There can be no contesting the fact that Nirvana secured a large fan base through a single song, "Smells Like Teen Spirit" (1991). At the turn of the millennium, the song was chosen as the third most significant pop song of the past forty years by *Rolling Stone* magazine and VH1 television. (Songs by the Beatles and the Rolling Stones took the number one and number two slots.)

Nirvana's recording of "Smells Like Teen Spirit" is a furious blast of rock and roll. It is also graced with an aching, sweet melody. Except for one or two songs and then the television broadcast and subsequent album, *MTV Unplugged in New York* (1994), Nirvana brought together elements of heavy metal and punk rock by accompanying every song with the rapid strumming of feedback-drenched rhythm guitar. The vocals tended to be throaty, shouted rasps. The arrangements seem designed to disguise Kurt Cobain's flair for melody, yet it really was Cobain's way with melody that distinguished Nirvana from a thousand other punk-influenced bands and catapulted them into the ranks of major pop stars.

The melodic sense that is supposedly deficient in Nirvana is demonstrated by Tori Amos's version of "Smells Like Teen Spirit," recorded in 1992. Arranged only for piano and voice, it sits sandwiched on *Crucify* between similar reductions of songs by the Rolling Stones and Led Zeppelin. Presented by a classically trained pianist as if it were a piece of nineteenth-century German romanticism, the regularity of the accompanying piano figure recalls one of Schubert's most famous lieder, "Gretchen am Spinnrade." Amos sings the same words and melody as Cobain, but liberated from the distraction of the guitar and pounding drums, she highlights the way that the pauses in the melody express hesitancy, confusion, and forbearance. Amos's singing increases in projection and intensity at the end, so that the song's resolution on the anticipated tonic is a gesture of resignation. (In some of her own songs, Amos's reliance on modal—rather than tonal—progressions creates musical directionality that will be lost on those who favor tonal idioms.)[37]

All of these musical elements of the song are there to be heard in Nirvana's version of the song. What Nirvana's arrangement contributes is, in a word, noise. Amos emphasizes the song's melodic power. Nirvana makes listeners work to hear it. I suppose that nonfans will interpret this as incompetence or decadence. But if we return to our earlier insight that something might be happening here that is only constituted intentionally, then we must ask what we are to understand by Nirvana's continuing decision to put melody and accompaniment into such sharp conflict. This is not speculation about Cobain's personal intentions. Rather, it is an attempt to articulate the music's aesthetic appeal as something that includes noise, and not as music that is appealing despite the noise.

For listeners who hear the melody and the elements of noise as two parts of a musical complex, the refusal to let melody triumph can stand for a political refusal. As if intended to illustrate Attali's claims about music, noise, and political organization, Nirvana refuses to "normalize" its activity in conformity to the demand that tonality must govern music.[38] There is melodic gesture. But there is not the extreme subordination of discord that has been the price of tonality in European art music. At the same time, the group displays discipline in audible acts of repeatedly taming noise, of civilizing chaos, of controlling impulsive outburst of sound and energy. In live performance (documented on Nirvana's *From the Muddy Banks of the Wishkah*), virtually every Nirvana song began with a piercing wail of feedback that is suddenly interrupted by a burst of rhythmic strumming, establishing the song's pulse before the drums and bass guitar enter. Finally, we hear the voice that supplies the melody. Here, listeners are vividly reminded that music involves continuous discipline and suppression of noise. The transformation of noise into rhythm invokes Puritanism far more than decadence.

Sounding very much like Scruton, Attali believes that the "new noise" of both John Cage and the Rolling Stones represents the collapse of the old order of musical and social organization without announcing anything new.[39] I have proposed something different. Cage may be the pinnacle of a modernist movement that rejected the logic of tonal music, but the Rolling Stones and Nirvana were never part of that legacy and so their actions are not specifically a repudiation of it. Nirvana's music may be an illustration of the tensions of bourgeois life, but their musical balancing act of noise and melody is a stand against the degree of repression that we often assume everyone must accept as the price of modern life. This public gesture is directed at society at the end of the twentieth century, not at Europe in the nineteenth. Ten years later, Nirvana's style of music is out of fashion and, hip-hop excepted, "noisy" music has become a distinctly minority taste. We may hear the nonthreatening, best-selling music of Norah Jones, John Mayer, Shania Twain, Jack Johnson, Enya, and teen idols as gestures of conformity. But let's avoid the mistake of thinking that popular music that turns its back on music dominated by the intentional world of tones (tonality as in the Western classical system) is less musical.

Nirvana's arrangement of "Smells Like Teen Spirit" employs sound to elicit an intelligible experience. It displays musical intelligence. It may be interpreted as directing us back to facts about this world and as illustrating the brutal struggle involved in the pursuit of a perfect order. However, it would be a serious mistake to suppose that philosophy reveals a correlation between immutable, objective musical values and the ideal organization of human society. Philosophy of music may well tell us that the meaning of music lies in the sympathetic response of knowledgeable listeners. But we need something more than aesthetic theory to demonstrate that only a decadent musical taste approves of "D'Yer Mak'Er" and "Smells Like Teen Spirit."

7. Taste and Musical Identity

Haven't old people always tended to see too absolutely and too moralistically? . . .
And haven't they—we—always been puzzled by the enthusiasms of the young for
things that we have outgrown; and no less puzzled by their lack of sympathy for
things that we continue to feel enthusiastic about but that the times have outgrown?

—Igor Stravinsky, *Dialogues and a Diary*

Looking for an image to illustrate a document and vaguely recalling a photograph that I had seen some years before, I turned to my computer and
conducted an Internet image search. I wanted a photograph of the band
Talking Heads, a band that routinely engaged my interest from the appearance of their debut, *Talking Heads: 77*, until their final album, *Naked*, in
1988. Typing the prompt "Talking Heads" into the search engine, I was
rewarded with hundreds of images of the group. I soon located the shot I
wanted, an early concert photo of the band at the New York club CBGB's.
But at the very moment that I found it, I was hit with a gut response of
intense nostalgia. It was as if I had lost something that mattered very much
to me, forgotten it, and then had been reminded of it, and of its loss. Or it
felt as if I'd just been told of the death of someone I cared about but had not
thought about in a very long time. But who or what had I lost? What was I
recalling, and why? It was not a response to the image I'd been seeking. I'd
wanted a copy of a specific photograph, but there was nothing about that
image that meant anything special to me.

I surveyed the other tiny "thumbnail" images in their neat rows on my
computer screen. One seemed familiar, yet I did not consciously remember
having seen it before. It was a photograph of the four members of Talking
Heads, accompanied by some kind of block lettering. I clicked on the image
to enlarge it. It turned out to be a concert poster advertising a Talking
Heads show, carrying the words "Monday 8 PM/October 1/Freeborn

Hall/UC Davis." I had attended that very show in Freeborn Hall for performances by the B52s and then Talking Heads. The B52s were great fun. Talking Heads were absolutely riveting.

I must have seen that poster many times in the weeks leading up to the concert. Copies would have been all over the campus, stapled to kiosks and taped to doors and windows. A tiny digital image of a forgotten poster had stirred my memories, tapping into my emotional investment in a musical moment that I had not thought about for many years. It gripped me with a nostalgia and sense of loss for a musical identity that was once important to me—so important, we might say, that it is part of me.

Without denying that there might be other reasons for my gut response to long-unheard music, it points to a deep and intimate relationship to that music. This relationship is different from the developing realization that the music is genuinely good of its kind, for the music that we feel most intimately connected with is not necessarily music that, in hindsight, we regard as good. There is other music that I once enjoyed that has lost its luster and which, when I hear it, fails to move me. The amount of time that I once invested in specific music does not appear to be correlated with its having a particular quality of intimacy.

Presumably, my strong response indicates that this music played an important role in my personal identity. Studying the social construction of identity, many researchers examine music's role in the articulation of gender, class, ethnicity, and social status. There is strong agreement that musical taste is an important "badge of identity," particularly during adolescence.[1] Adolescence appears to be the age when people learn to judge others according to the styles of music they prefer—and consequently it is the age when most listeners narrow, rather than expand, their range of listening. Some cultural studies of music endorse this standpoint for every judgment about music: "Ultimately, judgments of music are judgments of people. [Music] analysis is not about structure; it is about people, because people make and perceive structures."[2]

I will address this idea by pushing it in a slightly different direction. Rather than stress how judgments of music are always judgments of *other* people, or about a listener's relationship to the larger society, I want to suggest that music's sense of emotional depth might stem from a different source, music's value in articulating the *concept* of "self" to each listener.

Music in Identities

Decades of research have made it clear that musicality is an innate drive, as fundamental as speech but prior to it in each infant's life.[3] This musicality first emerges in vocal games between infants and adults. Colwyn Trevarthen is almost apologetic when he notes that the pride taken in "advanced musicianship" is "not so far removed" from the pride a six-month-old takes in sharing a musical game.[4] Yet this interpretation of infant behavior, if correct, suggests the deep origins of the appreciative response.[5] But we also know that musical instinct can be smothered through conformity to social expectations about cultivated musical skill.

It is refreshing to read about the rich and varied modes of musicianship in children's lives. Patricia Shehan Campbell found that children engage in a wide variety of musical play and that singing is central to the self-identities of many children.[6] Spontaneous rhythmic music making is constantly present in children's lives—something already apparent to most people who work with small children in institutional situations, such as teachers who are expected to squelch such activity. Sadly, Western culture's emphasis on serious music and trained musicianship privileges the musical activities of a small (and shrinking) elite, frustrating the very search for community that underlies the human drive to make music. This trend toward musical specialization has resulted in the phenomenon of identities in music, where particular cultural roles are assigned differently to different individuals. Thus we think of Madonna and Elvis Presley as singers, but not musicians, and guitarists Jimi Hendrix and Eddie Van Halen as musicians, not singers.

When researchers move beyond the topics of infancy and trained musicianship, attention usually shifts to the issue of how music is used to construct social identities. Thus we distinguish *identities in music* (Madonna is a singer) from *music in identities,* where music is used to facilitate some aspect of nonmusical identity.[7] As we saw in chapter 2, there is a tendency to claim that music does the latter sort of work by excluding others from a group—ironically reversing music's function in infancy, where it serves as a vehicle for one-on-one social bonding. Music preferences become a vehicle for establishing or developing aspects of nonmusical identity (e.g., being female or belonging to an in-group). When it is noted that males tend to be collectors of music (i.e., of recorded music) in a way that females are not, it is assumed that modes of collecting reflect and reinforce gender. When it is noted that adolescent males are far more likely to spend time doing nothing but listening to music, this behavior is interpreted as time spent internalizing identity stereotypes associated with the music. There is no thought about the possibility that being a collector is itself a significant musical identity, that is, an identity in music, or that the activity of listening might itself be an important operation in the construction of self-identity.

For example, one research team used listening to popular and unpopular music styles as examples of positive and negative behaviors. Without labeling them as "positive" and "negative," the researchers counted on the tendency of adolescents to treat them as such. Indeed, English adolescents took the bait and regarded time spent with classical music as a very undesirable activity. The purpose of the study was to confirm that adolescents would create relatively favorable explanations for this listening activity if it was attributed to their friends, and unfavorable explanations for exactly the same activity when it was attributed to an "out-group." This result was confirmed. But the striking thing about the study is the researchers' warning not to read it as a study of music and musical taste: "we are confident that the current participants' response reflected underlying identity concerns," rather than anything related to music.[8]

So studies about music and identity formation are seldom about music. The controlling assumption is that "musical behavior is guided . . . by group identity needs."[9] If we examine the special case of music in adolescence, we are reassured that adolescent interest in music reflects psychological or anthropological patterns that explain intergroup behavior in general. It is assumed that there is nothing *special* about the relationship between music and identity. Like everyone else, adolescents use music as they use sports and entertainment, dress codes, and eating rituals, as a means for "obtaining security in one's own identity whilst simultaneously achieving knowledge and understanding of others."[10] So the trend is to deny that most people develop significant *musical* identities. We learn nothing at all about why *music* is so useful for finding, developing, and communicating aspects of social and personal identity. But isn't this one of the things that we want to understand about musical taste?

Many people report that adolescent encounters with music are among the most intense experiences of life, and males, in particular, turn to music specifically for intense experiences. Dave Evans, guitarist in the rock band U2, reports very typical adolescent behavior, less influenced by peers than by the experience he got from music when alone:

> I didn't go out an awful lot. Those are the years when I listened to the most music . . . between fourteen and sixteen. That was when album like *Horses,* by Patti Smith, came out. There were some good records around that time—Lou Reed, [David] Bowie, the first Talking Heads records. Nobody else was really listening to those records, but they really meant a lot to me. I always remember that when someone who's sort of fifteen or sixteen comes up to me and talks about our records. I remember how I felt about records at that age.[11]

Although he became a musician, he fits the typical pattern of narrowing his musical interests and, simultaneously, responding strongly to the music he prefers. But why music, more than any other artistic medium?

What I propose is not in conflict with psychological and cultural accounts of music and identity. Those accounts ask how we acquire the specific social and personal identities that we construct, and how different kinds of music correlate with various identities. But I am pursuing the very different question of why music (of *any* sort) seems more pertinent to identity than does one's food preferences or one's taste in fashion or most hobbies. Connections between identity and food or fashion are susceptible to precisely the same sort and level of analysis given to music and identity. But I suspect that these links are more pertinent with music than with most cultural signifiers, because music can be more central to identity than whether one likes extra pickles on a hamburger or even whether one hopes to become a doctor or a kindergarten teacher.

Even within a social constructionist paradigm, in which each individual's musical identities are seen to depend on contingent sociocultural vicissitudes, musical identity might prove to be a deep element of identity, so that the music one liked as an adolescent is more noteworthy than how one wore one's hair. Without romanticizing innate musical sensibilities, we should begin with the obvious point that musicality is an innate human drive. Then we might take notice of the fact that listening to music is the "most preferred leisure interest" for adolescents of both sexes.[12] We might then wonder whether music does any special work for us during adolescence and young adulthood.[13]

Adolescence and the Problem of Self-Identity

Against this backdrop, I would like to pursue the insight that adolescence and young adulthood is a distinctive stage of our *musical* lives, uniquely configured so that an individual's relationship to music plays a profound role in the formation of identity. Music may be exceptionally suited to serve as a tangible model for making sense of both self and self–identity.

It might seem that the centrality of music to adolescence is readily explained by citing the connection between music and expression of emotion. We can simply cite the increasing emotional sensitivity and turbulence that has become the norm during adolescence in Western and industrialized societies.

> The liminal period of adolescence, then, might be thought of as a period when a person has multiple and fragmented conceptions of who he or she is, *and* concurrently, a time when responsibility for emotional self-regulation is being transferred, albeit sometimes precariously, from parent to child. . . . In sum, the softening and fragmentation of the self contributes to fragmentation and more frequently pain in adolescents' daily emotional experience.[14]

The "emotional images of music" offer a package of intense emotions and identity scripts, which adolescents temporarily (and repeatedly) "assume" as a stabilizing mechanism.[15] Yet relatively little research substantiates the supposed connection. Furthermore, television, books, and films are probably more powerful than music in presenting and dealing with concrete human problems and their attendant emotions. More to the point, it does not seem to matter *what* music is chosen. When classical music takes the place of popular music in adolescence, it occupies the same role in listeners' private time.[16] On balance, the "emotional images of music" do not explain why *music* occupies so much more time—and seems so powerful—during adolescence. Perhaps there is some way that music itself helps adolescents to stabilize their fragmenting conceptions of self.

I will suggest a more fundamental attraction of music by drawing on an influential argument about personal identity in David Hume's philosophy. He was one of the first thinkers to argue that personal identity is not a matter of discovering the self through careful introspection: the idea of an "invariable and uninterrupted" self is an invented "fiction."[17] The fiction of a stable and unchanging self is a heuristically useful construct of memory and imagination, but there is never any experiential confirmation that such a self exists.

Here is Hume's famous summary of the thesis that one's self-identity is not a matter of locating an observable, stable self:

> For my part, when I enter most intimately into what I call *myself*, I always stumble on some particular perception or other, of heat or cold, light or shade, love or hatred, pain or pleasure. I never can catch *myself* at any time without a perception, and never can observe any thing but the perception. . . . If any one, upon serious and unprejudic'd reflection thinks he has a different notion of himself, I must confess I can reason no longer with him. All I can allow him is, that he may be in the right as well as I, and that we are essentially different in this particular. He may, perhaps, perceive something simple and continu'd, which he calls himself; tho' I am certain there is no such principle in me.[18]

Hume is making the important point that I find nothing in me that will even serve as a stable prototype of the concept of self. Seeking a stable, authentic self, each individual finds only "a bundle or collection of different perceptions, which succeed each other with an inconceivable rapidity, and are in a perpetual flux and movement."[19] The harder I look for my "self," the more fragmented I seem to be.

But if each person needs to attach content to the term *self*, constructing a concept to give meaning to the term, and if we do not find some stable core ready to be observed through introspection, where do we find the template for the concept we employ in constructing a self-identity?

> There are some philosophers, who imagine we are every moment intimately conscious of what we call our SELF; that we feel its existence and its continuance in existence; and are certain, beyond the evidence of a demonstration, both of its perfect identity and simplicity. . . . Unluckily all these positive assertions are contrary to that very experience, which is pleaded for them, nor have we any idea of self, after the manner it is here explain'd. For from what impression cou'd this idea be deriv'd? . . . If any impression gives rise to the idea of self, that impression must continue invariably the same, thro' the whole course of our lives; since self is suppos'd to exist after that manner. But there is no impression constant and

invariable. Pain and pleasure, grief and joy, passions and sensations succeed each other, and never all exist at the same time. It cannot, therefore,
be from any of these impressions, or from any other, that the idea of self
is deriv'd; and consequently there is no such idea.[20]

Whatever the self is, it is not *discovered*. It must be *constructed*. But this generates the obvious question of why each individual *seeks* a self, for Hume
claims that there is a natural "propensity" to attribute stable personal identity to the flux of perception and emotion. For an answer, Hume turns to
the workings of memory and imagination.[21]

Hume's positive proposal centers on the claim that we develop two distinct concepts of object identity. Drawing on new work on the psychology
of concept development and use, we can read him as proposing that there
are two basic schemata for object identity.[22] The first, virtually unknown in
experience beyond our short-term perception, is of a thing "invariable and
uninterrupted" over some period of time. An example might be a green
book sitting on my desk. Without moving it or myself, I observe its
unchanging shape and color for five seconds. In the absence of change, I
count it as the same book at the end of the process as at the start.

The second notion of identity is "of several different objects existing in
succession, and connected together by a close relation." Here, a collection
of things is treated as a single thing. For example, I regard a moving freight
train as single object although I do not actually observe the physical connections between the visibly distinct cars of the train. By imagining the
presence of unobserved connections between the cars, I regard the train as
one object. (It helps that I've previously observed the couplings that connect stationary freight cars, and my imagination supplies them to the moving freight cars.) Once we grasp that a succession of perceived objects can
be a single object, we apply the strategy more radically. We adopt concepts
by which we "imagine something unknown and mysterious, connecting
the parts." In the case of the train, I could go over to it and see the connections. But what if we cannot?

Imagination often corrects for observed "interruption or variation" by
constructing fictions, setting aside what we have observed in favor of an
unchanging object. So despite many changes in membership, we count this
year's senior class as identical with last year's junior class. Imagination often
postulates "mysterious," empirically inaccessible unity to a collection, and

jumps to the unverifiable conclusion that some invariant element underlies the limited similarities we actually observe.[23]

Socially constructed categories play an important role in the process of assigning identity. Based on the words that others use to categorize things, we learn that different types of objects are allowed to display different ranges of variation and diversity. If we see a very small dog and then a very much larger dog in the same place twenty-four hours later, we immediately conclude that it is a different dog. Dogs are not the sort of things that change that much, that quickly. In contrast, Hume notes, "the nature of a river consists in the motion and change of parts," and we count it as the same river although it changes dramatically over the same twenty-four hours. Following a heavy rain, I regard the local river as the same river even when I see that it has more than doubled in size. We learn that it is the "nature" of other things to preserve identity in other ways: if a brick church is destroyed and then replaced with a stone church, built in a different style, we treat them as the same church through "their relation to the inhabitants of the parish." Yet the two physical buildings have no direct connection to one another. We simply find it easier to ignore the complexity of lived experience. We set this complexity aside, and imagine that related objects are identical by hypothesizing an unconfirmed sameness.[24]

Imagining Music and Imagining Self

So how does Hume's proposal about imagination and two types of identity help us to understand adolescence and musical identities? Musical appreciation demands surprisingly complex decisions about identity. In developing the capacity to perceive a musical work in a specific sound event, listeners must learn to distinguish between what is unique to the sounds, considered as the material instantiation of the work, and the work itself. This point is often made by observing that there is a difference between the tokens (specific aural events) and the type (the musical composition).[25] In some ways, music is like Hume's example of the river. In other ways, music is more like the church. Like a river, it is the nature of a musical work to consist of a succession of perceptually successive and differing items. Like the church, we learn to count two perceptually and temporally distinct appearances as manifestations of the same object.

Yet most children understand these basic principles of musical work identity at a very early age, generally beginning around the age of eighteen months.[26] For purposes of illustration, I will cite my own experiences as a parent. One day I dropped a CD into the stereo system and pushed "play." Fifteen or twenty seconds later, my five-year-old looked up from his toys and said, "Hey, this is *Fantasia*."[27] It was Beethoven's sixth symphony and my son remembered the music from having seen the film twice, some months earlier. He had not yet received any formal musical training, yet he understood that this music (in an "authentic" performance instead of Leopold Stokowski's adaptation) was the same music that he'd heard twice before. The same year, he surprised me when he demonstrated further awareness of Beethoven, in this case the opening phrase of Beethoven's Symphony No. 5. Having head it a few times on the stereo in standard orchestral dress (conducted by John Eliot Gardiner), my son spontaneously taught himself how to play the opening four notes on the piano. He thus demonstrated that he already understood that the timbre of the strings and clarinet are not essential to the musical work, nor is the orchestral *fortissimo* that his index finger could not reproduce.

As Hume proposes, the involuntary operations of memory and imagination led my son to seek and impose identity in the face of perceptually and temporally distinct sets of perceptions. Nobody tried to get him to adopt these assumptions about musical identity. He imposed them on his experiences, suggesting that infants and children possess "innate psychological foundations of both musical behavior and musical awareness."[28] As a "willing and active candidate" in the socialization process, my son's musical behavior confirms that such behavior is a by-product of an "innate drive."[29]

This interpretation of childhood behavior distinguishes between innate drives and the subsequent habits formed on the basis of "observation and experience."[30] Equipped with the same innate instincts and cognitive faculties and exposed to similar circumstances, each individual spontaneously generates similar habits of response (including similar abstract thoughts about self and world). We thus explain how individuals agree on topics such as personal identity without postulating either innate ideas or behaviorism.[31]

Let's now leap from childhood recognition of musical work identity as a manifestation of innate drives to the identity issues that typically arise in human adolescence. Besides the more obvious physical changes associated with puberty and sexual maturation, adolescence is a time of intense cognitive maturation, including transition to genuine hypothetical, deductive, and abstract thinking.[32] Thinking that was previously tied to concrete cases gives way to analysis of concrete circumstances in light of abstract concepts and ideals. Expanding self-awareness is facilitated as adolescents learn to view themselves from multiple viewpoints, including that of their increasingly important peers. This period of life is particularly interesting to social constructionists, for this period is dominated by exploration of "multiple selves," that is, of the possibility that different and even antithetical principles may guide behavior at different times. Many adolescents struggle with the loss of any clear "core" self as personal identity becomes increasingly independent of identification with basic, rigid categories (e.g., "I'm a girl" or "I'm seven years old"). Adolescents differ widely in how many options they are willing to explore in attempting to construct a coherent identity.

While biological dispositions account for the strong interest in music displayed by infants and young children, why is an interest in music (particularly the "leisure" activity of *listening* to music) so important in the lives of adolescents, who no longer rely on it for communication with others? It may appear that musical taste and musical behavior are simply two more avenues to explore as adolescents sort through their "multiple selves," no different from nor more important than any other. But we should not forget that the adolescent search for identity is driven by enhanced cognitive abilities. Achieving a coherent self-understanding is a challenge *because* that self-understanding is no longer tied to concrete thinking. Abstract thinking equips the adolescent to question the meaning of life and the status of the self.[33] (Following Hume's model of analogical reasoning, we might note that dogs and horses also experience adolescence, but they do not appear to undergo any parallel period of identity crisis.) It is only upon developing abstract cognition that adolescents become aware of the diversity of their own choices and of the diversity of points of view that will evaluate and respond to those choices. The challenge of constructing a self-identity is driven by a Humean realization that nothing concrete—"no impression constant and invariable"—anchors the integration of self-identity. At this stage of life, even the physical body is in flux.

Music's power, particularly in adolescence, may stem from the manner in which it serves as an external model for the concept of self, anchoring the very process of identity formation. The process by which individuals stabilize a self-identity is remarkably like that for recognizing musical identity, such as the identity of the self-same piece of music in temporally separated and sonically distinct performances. As I've noted, most preadolescent children know how to identify musical works despite the fact that they are dealing with objects that count as "same" in multiple and very different concrete instantiations. Furthermore, because music is a temporal art, with works unfolding in time, this ability to recognize musical works involves the ability to project sequences of sounds in advance of actually hearing them.

I have endorsed the view that music must appeal to the imagination before it can appeal to the emotions. This is an old hypothesis. The "auditory imagination," proposes nineteenth-century music critic Eduard Hanslick, is the process of finding "mysterious bonds and affinities among tones," so that within its "continuous self-formation" we perceive "the organic, rational coherence of a group of tones."[34] This sense of coherence (or, in problematic cases, incoherence) arises only through the coordination of memory and imagination. This coordination both constructs and evaluates a single object in the succession of perceptually successive and differing sensations. Hanslick emphasizes the complexity of the achievement of enjoying music as a "mental" project: "its achievements are not static; they do not come into being all at once but spin themselves out sequentially before the hearer." Of course, many people never learn to integrate all the components of complex music, so "indolent" listeners focus on vocal melodies at the expense of harmonic complexity.[35]

Putting aside the dated aspects of Hanslick, it is interesting to notice that his theory of imaginative listening is motivated by issues that are strikingly similar to Hume's description of his attempts to sense himself through introspection. As we saw in our initial discussion of imagining, Hanslick invokes imagination just because the music must be constructed from the flow of sound: "It goes without saying that this mental streaming this way and that, this continual give and take, occurs unconsciously and at the speed of lightning. . . . Without mental activity, there can be no aesthetical pleasure whatever."[36] What we attend to in music is what we find when we engage in introspection. We follow a succession of local experiences that "spin themselves out sequentially." We do not perceive anything that remains the "same" from the beginning to the end that will distinguish one piece of music from another.

Theorists who emphasize the hierarchical organization of tonal music will dispute this point, insisting that when listening to such music, people can and should attend to the unifying level of the underlying harmony. Yet it is relatively clear that, even if one thinks people *should* listen for this unifying architecture, almost no one (if anyone) actually listens for it. Based on experimental studies, it is increasingly clear that listeners are relatively indifferent to music's tonal unity and global organization. Even highly trained adult musicians attend to local coherence and coherent succession rather than to any underlying architecture that unifies the music.[37] Hanslick and music theory to the contrary, it appears that our basic nature is that of "indolent" listeners.

Given these parallels between listening to music and introspecting for the self, there are four distinct ways that music may help adolescents to construct a concept of self as a scaffold for self-identity. Adolescent investment in music as a leisure activity may make several subtle contributions to the process of "discovering" one's identity.

First, because we are equipped with an innate disposition to recognize musical objects in advance of the adolescent challenge of constructing a self-identity, adolescents may be drawn to music for the opportunity to practice the mental task of integrating successive experiences into a coherent object. The important point is that we recognize a musical work only when we actively construct the appropriate object in the "auditory" imagination. The process may seem passive (one merely listens and hears, just as one simply looks at physical objects and sees them). But it is not. However "recreational" it may appear, informed listening to music always involves a complex synthesis and analysis of competing clusters of unfolding sensations.

In the same way that a successful musical performance enhances an individual's sense of self (as autonomous yet capable), the simpler activity of listening can provide the reassuring pleasure of finding a stable and coherent object within a "lively arabesque."[38] So listening to music of a familiar style involves an easily repeatable and generally successful exercise of the mental processes that are needed to construct a sense of self. Even the repetitive behavior of listening to the same song again and again may have far more to do with securing a needed a sense of stability (through satisfied anticipation) than with the specific emotional content of the piece of music.

Second, music is a powerful memory stimulus. Tia DeNora explores the implication that music's temporal quality gives it a unique capacity to integrate or "interlace" diverse experiences that happen to coincide with hearing the music. Rehearing the music (whether a song or a musical group or even a style of music) at a later date encourages us to vividly recall associated events. Through their association with music, memories of otherwise mundane events, times, and places seem unusually integrated and meaningful. So to the extent that a sense of self-identity literally begins with one's memories, music's power to enhance and integrate selected extra-musical memories contributes to the construction of self in unpredictable but powerful ways. Music serves as an unconscious principle of selection in the ongoing project of assembling an identity from the total sum of one's past.[39]

Third, musical works may themselves serve as a prototype of the elusive sort of *thing* that we seek in trying to establish personal identity.[40] Musical works offer a model of the *type* of intangible object that we seek when we seek ourselves.[41] Consider the major parallels. In order to grasp music, listeners must locate a distinctive kind of object. To use Hume's description, the listener must hypothesize "a close relation" that unites sounds delivered to the listener as "several different objects existing in succession." Even the simplest popular songs generally alternate vocal and instrumental passages and feature distinct verses and choruses. Furthermore, adolescents tend to narrow their listening to a single style of music. By comparing different heavy metal bands or the earlier and later work of a favorite vocalist, adolescents restrict their comparisons to a perceptually similar music, increasing their likelihood of finding some measure of coherence. An additional level of complexity faces music fans who listen to the "same" music in different interpretations. Before recordings, music was almost always heard with noticeable variation from performance to performance. Today, most adolescents will collect and compare many recordings by a few favorite musicians, and many fans will seek out multiple mixes of the same recording. Fans attend to small differences in a succession of similar objects, remembering earlier cases while comparing them (in the auditory imagination) with present cases.

Both musical works and musical styles are realized differently in many specific examples, each of which is apprehended as a unified object only because the listener has assembled that object in the act of listening. Each encounter with music has its own unique character, yet these multiple instantiations are recognizable as appearances of a common "thing." Similarly, the adolescent struggles to find a stable self that unites the multiple selves that emerge in diverse settings and contexts. In each case what is sought is relational, not concrete. With both music and the self, the object sought is a relational connection uniting a varied set of experiences.

Whether a listener enjoys the same recording again and again, recognizes a piece in a fresh interpretation, or hears a new song in a preferred style, what feels like a process of discovery is really a process of imaginative construction informed by memory. Of these three cases, constructing self-identity is less like rehearing a favorite record than it is like listening to many different interpretations of the same piece. Here, the musical object must be granted stability despite awareness that it can show very different faces to the world. Its stability is always postulated more than it is experienced. Yet what is more mundane than enjoying a piece of music? Music offers a daily reminder that an object as ontologically mysterious and complex as a piece of music is, after all, a perfectly familiar sort of thing.

Fourth, adolescence is also a time when listening genuinely qualifies as musical taste. Mere liking and disliking finally leads to appreciation. But how could the response of appreciation happen sooner? In advance of a developing capacity for self-awareness about the desirability of one's habits, preferences, and behaviors, we cannot evaluate our own listening with the requisite response. While many researchers concentrate on the heightened emotions of adolescence, appreciation demands the additional ability to ask whether one endorses the response. So in addition to rehearsing emotional "scripts" provided by the music, adolescents may be rehearsing their own newfound capacity for second-order responses, a cognitive capacity that becomes increasingly important as adolescents move into adult life.

In conclusion, the instinct guiding musical behavior in infancy may be equally valuable in adolescence. But where an infant receives benefits by engaging in music making with others, the self-aware adolescent may receive benefits from the seemingly "passive" activity of recreational listening. The mere act of listening to music can be a model for finding extramusical identity. One result is that the music that still resonates in memory and imagination can, decades later, revive experiences that are profoundly *of the self*, for they are echoes of the very experience of becoming ourselves.

Conclusion

One of the greatest joys I've yet found in life is to listen to Bobby Bland—it
doesn't have to have any further point than that, unless I want to tell someone else
they should perhaps check him out for themselves.
    —Elvis Costello, *Musician,* October 1983

Popular music serves many purposes in daily life. It is used for mood regu-
lation, memory enhancement, dancing and other synchronization of the
body, social construction and display of subcultural identity, and distraction
from boring routines. Because these uses go a long way toward explaining
patterns of popular music consumption, it is tempting to suppose that the
music's aesthetic value contributes little or nothing to the popularity of any
particular song, recording, or performer. As a result, standard analyses of
popular music have relatively little to say about its aesthetic strengths and
weaknesses. Ironically, many accounts of popular music end up reinforcing
elitist condemnations of the same music: popular music does not interest us
for its aesthetic value. Both defenders and detractors de-aestheticize most of
the music that dominates everyday life and ordinary culture.

Additional obstacles hinder recognition that popular music has aesthetic
value. Music is now so ubiquitous that we might suppose that most people
"turn off" their appreciative activity with most music, most of the time.
Furthermore, popular music is often incorporated into other activities or
experiences. When it functions as background music or as secondary object
of focus, there is little incentive to reflect on whether it is good or bad, better or worse, as the source of a particular experience.

In spite of all this, I've argued that aesthetic value plays an important part
in the experience of popular music. Popular music's many nonaesthetic
functions are frequently enhanced, not diminished, by our interest in aesthetically valuable experiences. To see how this can be so, it is necessary to
give up the idea that aesthetically valuable experiences are infrequent, or

beyond the reach of ordinary people, or reserved for reverential interactions with a few very special objects. As John Dewey argued decades ago, our understanding of aesthetic experience should be grounded in relatively ordinary lived experiences. I realize that my use of a small number of extended examples—Led Zeppelin, the Beach Boys, Bruce Springsteen, Queen, and Nirvana played important roles in my argument—invites criticism. But I consciously selected influential and immensely popular musicians whose music furnishes aesthetically valuable experiences to many millions of listeners who couldn't care less about the music's art status. Thinking about such music shows that music's aesthetic value is not always a matter of autonomous, timeless sonic structures. I leave it to others to decide if it's a mere coincidence that the rise of popular culture has coincided with increasing intellectual reconsideration of the doctrine that aesthetic value involves a distinct, cloistered realm of experience.

None of which implies that popular music is a completely unique case within the broad domain of popular culture. In the course of my argument I pointed to parallels with movie viewing and joke telling, and to ordinary activities such as taking a walk. More to the point, popular music is often present as a contributing element of ordinary activities. Its integration into everyday environments and other experiences speaks for, not against, its aesthetic importance. Once again, this admission involves giving up the stereotypical description of aesthetic value as autonomous and reserved for perceptual objects that lack significant relationships to other realms of value. But a few moments of attention paid to any older form of cultural expression challenge the autonomy model of aesthetic value. Twenty-five centuries ago, the ancient Greeks produced terra-cotta amphora vases to hold wine. The utility of this pottery does not detract from its considerable aesthetic value. We would be foolish to suppose that the people who made and used these things were so concerned with their utility that they were insensitive to their harmony and grace. The craftsmen who made them and the people who used them were people very much like us. That is to say, they had aesthetic sensibilities that extended to and informed the ordinary objects of daily life. Are we simply too close to the popular music of the last fifty years to see that it, too, is produced and consumed with a concern for its aesthetic dimension?

Despite my criticisms of traditional accounts of aesthetic value, I grant that some aesthetic experiences are remarkable for the way that they take us out of ourselves, suspend time, or transform our relation to the world around us. Twenty-five years ago, visiting the home of friends, I went down to the basement to fetch some beers. Retracing my steps through an empty room, I passed a radio that had been left on. It was playing Lou Reed's "Heroin." I stopped, transfixed. In what seemed mere seconds, thirteen minutes passed. Qualitatively, it was the same experience that I later had in response to a glorious performance of a Mozart piano sonata in the church of St. Martin in the Fields, in London. Walter Pater famously endorsed aestheticism, according to which the best life is a succession of these intense moments, each one burning with a "hard, gem-like flame." Setting aside the question of whether anyone has ever attained this ideal, I do not want to make too much of the fact that popular music sometimes transfixes us in a seemingly transcendent moment. Traditional aesthetics is overly concerned with such experiences. This fixation distracts us from the possibility that our less intense experiences of music are also aesthetically valuable. Intensity is not the only aesthetic property worth experiencing.

Working backward from the idea that aesthetic evaluation is most obviously present when we use evaluative predicates such as *beautiful* and *ugly*, I argued that aesthetic uses of language characteristically point to the presence of aesthetic evaluation. But evaluation is not simply a veneer of language that we learn to apply to our experiences. Language refers beyond itself. Aesthetic predicates are used to refer to perceptual properties that contribute to or detract from an experience when it is evaluated *as* an experience (as one worth experiencing for its own sake). It's often assumed that aesthetic principles guide our derivation of aesthetic evaluations from the presence of various musical and aesthetic properties. But this is doubtful. Aesthetic evaluation is fundamentally holistic and situational.

Once we allow that both objects and environments invite aesthetic evaluation, I am hard pressed to find a perceptual experience that lacks aesthetic properties. Granted, the cultural practices most strongly identified with the appreciation of fine art are ones that encourage attention to—and evaluation of—aesthetic properties. Those cultural practices include highly developed modes of criticism. Popular culture is too varied to encourage us to develop its own distinctive aesthetic vocabulary. Nonetheless, music enters into so many other practices of daily life—in many situations, by contributing to the lived environment—that most people have frequent opportunities to formulate aesthetic evaluations of music. Most of the time, it is popular music. Far from being insensitive to the situations in which musical experiences are embedded, aesthetic evaluation is a holistic evaluation of a particular experience within a broader framework. Given the extent to which aesthetic value contributes to the quality of human life, the aesthetic value of popular music deserves more attention than it receives.

At the same time, we should remember that many experiences with popular music yield limited aesthetic value. They are often unrewarding for the same reason that so many people are bored by so much of the music that is regarded, to stretch Matthew Arnold's characterization of high culture, as the best we have produced and heard. Inexperienced, uninformed listening usually produces a superficial and distorting perception of the music's aesthetic properties. The ever-increasing importance of mass media and the constant mutation of popular styles combine to provide frequent encounters with music that we superficially understand. So I have questioned the democratic impulse to think that any aesthetic response to any music is equally valid. Our mutual impulse to evaluate music is no evidence that a randomly chosen individual is positioned to offer a worthwhile evaluation of *cuarteto* music (an Argentinean popular form), the highlife music of Ghana and Nigeria, or a new trend in hip-hop. Substitute 1950s honky-tonk, the blues of Bessie Smith or another blues empress of the 1920s, or whichever album is number one in this week's popular music sales. The conclusion does not change. Each listening experience is shaped by the influence of previous listening and by our concurrent purposes. Our listening histories influence the way we hear music, and thus our listening habits can both reveal and obscure the aesthetic properties of any music, popular or "serious."

Notes

Introduction

1. Some scholars reserve the phrase *cultural studies* for scholarship arising from the British or Birmingham tradition. In the United States, the use is more open-ended. See Philip Smith, *Cultural Theory: An Introduction* (Oxford: Blackwell, 2001), 151–66.

2. This point encapsulates the argument of Janet Wolff, *Aesthetics and the Sociology of Art,* 2nd ed. (Ann Arbor: University of Michigan Press, 1993), 48–67.

3. I discuss naive listening in Theodore Gracyk, *I Wanna Be Me: Rock Music and the Politics of Identity* (Philadelphia: Temple University Press, 2001), 142–60.

4. The same thesis is defended for moral, rather than aesthetic, values in Kwame Anthony Appiah, *Cosmopolitanism: Ethics in a World of Strangers* (New York: Norton, 2006).

5. Two excellent accounts of the obstacles facing objective, nonsocial criteria for distinguishing between high and low are John A. Fisher, "High Art versus Low Art," in *The Routledge Companion to Aesthetics,* ed. Berys Gaut and Dominic Lopes (New York: Routledge, 2001), 409–21, and Richard Shusterman, *Pragmatist Aesthetics: Living Beauty, Rethinking Art* (Oxford: Blackwell, 1992), 183–200.

6. Although it was not assembled for this purpose, consider the impoverished vocabularies employed in most of the interviews collected in *My Music,* which provides a snapshot of popular thought about music in 1988. Susan D. Crafts, Daniel Cavicchi, and Charles Keil, *My Music* (Hanover, NH: Wesleyan University Press, 1993). My point mirrors Susan McClary and Robert Walser, "Start Making Sense! Musicology Wrestles With Rock," in *On Record: Rock, Pop, & the Written Word,* ed. Simon Frith and Andrew Goodwin (New York: Pantheon, 1990), 279.

7. Quoted in G. Barry Golson, ed., *The Playboy Interviews with John Lennon & Yoko Ono* (New York: Berkley Books, 1982), 101. Aeolian cadences are a type of harmonic progression establishing closure at the end of a piece of music. William Mann pointed out that "It Won't Be Long" ends with such a cadence.

8. Timothy Warner, *Pop Music Technology and Creativity: Trevor Horn and the Digital Revolution* (Aldershot: Ashgate, 2003), 3–17. See also Lucy Green, *Music on Deaf Ears* (Manchester: Manchester University Press, 1988), 102–20, and Deena Weinstein, "Art Versus Commerce: Deconstructing a (Useful) Romantic Illusion," in *Stars Don't Stand Still in the Sky: Music and Myth,* ed. Karen Kelly and Evelyn McDonnell (New York: New York University Press, 1999), 56–69.

9. Quoted in Jim Reeves, "To Hell with Country," *Connect Savannah,* http://www.connectsavannah.com/show_article.php?article_id=618.

10. David Hume, "Of the Standard of Taste," in *The Philosophical Works,* ed. Thomas Hill Green and Thomas Hodge Grose, vol. 3 (London: Smith, Elder, 1882; repr. Darmstadt: Scientia Verlag Aalen, 1964), 271.

11. Associated Press, "George Harrison is dead at age 58," November 30, 2001, www.msnbc.com/news.

12. Pierre Bourdieu, *Distinction: A Social Critique of the Judgement of Taste,* trans. Richard Nice (Cambridge: Harvard University Press, 1984), 56.

13. John A. Sloboda, *The Musical Mind: The Cognitive Psychology of Music* (Oxford: Oxford University Press, 1985), 17.

14. This formulation borrows from the distinction between deep and local background—a universal capacity and culturally specific ones, respectively—in John Searle, *Intentionality: An Essay in the Philosophy of Mind* (New York: Cambridge University Press, 1983), 143–44. Regarding music, see Jean-Jacques Nattiez, *Music and Discourse: Toward a Semiology of Music,* trans. Carolyn Abbate (Princeton, NJ: Princeton University Press, 1990).

15. Curiously, recognition of the importance and potential *universality* of many values has become a staple of recent sociology, yet the sphere of aesthetic values remains all but invisible. Although John Dewey's pragmatism is sometimes cited, Dewey's concern for aesthetic value is ignored. An illustration of both points is Steven Hitlin and Jane A. Piliavin, "Values: Reviving a Dormant Concept," *Annual Review of Sociology* 30 (August 2004): 364.

16. Jacques Attali, *Noise: The Political Economy of Music,* trans. Brian Massumi (Minneapolis: University of Minnesota Press, 1985), 105, and Theodor W. Adorno, *Introduction to the Sociology of Music,* trans. E. B. Ashton (New York: Seabury, 1976), 29, respectively. An earlier discussion is Theodore Gracyk, *Rhythm and Noise: An Aesthetics of Rock Music* (Durham, NC: Duke University Press, 1996), 149–73.

17. McClary and Walser, "Start Making Sense," 281.

18. See Shusterman, *Pragmatist Aesthetics,* xii.

19. George Orwell, *My Country Right or Left, 1940–1943,* vol. 2 of *Collected Essays, Journalism and Letters,* ed. Sonia Orwell and Ian Angus (New York: Harcourt Brace Jovanovich, 1968), 41.

20. Quoted in Timothy White, "Bono Vox," in *Music to My Ears: The Billboard Essays* (New York: Owl Books, 1997), 737.

21. Raymond Williams, *Keywords: A Vocabulary of Culture and Society* (London: Fontana, 1983), 237. See also Richard A. Peterson, "Popular Music is Plural," *Popular Music and Society* 21, no. 1 (1997): 53–58. The problem is pervasive in popular culture studies; see Colin MacCabe, "Defining Popular Culture," in *High Theory/Low Culture: Analysing Popular Television and Film,* ed. MacCabe (New York: St. Martin's Press, 1986), 1–10.

22. Elijah Wald documents that the blues musicians who were most popular in the 1920s and 1930s "are unfamiliar to present-day blues fans" (e.g., Walter Davis and Clara Smith were popular, but Robert Johnson was not). *Escaping the Delta: Robert Johnson and the Invention of the Blues* (New York: Amistad, 2004), 41.

23. For an informative overview of the issues involved here, see Fisher, "High Art versus Low Art." For an overview of the processes that continuously redefined "popular" taste in the United States, see Lawrence W. Levine, *Highbrow/Lowbrow: The Emergence of Cultural Hierarchy in America* (Cambridge: Harvard University Press, 1988), and Michael Kammen, *American Culture, American Tastes: Social Change and the 20th Century* (New York: Basic Books, 1999). They cover the nineteenth and twentieth centuries, respectively.

24. E.g., Gunther Schuller, *Early Jazz: Its Roots and Musical Development* (New York: Oxford University Press, 1968), and Walter Everett, *The Beatles as Musicians: The Quarry Men through "Rubber Soul"* (Oxford: Oxford University Press, 2001).

25. Noël Carroll argues that the crucial organizing concept is not that of popular art, but of mass art. See *The Philosophy of Mass Art* (New York: Oxford University Press, 1998).

26. See Jason Middleton, "D.C. Punk and the Production of Authenticity," in *Rock over the Edge: Transformations in Popular Culture,* ed. Roger Beebe, Denise Fulbrook, and Ben Saunders (Durham, NC: Duke University Press, 2002), 335–56.

27. This formulation is based on Anahid Kassabian, "Popular," in *Key Terms in Popular Music and Culture,* ed. Bruce Horner and Thomas Swiss (Oxford: Blackwell, 1999), 113–23.

28. Kassabian, "Popular," 117.

29. Morris Weitz, "The Role of Theory in Aesthetics," *Journal of Aesthetics and Art Criticism,* 15, no. 1 (1956): 27–35. Weitz argues that art is an open concept. For extended analysis and response, see Stephen Davies, *Definitions of Art* (Ithaca, NY: Cornell University Press, 1991), 4–22.

30. Carroll, *Philosophy of Mass Art,* 192–96, and Gracyk, *I Wanna Be Me,* 17–26.

Chapter 1

1. This phrase appears in a public announcement that P. T. Barnum placed in newspapers in 1850. The announcement is quoted in W. Porter Ware and Thaddeus C. Lockard, Jr., *P. T. Barnum Presents Jenny Lind: The American Tour of the Swedish Nightingale* (Baton Rouge: Louisiana State University Press, 1980), 4–5.

2. P. T. Barnum, printed circular, quoted in *Selected Letters of P. T. Barnum,* ed. A. H. Saxon (New York: Columbia University Press, 1983), 43.

3. Ware and Lockard, *Barnum Presents Lind,* 4.

4. Neil Harris, *Humbug: The Art of P. T. Barnum* (Boson: Little, Brown, 1973), 121.

5. Levine, *Highbrow/Lowbrow,* 96–99.

6. From the *New York Herald,* quoted in Joan Bulman, *Jenny Lind: A Biography* (London: James Barrie, 1956), 244.

7. Jim Fusilli, *Pet Sounds* (New York: Continuum, 2005), 120.

8. Ibid., 119.

9. Ibid., 118.

10. Jon Landau, "Rock and Art," in *It's Too Late to Stop Now: A Rock and Roll Journal* (San Francisco: Straight Arrow Books, 1972), 129–34. It should also be noted that Landau assumed that the closer the music remained to its African-American sources, the

more bodily and less pretentious it was. It does not seem to have occurred to him that Otis Redding and Jimi Hendrix engaged in highly calculated, staged performances. Furthermore, within three years Landau was using "art" as high praise for selected recordings, such as Joni Mitchell's *Blue* (ibid., 104).

11. Dick Hebdige, *Subculture: The Meaning of Style* (New York: Methuen, 1979), 129. Similar hostility toward "aesthetic discourse" is found in Tony Bennett, "Really Useless Knowledge: A Political Critique of Aesthetics," *Thesis Eleven* 12 (1984): 28–52.

12. The aesthetic theory of art, which posits a necessary or fundamental connection between aesthetics and art, has few exponents. Typically, a recent textbook account of it concentrates on authors who defended modernist painting and New Criticism in literature (Clive Bell and Monroe Beardsley, respectively). Noël Carroll, *Philosophy of Art: A Contemporary Introduction* (New York: Routledge, 1999), 156–204. See also Carolyn Korsmeyer, "On Distinguishing 'Aesthetic' from 'Artistic,'" *Journal of Aesthetic Education* 11, no 4 (1977): 45–57.

13. E.g., Arthur Danto, "The Artworld," *Journal of Philosophy* 61, no. 19 (1964): 571–84, and Arnold Berleant, "Aesthetics and the Contemporary Arts," *Journal of Aesthetics and Art Criticism* 29, no. 2 (1970): 155–68.

14. The broader case of elevating a whole field of music, jazz, is covered in Simon Frith, *Performing Rites: On the Value of Popular Music* (Cambridge: Harvard University Press, 1996), 43–46.

15. See also Gracyk, *Rhythm and Noise,* 207–26.

16. J. Niimi, *Murmur* (New York: Continuum, 2005), 99; Bill Janovitz, *Exile on Main St.* (New York: Continuum, 2005).

17. Gary Iseminger, *The Aesthetic Function of Art* (Ithaca: Cornell University Press, 2004), 31–35, and Denis Dutton, "'But They Don't Have Our Concept of Art'," in *Theories of Art Today,* ed. Noël Carroll (Madison: University of Wisconsin Press, 2000), 217–38.

18. Noël Carroll raises very similar concerns about trying "to compare all films with all other films." *Engaging the Moving Image* (New Haven: Yale University Press, 2003), 161.

19. Fusilli, *Pet Sounds,* 119. Neal Umphred similarly emphasizes that *Pet Sounds* is an important transition from producing chart hits to making "Rock's first true concept album." Neal Umphred, "Let's Go Away For Awhile: The Continuing Saga of Brian Wilson's *Pet Sounds,*" in *Back to the Beach: A Brian Wilson and The Beach Boys Reader,* ed. Kingsley Abbott (London: Helter Skelter, 1997), 32.

20. Preben Mortensen, *Art in the Social Order: The Making of the Modern Conception of Art* (Albany: State University of New York Press, 1997), 172.

21. E.g., Umphred, "Let's Go Away," 32.

22. Fusilli, *Pet Sounds,* 102.

23. Daniel Harrison, "After Sundown: The Beach Boys' Experimental Music," in *Understanding Rock: Essays in Musical Analysis,* ed. John Covach and Graeme M. Boone (Oxford: Oxford University Press, 1997), 39.

24. Umphred, "Let's Go Away," 32.

25. Quoted in Brad Elliott, liner notes to the Beach Boys, *Pet Sounds* (Capital Compact Disc, 1999), 24.

26. Harrison, "After Sundown," 38.

27. "The category of originality, which became in the late eighteenth century the definitive aesthetic authority, implies as the opposite of imitation and convention the postulate that a work of art worthy of the name must be substantially new." Carl Dahlhaus, *Analysis and Value Judgment,* trans. Siegmund Levarie (New York: Pendragon, 1983), 18. For an example of the earlier emphasis on a genius of imitation rather than originality, see Giorgio Vasari, "Life of Leonardo da Vinci," in *The Lives of the Artists,* trans. Julia Conaway Bondanella and Peter Bondanella (Oxford: Oxford University Press, 1991), 284–98.

28. Immanuel Kant, *Critique of Judgement,* trans. James Creed Meredith (Oxford: Oxford University Press, 1911), section 46.

29. Ibid.

30. The story is somewhat more complicated than I have suggested, in part because two different kinds of genius have been recognized since antiquity. An accessible history of the concept of musical genius is Peter Kivy, *The Possessor and the Possessed: Handel, Mozart, Beethoven, and the Idea of Musical Genius* (New Haven: Yale University Press, 2001).

31. Fusilli, *Pet Sounds,* 117.

32. R. G. Collingwood, *The Principles of Art* (Oxford: Oxford University Press, 1958).

33. The Romantic aesthetic is generally reactionary in this way. Raymond Williams, *Marxism and Literature* (New York: Oxford University Press, 1997), 151; and Mortensen, *Art in Social Order,* 155–56.

34. Friedrich Schiller, *On the Aesthetic Education of Man in a Series of Letters,* trans. E. M. Wilkinson and L. A. Willoughby (Oxford: Oxford University Press, 1967). Kant is often described as a formalist, but sections 43–54 of the *Critique of Judgement* make it clear that Kant does not value form over content. He assigns low value to instrumental music, compared to poetry, precisely because music lacks ideas.

35. David Novitz, *The Boundaries of Art* (Philadelphia: Temple University Press, 1992), 2.

36. The disjunctive definition of art is defended by Robert Stecker, *Artworks: Definition, Meaning, Value* (University Park: Pennsylvania State University Press, 1997), 48–65. To the extent that such analyses capture the truth about art, we must not expect to extract "an account of artistic value" from the concept of art. Malcolm Budd, *Values of Art: Painting, Poetry, and Music* (London: Penguin, 1995), 3.

37. A list of features shared by all "art" in all known societies is offered by Dutton, "But They Don't Have," 233–34.

38. Shusterman, *Pragmatist Aesthetics,* 200. Shusterman's positive argument requires a lengthy analysis of a single example of popular music. He uses Stetsasonic's "Talkin' All That Jazz" (Shusterman, 215–35).

39. Ellen Willis quoted in John Strausbaugh, *Rock 'Til You Drop: The Decline from Rebellion to Nostalgia* (New York: Verso, 2001), 114.

40. Shusterman, *Pragmatist Aesthetics,* 212.

41. Richard Shusterman, "Art Infraction: Goodman, Rap, Pragmatism," *Australasian Journal of Philosophy* 73, no. 2 (1995): 269 and 276.

42. Richard Shusterman, "Rap Remix: Pragmatism, Postmodernism, and Other Issues in the House," *Critical Inquiry* 22, no. 1 (1995): 151.

43. Danto, "The Artworld." In chapter 3, I argue that many aesthetic values are only available to listeners who are aware of this "weight of tradition." The additional task of worrying about how each of these categories intersects with the overarching category of art seems beside the point, an unnecessary epicycle in the argument.

44. Formal properties are often identified as being particularly relevant. I address this topic in chapter 5.

45. Robert Christgau, *Any Old Way You Choose It: Rock and Other Pop Music, 1967–1973* (Baltimore: Penguin, 1973), 128; from an article originally published in 1970.

46. Quoted in Robert Doerschuk, "Live: Topping Copper," *Musician,* April 1997, 55. For a detailed anaylsis of Young's music, see William Echard, *Neil Young and the Poetics of Energy* (Bloomington: Indiana University Press, 2005).

47. Frith, *Performing Rites,* 251–52.

48. Ibid., 277, 275.

49. Bourdieu, *Distinction,* 492.

50. Ibid., 486–87, 5.

51. Kant, *Critique of Judgement,* section 13. For a recent defense of a sharp distinction between the entertainment value of popular music and the specifically musical value of classical music, see Julian Johnson, *Who Needs Classical Music? Cultural Choice and Musical Value* (Oxford: Oxford University Press, 2002).

52. Bourdieu, *Distinction,* 66.

53. "Charles," in Crafts, Cavicchi, and Keil, *My Music,* 136.

54. E.g., Elbieta Szubertowska, "Education and the music culture of Polish adolescents," *Psychology of Music* 33, no. 3 (2005): 317–30.

55. The theory of fine art is in Kant, *Critique of Judgement,* sections 43–54.

56. Dahlhaus, *Analysis and Value Judgment,* 18.

57. Bourdieu, *Distinction,* 485. An excellent discussion of Bourdieu's methods and reasoning is John Frow, *Cultural Studies & Cultural Value* (Oxford: Oxford University Press, 1995), 27–59.

58. Kant, *Critique of Judgement,* section 53.

59. Some of this can be gleaned from Paul Mattick, *Art in Its Time: Theories and Practices of Modern Aesthetics* (New York: Taylor and Francis, 2003), 39–45 and 174–82, and Michael Bérubé's introduction to *The Aesthetics of Cultural Studies,* ed. Bérubé (Oxford: Blackwell, 2005), 1–27.

60. Bourdieu, *Distinction,* 41 and 32. The objection can be made that a failure to locate a broader notion of aesthetic value will endorse the status quo. For one response, see Barbara Herrnstein Smith, *Contingencies of Value: Alternative Perspectives for Critical Theory* (Cambridge: Harvard University Press, 1988), 156–66.

61. Kant, *Critique of Judgement,* section 9. In failing to consider alternative formulations, Bourdieu appears to be "condemning aesthetic experience as a tool of false essentialism" while he "falsely essentializes aesthetic experience." Richard Shusterman, *Surface and Depth: Dialectics of Criticism and Culture* (Ithaca, NY: Cornell University Press, 2002), 223.

62. David Cantwell, "Sammi Smith: The Art of Inauthenticity," *Oxford American* 50 (Summer 2005): 114.

63. Richard A. Peterson, "Understanding Audience Segmentation: From Elite and Mass to Omnivore and Univore," *Poetics* 21, no. 4 (1992): 243–58, and Bethany Bryson, "'Anything but Heavy Metal': Symbolic Exclusion and Musical Dislikes," *American Sociological Review* 61, no. 5 (1996): 884–99.

64. Peterson, "Understanding Audience Segmentation," 249, and Bryson, "Anything but Heavy Metal," 894.

65. Bourdieu, *Distinction,* 516.

66. Smith, *Contingencies of Value,* 76. A parallel argument is made about all "art" by Keith Moxey, *The Practice of Persuasion: Paradox and Power in Art History* (Ithaca, NY: Cornell University Press, 2001), 132.

67. McClary and Walser, "Start Making Sense," 281.

68. Wolff, *Aesthetics and Sociology of Art,* 17. However, Wolff's recommendation to pay more attention to the specificity of art does little to shed light on *aesthetic* value. If we begin with a specific social institution, we cannot generate a general account of aesthetic value. The same problem arises for Frith's proposal that "we can use a sociology of music as the basis of aesthetic theory," moving "from a description of popular music as a social institution to an understanding of how we can and do value it" (*Performing Rites,* 276). See also Austin Harrington, *Art and Social Theory: Sociological Arguments in Aesthetics* (Cambridge: Polity, 2004).

69. One exception is James C. Anderson, "Aesthetic Concepts of Art," in Carroll, *Theories of Art Today,* 65–92.

70. E.g., Friedrich Nietzsche, *The Birth of Tragedy & On the Genealogy of Morals,* trans. F. Golffing (Garden City, NY: Doubleday, 1956), 238.

71. Crispin Sartwell, *Six Names of Beauty* (New York: Routledge, 2004), 150.

72. Shusterman, *Surface and Depth,* 223.

73. Arnold Berleant, *Rethinking Aesthetics: Rouge Essays on Aesthetics and the Arts* (Aldershot: Ashgate, 2004), 35.

74. Arnold Isenberg, "Critical Communication," *Philosophical Review* 58, no. 4 (1949): 330–44.

75. Paul Ziff, "Reasons in Art Criticism," in *Philosophy Looks at the Arts,* ed. Joseph Margolis (New York: Charles Scribner's Sons, 1962), 158–78.

76. Edward Bullough, "Psychical Distance as a Factor in Art and an Aesthetic Principle," *British Journal of Psychology* 5, no. 2 (1912): 88–89.

77. See Yuriko Saito, "The Aesthetics of Weather," in *The Aesthetics of Everyday Life,* ed. Andrew Light and Jonathan M. Smith (New York: Columbia University Press, 2005), 156–76, and Barbara Sandrisser, "Fine Weather—the Japanese View of Rain," *Landscape* 26 (1982): 42–47.

78. Tom Leddy, "The Nature of Everyday Aesthetics," in Light and Smith, *Aesthetics of Everyday Life,* 3–22, and Arto Haapla, "On the Aesthetics of the Everyday: Familiarity, Strangeness, and the Meaning of Place," in Light and Smith, 39–55.

79. Leddy, "Nature of Everyday Aesthetics," 18.

80. Thus, the expression "sounds fun" has a use that describes and positively evalu-

ates an immediate experience. Although Leddy regards "fun" as an aesthetic term of everyday life, he cannot think of a case in which "sounds fun" has immediate application, as opposed to expressing an expectation of future fun. Ibid., 12.

81. Ibid., 12–14.

82. My account draws on Iseminger, *Aesthetic Function of Art,* 31–61. For a division of aesthetic properties into eight broad categories—formal, historical, representational, behavioral, emotionally expressive, evocative, second-order (e.g., "vivid"), and purely evaluative—see Alan H. Goldman, *Aesthetic Value* (Boulder, CO: Westview Press, 1995), 17–44. More stringent analyses treat some categories as artistic but not aesthetic, as in Nick Zangwill, *The Metaphysics of Beauty* (Ithaca, NY: Cornell University Press, 2001).

83. This formulation adapts Goldman, *Aesthetic Value,* 21. This criterion is epistemological, not phenomenological. It permits neutrality about the metaphysical status of aesthetic properties and avoids "armchair" psychological speculation. See Gary Iseminger, "Aesthetic Experience," in *The Oxford Handbook of Aesthetics,* ed. Jerrold Levinson (Oxford: Oxford University Press, 2003), 99–116.

84. Allan F. Moore, introduction to *Analyzing Popular Music,* ed. Moore (Cambridge: Cambridge University Press, 2003), 6.

85. Gary Iseminger, "The Aesthetic State of Mind," in *Contemporary Debates in Aesthetics and the Philosophy of Art,* ed. Matthew Kieran (Oxford: Blackwell, 2006), 100.

Chapter 2

1. The dancing metaphor is similarly employed by Lawrence Grossberg, *Dancing in Spite of Myself: Essays on Popular Culture* (Durham, NC: Duke University Press, 1997).

2. Theodor W. Adorno, "On Popular Music," in Frith and Goodwin, *On Record,* 311.

3. Quoted in Eric Alterman, *It Ain't No Sin to Be Glad You're Alive: The Promise of Bruce Springsteen* (Boston: Little, Brown, 1999), 148.

4. Dave Marsh, *Glory Days: Bruce Springsteen in the 1980s* (New York: Pantheon, 1987), 179.

5. Ibid., 185–86.

6. Ibid., 257.

7. Ibid., 260.

8. Roy Shuker, *Understanding Popular Music,* 2nd ed. (London: Routledge, 2001), 146. For evidence that the majority of the audience misunderstood the song, see Patricia M. Greenfield et al., "What Is Rock Music Doing to the Minds of Our Youth? A First Experimental Look at the Effects of Rock Music Lyrics and Music Videos," *Journal of Early Adolescence* 7, no. 3 (1987): 315–29.

9. Another possibility is that the song has two or more equally good interpretations, and some people misunderstand it by failing to acknowledge this possibility. See Stecker, *Artworks,* 133–55.

10. Quoted in Alterman, *It Ain't No Sin,* 163. See also Ray Pratt, *Rhythm and Resistance: Explorations in the Political Use of Popular Music* (New York: Praeger, 1990), 177.

11. Grossberg, *Dancing in Spite of Myself,* 30. Grossberg recognizes that many listeners do not find "cultural significance" in the music they like: "the experience was purely

affective" (29). See also Kathleen Higgins, "Musical Idiosyncrasy and Perspectival Listening," in *Music and Meaning,* ed. Jenefer Robinson (Ithaca, NY: Cornell University Press, 1997), 83–102.

12. Ironically, in 1984, when the White House staff considered actions favorably linking President Reagan and Michael Jackson, legal advisor John G. Roberts Jr. counseled against official actions connecting them. He warned that Jackson's popularity should not obscure the questionable values represented by Jackson and his music. Richards, elevated to chief justice of the United States Supreme Court in 2005, saw that those values were difficult to reconcile with Reagan's political values.

13. McClary and Walser, "Start Making Sense," 277.

14. The poster is reproduced in Mark Zwonitzer with Charles Hirshberg, *Will You Miss Me When I'm Gone? The Carter Family and Their Legacy in American Music* (New York: Simon and Schuster, 2002), 169.

15. Quoted in Stanley Booth, *The True Adventures of the Rolling Stones* (New York: Vintage, 1985), 146. Jerry Garcia mentions a similar attitude informing his decision to perform some songs, and Bruce Springsteen reports a similar response to Bob Dylan's music from 1965 to 1968 ("it had incredible sound and that was what got me"). Springsteen reports that he had no other interest in Dylan or in "the folk boom." Garcia quoted in Blair Jackson, *Goin' Down the Road: A Grateful Dead Traveling Companion* (New York: Harmony Books, 1992), 17; Springsteen quoted in Paul Williams, "Lost in the Flood," in *Backstreets: Springsteen: The Man and His Music,* ed. Charles R. Cross (New York: Harmony Books, 1989), 57.

16. Quoted in Timothy White, "Harrison Live: Here Comes the Fun," in *Music to My Ears: The Billboard Essays* (New York: Owl Books, 1997), 31.

17. Quoted in Bob Guccione, Jr., "Live to Tell," *Spin,* January 1996, 94.

18. Wolff, *Aesthetics and Sociology of Art,* 72. Wolff argues that all but the most "banal" art is political, yet aesthetic grounds of assessment can be distinguished from its social relevance. However, because she does not clearly differentiate between aesthetic value and artistic value, one can challenge her arguments as limited to fine art without extending them to popular culture (64–66).

19. When a listener thinks that music can be found valuable for its own sake, she is usually diagnosed as having internalized the "*ideological* baggage" of modernism. Frith, *Performing Rites,* 95. This position is most strongly associated with Bourdieu, *Distinction.* For criticisms, see Harrington, *Art and Social Theory,* 94–111.

20. Frith, *Performing Rites,* 102. Frith approvingly cites Philip Tagg, "'Universal' Music and the Case of Death," *Critical Quarterly* 35, no. 2 (1993): 76. See also Richard Middleton, "Popular Music Analysis and Musicology: Bridging the Gap," in *Reading Pop: Approaches to Textual Analysis in Popular Music,* ed. Middleton (New York: Oxford University Press, 2000), 104–21.

21. Robert Walser, "Popular Music Analysis: Ten Apothegms and Four Instances," in Moore, *Analyzing Popular Music,* 36.

22. Williams, *Marxism and Literature,* 155.

23. George Lipsitz, foreword to Crafts, Cavicchi, and Keil, *My Music,* xviii.

24. Gordon Graham, *Philosophy of the Arts: An Introduction to Aesthetics* (New York: Routledge, 1997), 62. The discipline of popular music studies largely ignores the varia-

tion of aesthetic cognitivism that regards cultural objects as valuable to the degree that they teach us about a community's nonaesthetic values. For this version of cognitivism, see Berys Gaut, "Art and Cognition," in *Contemporary Debates in Aesthetics and The Philosophy of Art,* ed. Matthew Kieran (Oxford: Blackwell, 2006), 115–26.

25. Graham, *Philosophy of the Arts,* 147. For a reply, see Peter Lamarque, "Cognitive Value in the Arts: Marking the Boundaries," in Kieran, *Contemporary Debates,* 127–39. Lamarque's reply is likely to be rejected by many readers for his appeal to art's capacity to capture something universal and timeless.

26. John Guillory, *Cultural Capital: The Problem of Literary Canon Formation* (Chicago: University of Chicago Press, 1993), 22. See also Wolff, *Aesthetics and Sociology of Art,* 33.

27. Gillory, *Cultural Capital,* 279. Frith endorses this view: "value judgments only make sense as part of an argument" and thus as "social events" (*Performing Rites,* 95).

28. Walser, "Popular Music Analysis," 36.

29. Mark Everist, "Reception Theories, Canonic Discourses, and Musical Value," in *Rethinking Music,* ed. Nicholas Cook and Mark Everist (Oxford: Oxford University Press, 1999), 378–402. See also Walser, "Popular Music Analysis," 37–38.

30. Wolff, *Aesthetics and Sociology of Art,* 15. See also Pierre Bourdieu and Alain Darbel, *The Love of Art: European Art Museums and Their Public,* trans. Caroline Beattie and Nick Merriman (Stanford: Stanford University Press, 1990), 59, and Nicholas Cook, *Music, Imagination, and Culture* (Oxford: Clarendon Press, 1990), 6–7. Cook argues that because different cultures position people to hear the same sounds differently, an aesthetic response is merely a Western cultural value.

31. This argument derives from Tony Hincks, "Aesthetics and the Sociology of Art: A Critical Commentary on the Writings of Janet Wolff," *British Journal of Aesthetics* 24, no. 4 (1984): 342. Wolff subsequently offers her own version of the argument in *Aesthetics and Sociology of Art,* 113.

32. Wilfred Dolfsma, *Valuing Pop Music: Institutions, VALUES, and Economics* (Delft, Netherlands: Eburon, 1999), 48.

33. Ibid., 49.

34. Ibid., 99.

35. Ibid., 51–52.

36. Ibid., 53.

37. Ibid., 133–34.

38. Ibid., 133.

39. Ibid., 55.

40. Ibid., 101–25.

41. Ibid., 139.

42. Ibid., 139–40. Facing the same problem, others have concluded that the answer must be in the musical details of the new style that was being embraced: "On the purely musical level, there was something that was, quite simply, highly satisfying about the blues." Peter van der Merwe, *Origins of the Popular Style: The Antecedents of Twentieth-Century Popular Music* (Oxford: Clarendon Press, 1989), 215.

43. E.g., Peter Wicke, *Rock Music: Culture, Aesthetics, and Sociology,* trans. Rachel Fogg (Cambridge: Cambridge University Press, 1991), ix. For a general account, see John Storey, *Cultural Studies and the Study of Popular Culture,* 2nd ed. (Edinburgh: Edinburgh University Press, 2003), 130–51.

44. Angela A. McRobbie, *Feminism and Youth Culture* (London: Macmillan, 1991), 134–44, 195–97.

45. I am focusing on reception, but a parallel problem arises with the production of cultural products; Paul Crowther, "Defining Art, Defending the Canon, Contesting Culture," *British Journal of Aesthetics* 44, no. 4 (2004): 361–77. Complementary arguments are advanced by Denis Dutton, "Aesthetic Universals," in Gaut and Lopes, *Routledge Companion to Aesthetics,* 203–14, and Virginia Postrel, *The Substance of Style: How the Rise of Aesthetic Value is Remaking Commerce, Culture, and Consciousness* (New York: Harper-Collins, 2003).

46. Dolfsma, *Valuing Pop Music,* 140. His criticism is independently argued by René Boomkens, "Uncanny Identities: High and Low and Global and Local in the Music of Elvis Costello," *European Journal of Cultural Studies* 7, no. 1 (2005): 62. A similar point is advanced by Simon Frith, *Sound Effects: Youth, Leisure, and the Politics of Rock'n'Roll* (New York: Pantheon, 1981), 165.

47. Dolfsma, *Valuing Pop Music,* 140. I find it misleading to say that people experience music as intrinsically valuable. If the point is that *music* is sometimes valued for providing a valuable experience (and the experience is valued for its own sake), then the music is valued instrumentally. See Stecker, *Artworks,* 251–58, and Christine M. Korsgaard, "Two Distinctions in Goodness," *Philosophical Review* 92, no. 2 (1983): 169–95.

48. Bakari Kitwana, *Why White Kids Love Hip-Hop: Wankstas, Wiggers, Wannabes, and the New Reality of Race in America* (New York: Basic Civitas, 2005), 36–37.

49. Ibid., 30.

50. Ibid., 7–8, 56–58. Kitwana loosely separates listeners into categories according to the depth of their political investment (53–79). He draws on William Wimsatt, *Bomb the Suburbs: Graffiti, Race, Freight-Hopping and the Search for Hip Hop's Moral Center* (New York: Soft Skull Press, 1993). For a more general account of levels of engagement, see Gracyk, *I Wanna Be Me,* 142–60.

51. For a more academic treatment of related issues, with somewhat more attention to aesthetics and hip-hop, see Cheryl L. Keyes, *Rap Music and Street Consciousness* (Urbana: University of Illinois Press, 2001). Consistent with the social relevance thesis, Keyes says, "people who react negatively to this music are often unable to decode its lyrics, style, and message" (123). However, she never asks whether everyone who favors the music have a genuine facility to decode it, nor does she consider the frequency with which children and teens listen but do not understand.

52. Robert Walser, *Running With the Devil: Power, Gender, and Madness in Heavy Metal Music* (Hanover, NH: Wesleyan University Press, 1993), xi and xiv.

53. Ibid., xvii. Walser also describes the music a "social signifying system" that he found "persuasive" (xiv).

54. Walser, "Popular Music Analysis," 37. Simon Frith defends augmented subjectivism. Frith, *Performing Rites,* 21. He draws on Smith, *Contingencies of Value,* 13. For an interesting discussion of listening that is personal and yet enriched by associated memories, see James R. McDonald, "Rock and Memory: A Search for Meaning," *Popular Music and Society* 17, no. 3 (1993): 1–17.

55. Walser, *Running with the Devil,* 39.

56. Ibid. The survey form is reproduced in an appendix (175–77).

57. By granting that music's aesthetic value depends on the presence of culturally

emergent aesthetic properties, we dodge Walser's charge that an appeal to aesthetic value tries to "establish value" without properly "historicizing . . . the particular pleasures offered." Walser, "Popular Music Analysis," 19–20.

58. Peg Brand argues that we can "toggle" or switch between two modes of valuing the same work of art, but I am concerned that this either/or model treats the art object as a fragmented entity. Peg Brand, "Can Feminist Art Be Experienced Disinterestedly?" in *Aesthetics: A Reader in Philosophy of the Arts,* ed. David Goldblatt and Lee B. Brown (Upper Saddle River, NJ: Prentice Hall, 1996), 532–35.

59. For a sample of American politicians attacking hip-hop, see Kitwana, *Why White Kids,* 19–23, and Keyes, *Rap Music,* 104–6. In chapter 3, I explore reasons why limited exposure to a musical style reinforces a lack of aesthetic appreciation.

60. Zeth Lundy, "Instinct or: My Alleged Musical Taste," *PopMatters,* November 10, 2005, http://www.popmatters.com/music/features/music-in-me/lundy-051110.shtml.

61. This situation is often explained by invoking psychoanalytic theory. However, I endorse Noël Carroll's criticisms of that strategy. See Noël Carroll, *Mystifying Movies: Fads and Fallacies in Contemporary Film Theory* (New York: Columbia University Press, 1988), and Wolff, *Aesthetics and Sociology of Art,* 101.

62. Patti Smith, "To find a voice," *Complete: Lyrics, Reflections & Notes for the Future* (New York: Doubleday, 1998), xviii–xix.

63. Quoted in Victor Bockris and Roberta Bayley, *Patti Smith: An Unauthorized Biography* (New York: Simon and Schuster, 1999), 23.

64. Quoted in David Fricke, "Patti Smith," *Rolling Stone,* July 11–25, 1996, 48.

65. In contrast, Wolff defends a difference between art and politics by noting that some art is valued "through changes of interpretation as to its political interest or implications." This parallels the case where both conservatives and liberals embrace Springsteen's music; it demonstrates nothing about aesthetic interest. Wolff, *Aesthetics and Sociology of Art,* 65.

66. Frank Sibley, *Approach to Aesthetics: Collected Papers on Philosophical Aesthetics,* ed. John Benson, Betty Redfern, and Jeremy Roxbee Cox (Oxford: Clarendon Press, 2001), 21.

67. Winfried Fluck, "Aesthetics and Cultural Studies," in *Aesthetics in a Multicultural Age,* ed. Emory Elliott, Louis F. Caton, and Jeffrey Rhyne (Oxford: Oxford University Press, 2002), 87.

68. Hebdige, *Subculture,* 18.

69. John P. Robinson and Paul Hirsch, "It's the Sound That Does It," *Psychology Today,* October 1969, 3, 42–45; Frith, *Sound Effects,* 63; Emily D. Edwards and Michael Singletary, "Mass Media Images in Popular Music," *Popular Music and Society* 9, no. 4 (1984): 17–26; Roger Jon Desmond, "Adolescents and Music Lyrics: Implications of a Cognitive Perspective," *Communications Quarterly* 35 (1987): 278; Jill Rosenbaum and Lorraine Prinsky, "Sex, Violence and Rock 'n' Roll: Youths' Perceptions of Popular Music," *Popular Music and Society* 11, no. 2 (1987): 85; David Shumway, "Rock & Roll as a Cultural Practice," *South Atlantic Quarterly* 90, no. 4 (1991): 760; and Peter G. Christenson and Donald F. Roberts, *It's Not Only Rock & Roll: Popular Music in the Lives of Adolescents* (Cresskill, NJ: Hapton Press, 1998), 151–79.

70. In fact, this proposal may correspond to Kant's view, as opposed to the tradi-

tional understanding of Kant's view. For an account of Kant's "instrumental autonomism," see Casey Haskins, "Kant and the Autonomy of Art," *Journal of Aesthetics and Art Criticism* 47, no. 1 (1989): 43–54.

71. In one study, audiences were shown a film clip featuring an argument between two characters. The audience was more likely to believe that the characters had a subsequent reconciliation when the soundtrack music had a satisfying resolution on a major chord. For a summary of relevant studies, see Annabel J. Cohen, "Music as a Source of Emotion in Film," in *Music and Emotion: Theory and Research,* ed. Patrik N. Juslin and John A Sloboda (Oxford: Oxford University Press, 2001): 249–72.

72. Gracyk, *I Wanna Be Me,* 230.

73. This phrase is Guillory's summary (*Cultural Capital,* 334) of Pierre Bourdieu's position on popular culture.

74. Harrington, *Art and Social Theory,* 53. Reworded as an issue about moral and aesthetic value, this position is known as moderate moralism, and it is defended by several prominent aestheticians. See Noël Carroll, "Moderate Moralism," in *Beyond Aesthetics: Philosophical Essays* (Cambridge: Cambridge University Press, 2001), 293–306.

75. This point is adapted from Stephen Davies, "Non-Western Art and Art's Definition," in Carroll, *Theories of Art Today,* 200.

76. Guillory, *Cultural Capital,* 286.

77. John Dewey, *Art as Experience* (New York: Capricorn Books, 1958), 325.

78. Tricia Rose, *Black Noise: Rap Music and Black Culture in Contemporary America* (Hanover, NH: Wesleyan University Press, 1994), 182.

79. Ibid.

80. Harrington, *Art and Social Theory,* 53.

81. Fluck, "Aesthetics and Cultural Studies," 93.

82. Roger Scruton, *The Aesthetics of Music* (Oxford: Clarendon Press, 1997), 379. Scruton goes very wrong in proposing that a "person with good taste turns instinctively away from certain things," including the music of Nirvana (499). Scruton confuses habit with instinct.

Chapter 3

1. Frith, *Performing Rites,* 19.

2. However, our assessments appear to identify more nuances than our discourse. See Diana Raffman, *Language, Music, and Mind* (Cambridge: MIT Press, 1993).

3. Monroe C. Beardsley, "The Generality of Critical Reasons," in *The Aesthetic Point of View: Selected Essays,* ed. Michael J. Wreen and Donald M. Callen (Ithaca, NY: Cornell University Press, 1982), 210–11. The qualification "of the relevant sort" is addressed later in this chapter.

4. For similar reservations about ethical principles, see Gerald Dworkin, "Unprincipled Ethics," in *Moral Concepts,* ed. Peter French, Theodore E. Uehling, Jr., and Howard K. Wettstein (Notre Dame, IN: University of Notre Dame Press, 1995), 230.

5. Kant, *Critique of Judgement,* section 17. See also Mary Mothersill, *Beauty Restored* (Oxford: Clarendon Press, 1984), 145–76, and William E. Kennick, "Does Traditional Aesthetics Rest on a Mistake?" *Mind* 67, no. 267 (1958): 317–34.

6. Wilfried van Damme observes that some *stimulus properties* appear to have a uni-

versal appeal (e.g., visual features such as balance and symmetry), whereas no parallel universality holds for evaluative principles related to these properties. "Universality and Cultural Particularity in Visual Aesthetics," in *Being Humans: Anthropological Universality and Particularity in Transdisciplinary Perspectives,* ed. Neil Roughley (Berlin: Waler de Gruyter, 2000), 258.

7. Notice the restriction to evaluative principles. Particularism does not imply any skepticism about nonevaluative principles that underlie the interpretation and appreciation of music (e.g., musical syntax might involve principles).

8. A recent introduction to "global music" spends a few paragraphs on the importance of "a set of artistic values referred to as aesthetics," but beauty is the only aesthetic value cited. "Aesthetics" is otherwise undefined, and it is almost immediately collapsed into functional utility. Bonnie C. Wade, *Thinking Musically: Experiencing Music, Expressing Culture* (Oxford: Oxford University Press, 2004), 6–9.

9. Robert S. Hatten, *Musical Meaning in Beethoven: Markedness, Correlation, and Interpretation* (Bloomington: Indiana University Press, 1994), 29–32.

10. Aaron Ridley employs Hatten to make a similar point. Aaron Ridley, *The Philosophy of Music: Theme and Variations* (Edinburgh: Edinburgh University Press, 2004), 41. Where it is central to Ridley's argument that pieces of music are works of art, I see this point as irrelevant.

11. William C. Handy, *Father of the Blues: An Autobiography* (New York: Macmillan, 1941), 74.

12. Ibid., 76–77. There is debate about categorizing what Handy heard as blues music. See Wald, *Escaping the Delta,* 10–13. On the question of whether Handy ever escaped his condescension to the blues, see Adam Gussow, "Racial Violence, 'Primitive' Music, and the Blues Entrepreneur: W. C. Handy's Mississippi Problem," *Southern Cultures* 8, no. 3 (2002): 56–77.

13. William C. Handy, "The Heart of the Blues," *Etude Music Magazine,* March 1940, 152, 193–94, reprinted in *Readings in Black American Music,* ed. Eileen Southern (New York: Norton, 1971), 202–7.

14. Dorothy Scarborough, *On the Trail of Negro Folk-Songs* (Cambridge: Harvard University Press, 1925), 264.

15. "By 1924, the basic style of the blues queens was thoroughly established." Wald, *Escaping the Delta,* 27.

16. This rhetoric is deconstructed by Barry Lee Pearson and Bill McCulloch, *Robert Johnson: Lost and Found* (Urbana: University of Illinois Press, 2003), and Wald, *Escaping the Delta,* 3–42.

17. This harmonic formula is the most dispensable element of the blues. See van der Merwe, *Origins of Popular Style,* 129.

18. Ibid., 199. Antecedents for this pattern are discussed at length (199–204).

19. Tilford Brooks, *America's Black Musical Heritage* (Englewood Cliffs, NJ: Prentice-Hall, 1984), 55.

20. Scarborough, *On the Trail,* 207.

21. Bob Dylan, *Chronicles: Volume One* (New York: Simon and Schuster, 2004), 282.

22. Ibid., 284–85.

23. Pearson and McCulloch, *Robert Johnson,* 34–35.

24. Ibid., 76–78.

25. Handy, *Father of the Blues,* 76.

26. Hatten, *Musical Meaning in Beethoven,* 63–64. See also Ridley, *The Philosophy of Music,* 39–41.

27. Kant, *Critique of Judgement,* section 17. Hatten offers his theory as a restricted explanation of "expressive meaning" (*Musical Meaning in Beethoven,* 227).

28. The second album was by the Delmore Brothers. Dylan, *Chronicles,* 280–81.

29. Jonathan Dancy calls this body of experience our "epistemic enablers." *Ethics Without Principles* (Oxford: Clarendon Press, 2004), 49.

30. If their different reasons point to different principles, one might appeal to the presence of "deeper" principles from which these different ones consistently arise. But a unifying principle would have to be very abstract, along the lines of "It is good if it has positive aesthetic properties." However, this is too vague to guide inferences. R. A. Sharpe, *Philosophy of Music: An Introduction* (Montreal: McGill-Queen's University Press, 2004), 164.

31. David Hume argues that there must be such principles, yet most commentaries on Hume note that such principles have no useful function in his theory of taste. See Alan H. Goldman, "There Are No Aesthetic Principles," in *Contemporary Debates in Aesthetics and the Philosophy of Art,* ed. Matthew Kieran (Oxford: Blackwell, 2006), 306–7.

32. The objection and the general response are found in Hatten, *Musical Meaning in Beethoven,* 32–22.

33. Roosevelt Porter, "Some Peculiarities about Musical Aesthetic Qualities," *Review of Metaphysics* 48 (March 1995): 487.

34. Oliver Conolly and Bashshar Haydar, "Aesthetic Principles," *British Journal of Aesehtetics* 43, no. 2 (April 2003): 118. See also John McDowell, "Aesthetic Value, Objectivity, and the Fabric of the World," in *Pleasure, Preference and Value: Studies in Philosophical Aesthetics,* ed. Eva Schaper (Cambridge: Cambridge University Press, 1983), 1–15.

35. Leddy, "Nature of Everyday Aesthetics," 14.

36. Although this relation is often described as supervenience, it may be something less, namely a resultance relation. Dancy, *Ethics Without Principles,* 85–89.

37. Ibid., 86.

38. Such principles are defended by George Dickie, *Evaluating Art* (Philadelphia: Temple University Press, 1988).

39. Robert Santelli, *The Best of the Blues: The 101 Essential Albums* (New York: Penguin, 1997), 10.

40. I often demonstrate the effect for students, fewer and fewer of whom have access to variable speed playback. However, digital music files can be altered in the same way.

41. Monroe C. Beardsley, *Aesthetics: Problems in the Philosophy of Criticism,* 2nd ed. (Indianapolis: Hackett, 1981), 454–89.

42. George Dickie responds to Goldman's version of this objection, but Dickie incorrectly treats the objection as saying that the polarity can be reversed for an isolated property (e.g., that gracefulness, considered apart from everything else, could be ugly). The objection is that its contribution to the overall verdict could have a reversed polar-

ity (e.g., that gracefulness is a defect in this case, all things considered). Goldman, "No Aesthetic Principles," 299–312, and Dickie, "Iron, Leather, and Critical Principles," in Kieran, *Contemporary Debates in Aesthetics and Philosophy,* 313–26.

43. Guy Sircello argues that an object is beautiful when a property that cannot be quantitatively measured is present in a very high degree, and the presence of the property gives us pleasure. An intensely yellow lemon can be beautiful, although an intensely sour one is not. Guy Sircello, *A New Theory of Beauty* (Princeton, NJ: Princeton University Press, 1975). Emotional intensity has been an important value for many popular music critics. For discussion of one strand of such criticism, see David Sanjek, "Valuing Popular Music," in Bérubé, *Aesthetics of Cultural Studies,* 117–39.

44. These properties are, in Noël Carroll's phrase, "implicitly connected to the reception side of things" (*Philosophy of Art,* 158). See also Alan H. Goldman, "The Experiential Account of Aesthetic Value," *The Journal of Aesthetics and Art Criticism* 64, no. 3 (2006): 333–42.

45. Kant, *Critique of Judgement,* section 8.

46. Ibid., section 16. Free beauties involve "pure" judgments of taste. Dependent beauty requires judgment that is "applied intentionally."

47. Handy, *Father of the Blues,* 77.

48. Allan F. Moore, *Rock, the Primary Text: Developing a Musicology of Rock,* 2nd ed. (New York: Ashgate, 2001), 6–7.

49. Kendall Walton, "Categories of Art," *Philosophical Review* 79, no 3 (1970): 350. For a precursor, see Aaron Copland, *Music and Imagination* (Cambridge: Harvard University Press, 1952), 28–29.

50. Walton, "Categories of Art," 339. Walton speaks of an "art-historical category," but nothing in his argument restricts the thesis to artworks, so I will use *musical category.* Frith offers a similar point about "genre rules and histories." Simon Frith, "The Cultural Study of Popular Music," in *Cultural Studies,* ed. Lawrence Grossberg, Cary Nelson, and Paula Treichler (New York: Routledge, 1992), 174. See also Ridley, *The Philosophy of Music,* 13, 64–67.

51. Walton, "Categories of Art," 337. The standard features that Walton discusses are perceptually distinguishable features of music. Walton's position is very different from Simon Frith's analysis (*Performing Rites,* 91–95) of musical genre as a set of socially governed rules. Walton's position is similar to Jan Mukaovský's earlier, neglected proposal that "the aesthetic is neither an attribute of objects nor a transcendental realm." Instead, any object has a capacity to perform an "aesthetic function" when it appears in "a certain social context." Unfortunately, Mukaovský so severely limits "the aesthetic" that he believes that aesthetic evaluation only emerged a few hundred years ago. *Aesthetic Function, Norm, and Value as Social Facts,* trans. Mark E. Suino (Ann Arbor: University of Michigan Press, 1970), 3.

52. Jerrold Levinson, "Musical Literacy," in *The Pleasures of Aesthetics: Philosophical Essays* (Ithaca, NY: Cornell University Press, 1996), 36–37.

53. Charles Keil, *Urban Blues* (Chicago: University of Chicago Press, 1966). In appendix C, Keil provides a detailed outline of standard features of twenty-nine distinct blues categories, including "phony folk blues" (217–24).

54. Walton, "Categories of Art," 347. Walton's example is a more famous piece of

antiwar protest, Pablo Picasso's *Guernica*. Walton asks us to reimagine it relative to the category *guernicas,* whose "surfaces are molded to protrude from the wall like relief maps of different kinds of terrain" (347).

55. Zangwill, *The Metaphysics of Beauty,* 98. For arguments supporting the weaker claim that familiarity with the specific style is unnecessary for the perception of some aesthetic qualities, see Davies, "Non-Western Art."

56. Walton, "Categories of Art," 366. For arguments supporting the indispensability of appropriate experience (and the limited value of music-theoretical knowledge), see Cook, *Music, Imagination, and Culture,* 143–52.

57. E. H. Gombrich, *Art and Illusion: A Study in the Psychology of Pictorial Representation* (Oxford: Phaidon Press, 1960), 8. See also Nelson Goodman, *Languages of Art: An Approach to a Theory of Symbols,* 2nd ed. (Indianapolis: Hackett, 1976), 7–8.

Chapter 4

1. Aaron Meskin, "Aesthetic Testimony: What Can We Learn From Others About Beauty and Art?" *Philosophy and Phenomenological Research* 69, no. 1 (2004): 65–91.

2. Greil Marcus, *Like a Rolling Stone: Bob Dylan at the Crossroads* (New York: Public Affairs, 2005).

3. Ibid., 29.

4. Ibid., 97–98.

5. Such value has traditionally been called "intrinsic value," but this is not a particularly useful way of thinking about it. Stecker, *Artworks,* 251–58.

6. See Philip Auslander, "Performance Analysis and Popular Music: A Manifesto," *Contemporary Theatre Review* 14, no. 1 (2004): 1–14, and Nicholas Cook, "Between Process and Product: Music and/as Performance," *Music Theory Online* 7, no. 2 (2001): http://societymusictheory.org/mto.html.

7. One could endorse it as instrumentally good for providing idiosyncratic responses, but such an endorsement confers roughly the same value on everything. See Higgins, "Musical Idiosyncrasy."

8. The transition from "I like this music" to "This music is aesthetically good" presupposes that aesthetic properties emerge from a resultance base in the music. Unlike the former, the latter judgments "aspire to be correct and they run the risk of failure." Zangwill, *The Metaphysics of Beauty,* 26.

9. "It is thus no refutation of the specificity of the aesthetic that a work of art might be used in some nonaesthetic context." Guillory, *Cultural Capital,* 295.

10. H. L. A. Hart, *The Concept of Law,* 2nd ed. (Oxford: Clarendon Press, 1994), 89. There is also a mixed, hermeneutic point of view, in which a nonparticipant attempts to understand the internal point of view of others.

11. David Yaffe, "Tangled Up In Bob," *The Nation,* April 25, 2005, 108, and http://www.thenation.com/doc/20050425/yaffe.

12. Marcus, *Like a Rolling Stone,* 215–21.

13. These evaluative judgments reflect Pierre Bourdieu's much-cited insight that taste classifies, and what it classifies is the classifier (*Distinction,* 6). Bourdieu ignores the possibility of internal evaluation of another person's tastes.

14. For examples and analysis of both cases, see Keyes, *Rap Music,* 162–71.

15. Frow, *Cultural Studies,* 168–69.

16. See Robert Kraut, "Perceiving the Music Correctly," in *The Interpretation of Music: Philosophical Essays,* ed. Michael Krausz (Oxford: Clarendon Press, 1993), 103–16.

17. It is the only Elvis Costello album to which Marsh gives five of five stars; see *The New Rolling Stone Record Guide,* ed. Dave Marsh and John Swenson (New York: Random House/Rolling Stone Press, 1983), 115. In a more recent version of the guide, other critics evaluate Costello's career and award five stars to the first two albums, but only four to *Armed Forces.*

18. "The pleasure of appreciating music is not some *frisson* to which the musical work stands *merely* as the cause or occasion, for, whereas such pleasure is indifferent to its cause, the pleasure of appreciating a musical work . . . is not indifferent to the individuality of its object." Stephen Davies, "The Evaluation of Music," in *What Is Music? An Introduction to the Philosophy of Music,* ed. Philip Alperson (New York: Haven, 1987), 316. Perhaps it would be better to speak of one's interest in the music, and how rewarding it is to appreciate it, with pleasure one aspect of that reward.

19. For a parallel distinction, see Sibley, *Approach to Aesthetics,* 90. If the necessity of the distinction is doubted, consider that x facilitating result y is not equivalent to x being instrumentally valuable for y (e.g., poor sanitation facilitates the spread of communicable disease, but that does not confer instrumental value on poor sanitation). In order for x to be instrumentally valuable for $y,$ y must be valuable. To contend that music is instrumentally valuable for aesthetic reasons, it must facilitate something valuable. I propose that it is an experience that is valuable, and the process of determining whether a particular experience is appropriately valuable is being called "appreciation."

20. Dahlhaus, *Analysis and Value Judgment,* 13.

21. J. O. Urmson, "On Grading," *Mind* 59 (1950): 145–69.

22. Pete Welding, review of *Johnny Winter, Rolling Stone,* August 9, 1969, 35.

23. Landau, *It's Too Late,* 100. Writing in 1971, Landau predicts that the group will never "make it over the long haul" (99).

24. The listener is "concerned with the particular without being concerned with other particulars." T. J. Diffey, *The Republic of Art and Other Essays* (New York: Peter Lang, 1991), 186.

25. Calling it "appraisal" rather than "appreciation," Diffey observes, "we can only look to see what excellence is embodied in a work" (ibid., 193).

26. If appreciation is understood in this way, there should be no confusion of the activity of appreciation with the aesthetic attitude, a psychological state that was formerly thought to be a necessary condition for aesthetic engagement. For strong criticisms of the older, "psychological" tradition, see George Dickie, *Art and the Aesthetic: An Institutional Analysis* (Ithaca, NY: Cornell University Press, 1974).

27. Peter Kivy, "What Makes Aesthetic Terms *Aesthetic?" Philosophy and Phenomenological Research* 36, no. 2 (1975): 201.

28. Stephen Davies's position has had considerable influence on my description of aesthetic interest. Davies, "The Evaluation of Music," 314 and 316. Some texts are highly unsuitable for appreciation. Provided they do their job, there is not much to appreciate about a telephone book's pages of residential telephone numbers. But indi-

viduals with the proper knowledge base, such as graphic designers, aesthetically evaluate them.

29. Paul Williams, *Bob Dylan: Performing Artist. The Middle Years: 1974–1986* (Novato: Underwood Miller, 1992), 253–54. Williams's aesthetic criteria are basically those defended by Collingwood in *The Principles of Art.*

30. Clinton Heylin, *Bob Dylan Behind the Shades: A Biography* (New York: Summit Books, 1991), 246.

31. Clinton Heylin, *Bob Dylan: The Recording Sessions, 1960–1994* (New York: St. Martin's Griffin, 1995), 107.

32. Goodman, *Languages of Art,* 252.

33. Berys Gaut, "Art and Knowledge," in Levinson, *Oxford Handbook of Aesthetics,* 448.

34. Claims that this is the primary function of some styles of popular music are advanced by John Blacking, "Towards an Anthropology of Body," in *The Anthropology of the Body,* ed. Blacking (London: Academic Press, 1977), 1–28.

35. Kassabian, "Popular," 117.

36. See Joseph Lanza, *Elevator Music: A Surreal History of Muzak, Easy-Listening, and other Moodsong* (New York: Picador, 1994), 6–66 and 167–81.

37. Kassabian, "Popular," 121.

38. Peter Kivy, "The Fine Art of Repetition," in *The Fine Art of Repetition: Essays in the Philosophy of Music* (Cambridge: Cambridge University Press, 1993), 327–59.

39. Goldman, *Aesthetic Value,* 81.

40. Greil Marcus, *Ranters & Crowd Pleasers: Punk in Pop Music, 1977–92* (New York: Doubleday, 1993), 34–35. Roger Scruton regards the melodically sophisticated pop of Buddy Holly and the Beatles as different in kind from the "dehumanizing" music of Nirvana, R.E.M., and U2, so he might regard Elvis Costello as likewise on the proper side of "the divide between popular and classical culture." Scruton, *The Aesthetics of Music,* 501. Since I do not want to beg any questions by my choice of examples, note that Marcus applies the same critical practices to music that Scruton would surely damn; e.g., discussions of the Clash, Gang of Four, and the Au Pairs are included in *Ranters & Crowd Pleasers.* I pursue this issue at greater length in chapter 6.

41. Marcus, *Ranters & Crowd Pleasers,* 35–36. Contrast this with another Costello record, *Goodbye Cruel World* (1984), in which an uneven collection of songs is ruined by a series of cluttered arrangements and weak vocal performances.

42. Moore, *Rock,* 186. Moore is responding to a critic who would prefer the song if it were ironic, but finds no irony in the lyrics.

43. My position agrees with Sibley (*Approach to Aesthetics,* 89–90) and contrasts with that of Malcolm Budd, for whom artistic value is the intrinsic value of the experience a work offers, where aesthetic value is simply one *way* of realizing artistic value. Budd assumes but does not defend the thesis that there is an essence of artistic value. See Budd, *Values of Art,* 1–3.

44. Nelson Goodman, *Languages of Art* (Indianapolis: Hackett, 1976), 258, and *Ways of Worldmaking* (Indianapolis: Hackett, 1978), 57–70. Significant criticisms are offered by Dickie, *Evaluating Art,* 106–11.

45. This position is very close to that of Rose Rosengard Subotnik: "what the pub-

lic hears in [popular] music is what is always heard, not autonomous structure but the sensuous manifestation of particular cultural values." *Developing Variations: Style and Ideology in Western Music* (Minneapolis: University of Minnesota Press, 1991), 288. I do not endorse her position that all popular music expresses the same "general values" of Western culture.

46. Some critics of aesthetic valuation think that they presuppose a nonexistent homogeneity of experience. But they need not do so. Far from endorsing this homogeneity, foundational figures in traditional aesthetics warn that it is fundamentally problematic. See Guillory, *Cultural Capital,* 276.

47. In contrast, the assumption is central to the case against popular music in Johnson, *Who Needs Classical Music?*

48. "The rapt attention that features in some instances of accounts of the aesthetic state of mind undoubtedly characterizes some instances of it, but it is by no means a necessary condition of appreciation as I conceive it." Iseminger, "Aesthetic State of Mind," 100.

49. Arnold Berleant, "Ideas for a Social Aesthetic," in Light and Smith, *Aesthetics of Everyday Life,* 23–38.

50. Dahlhaus, *Analysis and Value Judgment,* 26.

51. Evaluations of a work's function(s) are contingent upon assumptions about an implicitly defined audience in implicitly defined circumstances. Smith, *Contingencies of Value,* 13–16. For extended criticisms of Smith, see Guillory, *Cultural Capital,* 269–325.

52. Wicke, *Rock Music,* 11.

53. See Lisa A. Lewis, *Gender Politics and MTV: Voicing the Difference* (Philadelphia: Temple University Press, 1990), 152–55.

54. Marcus, *Ranters & Crowd Pleasers,* 174, and *Like a Rolling Stone,* 98–99.

55. Gordon Graham, "The Value of Music," *The Journal of Aesthetics and Art Criticism* 53, no. 2 (1995): 151.

56. A detailed and compelling explanation of the underlying argument is Rafael De Clercq, "The Aesthetic Peculiarity of Multifunctional Artefacts," *British Journal of Aesthetics* 45, no. 4 (2005): 412–25. Similar arguments underlie Guillory, *Cultural Capital,* 295.

57. Langdon Winner, "Trout Mask Replica," in *Stranded: Rock and Roll for a Desert Island,* ed. Greil Marcus (New York: Alfred A. Knopf, 1979), 59.

58. These two functions are suggested by Susan McClary, *Feminine Endings: Music, Gender, and Sexuality* (Minneapolis: University of Minnesota Press, 1991), 148–66.

59. Simon Frith, "Towards an Aesthetic of Popular Music," in *Music and Society: The Politics of Composition, Performance and Reception,* ed. Richard Leppert and Susan McClary (Cambridge: Cambridge University Press, 1987), 144.

60. Goldman, *Aesthetic Value,* 172. I focus on Goldman because I share many assumptions with him, e.g., that we cannot specify principles that map nonaesthetic properties of musical works to the value of the resultant experiences.

61. A parallel argument is advanced by Herbert J. Gans, *Popular Culture and High Culture: An Analysis and Evaluation of Taste* (New York: Basic Books, 1999), 125 and 171n.

62. Goldman, *Aesthetic Value,* 21–30.

63. Jackson, *Goin' Down the Road,* 17.

64. If the hypothesis is supposed to imply that the ideal critic has no partiality to set aside, we might wonder what it means to say that critic assigns value to anything. Sharpe, *Philosophy of Music,* 134–35.

65. Samuel Lipman, *Music and More: Essays, 1975–1991* (Evanston, IL: Northwestern University Press, 1992), 17.

66. See Aaron Ridley, *Music, Value and the Passions* (Ithaca, NY: Cornell University Press, 1995), 51–72, and Stephen Davies, *Musical Meaning and Expression* (Ithaca, NY: Cornell University Press, 1994), 321–80.

67. See George H. Lewis, "Who Do You Love? The Dimensions of Musical Taste," in *Popular Music and Communication,* 2nd ed., ed. James Lull (Newbury Park, CA: Sage, 1992), 134–51. Because such codes are also acquired to operate within subcultures that have limited social status, we can also speak of subcultural capital; see Sarah Thornton, *Club Cultures: Music, Media and Subcultural Capital* (Hanover, NH: Wesleyan University Press, 1996).

68. Patricia Herzog, "Music Criticism and Musical Meaning," *Journal of Aesthetics and Art Criticism* 53, no. 3 (1995): 300. Compare: "Our interpretation of a work and our experience of its value are mutually dependent . . . simultaneously causing and validating themselves *and* causing and validating each other." Smith, *Contingencies of Value,* 10–11.

69. Goldman, *Aesthetic Value,* 150.

70. Elizabeth Anderson, *Value in Ethics and Economics* (Cambridge: Harvard University Press, 1993), 7, 23, 48–49. Anderson's distinction parallels the distinction between internal and external judgments of value.

71. Dave Marsh, *The Heart of Rock & Soul: The 1001 Greatest Singles Ever Made* (New York: Plume, 1989), xv.

72. See Anita Silvers, "Aesthetic 'Akrasia': On Disliking Good Art," *Journal of Aesthetics and Art Criticism* 31, no. 2 (1972): 227–34.

73. Marsh, *Heart of Rock,* xv.

74. Elizabeth Anderson, "Replies to Sturgeon and Piper," *Ethics* 106, no. 3 (1996): 549. Appreciating music does not invoke standards, so appreciating music does not mean endorsing it as a vehicle for the appreciative activities of everyone else. As such, appreciation does not directly invite reflection on our standards. In shifting the focus from a determination of the work's value to a reasonableness of valuing it, we avoid a debate about the ontological status of the values perceived by knowledgeable listeners.

75. Anderson, *Value in Ethics,* 7. An excellent introduction to "blameless differences" is Matthew Kieran, *Revealing Art* (New York: Routledge, 2005), 226–30.

76. Will Kymlicka, *Liberalism, Community, and Culture* (Oxford: Clarendon Press, 1989), 165.

77. Kivy, *Fine Art of Repetition,* 11–31 and 360–73, and *Philosophies of Art: An Essay in Differences* (Cambridge: Cambridge University Press, 1997), 179–217. With their emphasis on instrumental music in the tonal tradition, Julian Johnson and Roger Scruton generally agree.

78. Mary Mothersill, "Reply to Barrie Falk," *Philosophical Books* 27 (January 1986): 13.

79. Ibid., 13–14.
80. Scruton, *The Aesthetics of Music,* 370.
81. See Lipman, *Music and More,* particularly the introduction ("classical music today is in deep trouble" [25]), and Subotnik, *Developing Variations,* 87–97.

Chapter 5

1. The paucity of reliable experimental data on this topic creates an environment in which absurd claims about popular taste can flourish. Most empirical studies of music are directed by assumptions about art music, frequently by adopting claims made by Heinrich Schenker or Leonard B. Meyer. Little has been done to determine how listeners actually hear other types of music. See David J. Hargreaves, *The Developmental Psychology of Music* (Cambridge: Cambridge University Press, 1986), 7–8.

2. Howard D. McKinney and W. R. Anderson, *Discovering Music,* 4th ed. (New York: American Book Company, 1962), 27–28.

3. Quoted in Tom Moon, "The Black Saint's Epitaph," *Musician,* June 1989, 122.

4. Eduard Hanslick, *On the Musically Beautiful,* trans. Geoffrey Payzant (Indianapolis: Hackett, 1986), 60.

5. Ibid., 58–59.

6. Rechristened *concatenationism,* this position has been recently defended by Jerrold Levinson, *Music in the Moment* (Ithaca, NY: Cornell University Press, 1997).

7. Edmund Gurney, *The Power of Sound* (1880; repr., New York: Basic Books, 1966), 306. For a summary and analysis of Gurney's position, see Malcolm Budd, *Music and the Emotions: The Philosophical Theories* (London: Routledge and Kegan Paul, 1985), 52–75.

8. Robert Motherwell cites Prall as "a great aesthetician," and Leonard Bernstein dedicates *The Unanswered Question* to Prall. See Paul Cummings, "Interview with Robert Motherwell," *Smithsonian Archives of American Art,* Jan. 21 2003, http://artarchives.si.edu/oralhist/mother71.htm; and Leonard Bernstein, *The Unanswered Question: Six Talks at Harvard* (Cambridge: Harvard University Press, 1976), 3.

9. David W. Prall, *Aesthetic Judgment* (New York: Thomas Y. Crowell, 1929; repr., New York: Apollo Edition, 1967), 63–68. Prall's position is reminiscent of Hanslick's idea (*On the Musically Beautiful,* xxii) that emotions cannot be the "content" of music because their apprehension does not depend on our knowledge of musical laws.

10. For a response to Prall's position on taste and smell, see Carolyn Korsmeyer, *Making Sense of Taste: Food and Philosophy* (Ithaca, NY: Cornell University Press, 1999), 104–15.

11. Prall, *Aesthetic Judgment,* 210–11.

12. W. Jay Dowling, "The Development of Music Perception and Cognition," in *The Psychology of Music,* ed. Diana Deutsch, 2nd ed. (San Diego: Academic Press, 1999), 603–25.

13. Beardsley, *Aesthetics,* 97–113.

14. Ibid., 98.

15. Ibid., 337.

16. Leonard B. Meyer, *Emotion and Meaning in Music* (Chicago: University of Chicago Press, 1956), 40.

17. Scruton, *The Aesthetics of Music*, 500. To read the argument in a condensed form, see Roger Scruton, "The Decline of Musical Culture," in *Arguing about Art: Topics in Contemporary Philosophical Aesthetics*, ed. Alex Neill and Aaron Ridley, 2nd ed. (New York: Routledge, 2001), 119–34.

18. Regarding the contributing role of the European music concert in the eighteenth and nineteenth centuries, see David Gramit, *Cultivating Music: The Aspirations, Interests, and Limits of German Musical Culture, 1770–1846* (Berkeley and Los Angeles: University of California Press, 2002), 125–60.

19. The argument is made that the popular music fan is attending only to trivial customizations of otherwise banal and interchangeable tunes. For my response, see Theodore Gracyk, "Adorno, Jazz, and the Aesthetics of Popular Music," *Musical Quarterly* 76, no. 4 (1992): 526–42.

20. Ridley, *Music, Value and the Passions*, 54. For an explanation of why overreliance on structural listening limits perception of musical particularity, see Eugene Narmour, "Hierarchical Expectation and Musical Style," in Deutsch, *The Psychology of Music*, 441–72.

21. Hanslick, *On the Musically Beautiful*, 60.

22. Robert Cantrick, "Commentary on Nicholas Cook," *Music Theory Online* 8, no. 2 (2002), http://www.societymusictheory.org/mto/issues/mto.02.8.2/mto.02.8.2 .cantrick.html.

23. Nonstructural properties play a major role in the impact of many rock recordings. See Gracyk, *Rhythm and Noise*, 61–67, 99–124, and Albin J. Zak III, *The Poetics of Rock: Cutting Tracks, Making Records* (Berkeley and Los Angeles: University of California Press, 2001), 48–96.

24. Noël Carroll, *Philosophical Problems of Classical Film Theory* (Princeton, NJ: Princeton University Press, 1988), 82–83.

25. Edward Cone, "Music and Form," in Alperson, *What Is Music?* 134.

26. Carroll, *Classical Film Theory*, 86.

27. Fisher, "High Art versus Low Art," 413.

28. Those who favor analytical listening and who are unfamiliar with the extended improvisations of the Grateful Dead might consult the transcriptions and analysis of one such improvisation in Graeme M. Boone, "Tonal and Expressive Ambiguity in 'Dark Star,'" in Covach and Boone, *Understanding Rock*, 171–210.

29. Arlette Zenatti, "Children's Musical Cognition and Taste," in *Psychology and Music: The Understanding of Melody and Rhythm*, ed. Thomas J. Tighe and W. Jay Dowling (Hillsdale, NJ: Erlbaum, 1993), 185. The chief exception is listeners with higher education and occupational status, who develop broader musical tastes and who regard multiple musical styles as equally valuable. Listeners with the lowest levels of education and occupational status display the narrowest taste and most strongly deny any value to music they dislike. Peterson, "Understanding Audience Segmentation"; Bryson, "Anything but Heavy Metal." Sudden, radical change in an adult's musical taste or musical ability correlates with dementia. "Dementia 'Affects Musical Taste,'" *BBC News Online*, December 25, 2000, http://news.bbc.co.uk/1/hi/health/1082841.stm.

30. A prototype for this argument is Gurney, *The Power of Sound*, 403.

31. Colwyn Trevarthen, "Origins of Musical Identity: Evidence from Infancy for Musical Social Awareness," in *Musical Identities*, ed. Raymond MacDonald, David Hargreaves, and Dorothy Miell (Oxford: Oxford University Press, 2002), 25.

32. Wendy L. Magee, "Disability and Identity in Music Therapy," in *Musical Identities,* 182.

33. Always alert to the centrality of music to life, Oliver Sacks notes that hearing or even imagining music can "unfreeze" a musically sensitive Parkinsonian patient, and he invites us to generalize from the way "that patients' own kinetic melodies *can* be given back to them, albeit briefly, by the appropriate flow of *music.*" Oliver Sacks, *Awakenings* (New York: Harper Perennial, 1990), 348. However, Sacks warns that it must be music that the individual patient enjoys (62n) and it must have a rhythmic impetus "'embedded' in melody" (61n). For music in Sacks's case histories, see 60, 117, 125.

34. Ola Stockfelt, "Adequate Modes of Listening," in *Keeping Score: Music, Disciplinarity, Culture,* ed. David Schwarz, Anahid Kassabian, and Lawrence Siegel (Charlottesville: University Press of Virginia, 1997), 142. See also Moore, *Rock,* 24–28.

35. Even with food, physiology does not account for everything. Beliefs about food can contribute to phenomenal differences. Knowing which part of an animal (or even which animal) is on one's plate can have a profound effect on how it tastes.

36. What are those instincts? Above all, to notice changes in intervals and pitch levels of melodies, and to notice and remember melodic contours. Evidence strongly denies any instinctive preference for "Western" musical patterns. For a summary of the relevant recent research, see Dowling, "Development of Music Perception," 604–10.

37. Michael R. D'Amato, "A Search for Tonal Pattern Perception in Cebus Monkeys: Why Monkeys Can't Hum a Tune," *Music Perception* 5, no. 4 (1988): 478.

38. Peter Kivy, *Music Alone: Philosophical Reflections on the Purely Musical Experience* (Ithaca, NY: Cornell University Press, 1990), 41. As Moore puts it, "until we cognize the sounds, until we have created an internal representation on the basis of their assimilation, we have no musical entity to care about, or which to give value." Moore, *Rock,* 17; emphasis omitted.

39. Martyn Evans observes that cases of cross-cultural exposure seem to be our only genuine instances of an adult whose listening can be characterized as naive. *Listening to Music* (London: Macmillan, 1990), 11.

40. With most listeners, seven seems to be the pivotal age for grasping the syntax of the tonal system. See John A. Sloboda, "Music as a Language," in *Music and Child Development,* ed. Frank R. Wilson and Franz L. Roehmann (St. Louis: Biology of Making, 1990), 28–43.

41. The crucial years for developing sensitivity to harmonic cadences and closure are seven to eleven, but learning generally continues until the age of seventeen. Even expert adult musicians have considerable difficulty identifying concurrent voices in a complex fugue. Rosamund Shuter-Dyson, "Musical Ability," in Deutsch, *The Psychology of Music,* 635–36.

42. Some researches have concluded that music and language begin in the same instinct to organize the aural environment into distinct events according to musical qualities. See Christoph Fassbender, "Infants' Auditory Sensitivity Towards Acoustic Parameters of Speech and Music," in *Musical Beginnings: Origins and Development of Musical Competence,* ed. Irène Deliège and John Sloboda (Oxford: Oxford University Press, 1996), 56–87. See also Albert S. Bregman, *Auditory Scene Analysis* (Cambridge: MIT Press, 1990); Stephen Handel, *Listening* (Cambridge: MIT Press, 1990); Carol L.

Krumhansl and Peter Jusczyk, "Infants' Perception of Phrase Structure in Music," *Psychological Science* 1, no. 1 (1990): 70–73; and Sandra Trehub, E. Glenn Schellenberg, and D. Hill, "The Origins of Music Perception and Cognition: A Developmental Perspective," in *Perception and Cognition of Music,* ed. Irène DeLiège and John A. Sloboda (Hove, East Sussex: Psychology Press, 1997), 103–28.

43. Hanslick, *On the Musically Beautiful,* 69–70. But in the same passage, he denies that a rhythm by itself is genuinely "artistic" music, that is, music beyond what is natural and instinctive.

44. Ibid., 74.

45. For examples of audience engagement at the height of the classical age, see Lydia Goehr, *The Imaginary Museum of Musical Works* (Oxford: Clarendon Press, 1992), 191–93 and 236–39.

46. Listeners' expectations about when a musical segment will end are "fairly precisely synchronized" with what subsequently happens. Complex metrical structures alter those expectations in predictable ways. See Mari Riess Jones, "Attending to Musical Events," in *Cognitive Bases of Musical Communication,* ed. Mari Riess Jones and Susan Holleran (Washington, DC: American Psychological Association, 1992), 91–110.

47. Lawrence M. Zbikowski, *Conceptualizing Music: Cognitive Structure, Theory, and Analysis* (New York: Oxford University Press, 2002), 111.

48. Ibid., 96–134.

49. George Martin, *All You Need Is Ears* (New York: St. Martin's Press, 1979), 34–35.

50. One reason is that the average listener does not construct an abstract representation of a musical work: "memory for music typically operates in terms of more precise representations of particular stimuli than has been generally thought." Dowling, "Development of Music Perception," 620. It seems likely that unfamiliar styles introduce distracting stimuli that limit comparisons with remembered music.

51. Although Scruton praises the Beatles, he makes just this complaint about fans of the rock group Nirvana (*The Aesthetics of Music,* 500).

52. See Roger Scruton, *The Aesthetic Understanding* (New York: Methuen, 1983), 41.

53. Carol L. Krumhansl, "Internal Representations for Music Perception and Performance," in *Cognitive Bases,* 198.

Chapter 6

1. Johnson, *Who Needs Classical Music?* 14.

2. In a recent study of adult music listening, "the most outstanding feature . . . was the perceived stability of respondents' tastes." Vernon Pickles, "Music and the Third Age," *Psychology of Music* 32, no. 4 (2003): 420.

3. See Davies, *Musical Meaning and Expression,* 369, and Cook, *Music, Imagination, and Culture.*

4. See John Stuart Mill, "Inaugural Address Delivered to the University of St. Andrews," February 1st, 1867 (London: Longmans, Green, Reader and Dyer, 1867), and Gans, *Popular Culture,* 171. On the difficulty of justifying music's place in the curriculum, see Peter Kivy, "Music in the Liberal Education," in *Fine Art of Repetition,* 11–31.

5. Kenneth M. Steele, Joshua D. Brown, and Jaimily A. Stoecker, "Failure to confirm the Rauscher and Shaw description of recovery of the Mozart effect," *Perceptual and Motor Skills* 88, no. 3, part 1 (1999): 843–48, and Kenneth M. Steele, Karen E. Bass, and Melissa D. Crook, "The mystery of the Mozart effect: Failure to replicate," *Psychological Science* 10, no. 4 (1999): 366–69.

6. Because its implicit aims are questionable, music education frequently encourages alienation. Green, *Music on Deaf Ears,* 52–54 and 137–41.

7. Scruton, *The Aesthetics of Music.*

8. Ibid., 391.

9. Ibid., 354–59.

10. Ibid., 157. The Beatles and Buddy Holly are Scruton's exceptions in rock music. With Andrew Lloyd Weber, their melodies are in the same category as those of George Gershwin and Cole Porter (500–501).

11. Ibid., 502. The same opposition of intellectual and physical response grounds the argument against rock music in Johnson, *Who Needs Classical Music?*

12. Johnson, *Who Needs Classical Music?* 60.

13. For an extended discussion of this core idea, see Meyer, *Emotion and Meaning.*

14. Echard, *Neil Young,* 137. Echard draws on Edward T. Cone, *The Composer's Voice* (Berkeley and Los Angeles: University of California Press, 1974).

15. Echard, *Neil Young,* 137.

16. Ibid., 140.

17. Ibid., 190–91.

18. Ibid., 182.

19. For my earlier thoughts on the importance of timbre, see Gracyk, *Rhythm and Noise,* 118–24.

20. Although Echard approvingly cites the work of Susan McClary, he is much less concerned than she about the sociopolitical agendas in musical gestures. See McClary, *Feminine Endings.*

21. Susan Fast similarly observes that her scholarly research about Led Zeppelin arose from a radio encounter with "Whole Lotta Love." However, whereas Fast notes that she renewed her love of the music after "several years," I had not been a fan of their music. Susan Fast, *In the Houses of the Holy: Led Zeppelin and the Power of Rock Music* (Oxford: Oxford University Press, 2001), 56.

22. Because the drum roll is a rapid volley that disrupts the initial pulse, the rhythmic introduction consists of two competing phrases of equal length. Neither precisely reappears. So the opening two seconds of solo drumming are a musical tease, establishing and immediately shattering expectations. Where the opening of Led Zeppelin's "Custard Pie" exploits an ambiguous relationship between guitar and drums, "D'Yer Mak'Er" features overt misdirection.

23. McDowell, "Aesthetic Value," 5.

24. Fast, *Houses of the Holy,* 4. So Led Zeppelin is offering a variation of the same joke that informs Mozart's "A Musical Joke" (*Ein musikalischer spass,* KV 522).

25. As evidenced by his liner notes for *Freak Out!* (Verve, 1966), Frank Zappa knew from the outset that most of his audience didn't grasp much of what was interesting in the music. One of his droll explanations of what to listen for (to a Swedish audience,

September 30, 1967) is preserved on a live recording subsequently released as *'Tis the Season to be Jelly*.

26. Robert Plant quoted in Michael Odell, "The Greatest Songs Ever: Led Zeppelin," *Blender* (January/February 2005), 57.

27. Fast, *Houses of the Holy*, 122.

28. Page, Bonham, and Jones had to count silently to themselves during the *a cappella* passages, but this procedure did not work during live performance of the more complex arrangement. I owe this point about their live performances to John Brackett, "Examining Rhythmic and Metric Practices in Led Zeppelin's Musical Style," *Popular Music*, forthcoming 2007. Numerous Internet references to "Black Dog" speculate about its time signature or warn would-be performers of its difficulties.

29. One of the four musicians in Led Zeppelin, bass and keyboard player John Paul Jones, received some formal training in music and was briefly a church organist and choirmaster. Many rock bands have taken advantage of musical intelligence honed through the study of art music.

30. See Stan Godlovitch, *Musical Performance: A Philosophical Study* (London: Routledge, 1998), 52–78. Similarly, knowledge that music was improvised alters the experience and subsequent evaluation.

31. Popular music also employs the tradition of the final move to the tonic note. Led Zeppelin's "Stairway to Heaven" is a prime example. Musical organization in relation to the tonic is the hallmark of so-called progressive rock, which includes several other Led Zeppelin songs. See Edward Macan, *Rocking the Classics: English Progressive Rock and the Counterculture* (Oxford: Oxford University Press, 1997).

32. Fast, *Houses of the Holy*, 88–112.

33. For a discussion of the limits of paraphrase as evidence of understanding music, see Ridley, *The Philosophy of Music*, 26–44.

34. Tony Kirschner, "Studying Rock: Toward a Materialist Ethnography," in *Mapping the Beat: Popular Music and Contemporary Theory*, ed. Thomas Swiss, John Sloop, and Andrew Herman (Blackwell Publishers, 1998), 247–68. See also Ellen Willis, "Crowds and Freedom," in Kelly and McDonnell, *Stars Don't Stand Still in the Sky: Music and Myth*, 153–59.

35. Johnson, *Who Needs Classical Music?* 22.

36. Attali, *Noise*, 26. Bruno Nettl defends the similar idea that the organization of music expresses a culture's "relevant central values in abstracted forms." *The Study of Ethnomusicology: Twenty-Nine Issues and Concepts* (University of Illinois Press, 1983), 60. Several essays related to this theme appear in Swiss, Sloop, and Herman, *Mapping the Beat*.

37. Lori Burns, "Analytical Methodologies for Rock Music: Harmonic and Voice-Leading Strategies in Tori Amos's 'Crucify,'" in *Expression in Pop-Rock Music: A Collection of Critical and Analytical Essays*, ed. Walter Everett (New York: Garland, 2000), 213–46.

38. Attali, *Noise*, 59–62.

39. Ibid., 137. One of Attali's main proposals is that musical organization is prophetic in being a precursor to coming modes of political and economic organization; Cage and the Rolling Stones are merely a "liquidation of the old."

Chapter 7

1. Adrian C. North and David J. Hargreaves, "Music and Adolescent Identity," *Music Education Research* 1 (1999): 75–92.

2. Walser, "Popular Music Analysis," 38.

3. For a review and summary of five decades of research on music and infants, see Trevarthen, "Origins of Musical Identity."

4. Ibid., 35.

5. See Ellen Dissanayake, "Antecedents of the Temporal Arts in Early Mother-infant Interaction," in *The Origins of Music*, ed. Nils L. Wallin, Björn Merker and Steven Brown (Cambridge: MIT Press, 2000), 389–410, and Steven Mithen, *The Singing Neanderthals: The Origins of Music, Language, Mind and Body* (London: Weidenfeld and Nicolson, 2005).

6. Campbell draws on Christopher Small's catholic notion of "musicking" (a verb coined by Small to cover *any* activity relating to music). Patricia Shehan Campbell, *Songs in Their Heads: Music and its Meaning in Children's Lives* (Oxford: Oxford University Press, 1998); Christopher Small, *Musicking: The Meanings of Performing and Listening* (Middletown, CN: Wesleyan University Press, 1998).

7. David J. Hargreaves, Dorothy Miell, and Raymond A. R. MacDonald, "What Are Musical Identities, and Why Are They Important," in MacDonald, Hargreaves, and Miell, *Musical Identities*, 2.

8. Mark Tarrant, Adrian C. North, and David J. Hargreaves, "Adolescents' Intergroup Attributions: A Comparison of Two Social Identities," *Journal of Youth and Adolescence* 33, no. 3 (2004): 184.

9. Mark Tarrant, Adrian C. North, and David J. Hargreaves, "Youth Identity and Music," in MacDonald, Hargreaves, and Miell, *Musical Identities*, 145.

10. Göran Folkestad, "National Identity and Music," in *Musical Identities*, 160.

11. Quoted in James Henke, "The Edge: The Rolling Stone Interview," *Rolling Stone*, March 10, 1988, 53.

12. Michael Fitzgerald, Anil P. Joseph, Mary Hayes, and Myra O'Regan, "Leisure Activities of Adolescent Schoolchildren," *Journal of Adolescence* 18, no. 3 (1995): 350. This study was conducted in Ireland, but it confirms numerous earlier studies conducted elsewhere, e.g., James S. Leming, "Rock Music and the Socialization of Moral Values in Early Adolescence," *Youth and Society* 18, no. 4 (1987): 363–83.

13. The arguments that follow are not intended to challenge the idea that music plays multiple roles in lives of adolescents, as described by Tarrant, North, and Hargreaves, "Youth Identity and Music," 135.

14. Reed Larson, "Secrets in the Bedroom: Adolescents' Private Use of Media," *Journal of Youth and Adolescence* 25, no. 5 (1995): 538–39.

15. Ibid., 538–39, 544–47.

16. Ibid., 545.

17. David Hume, *A Treatise of Human Nature*, ed. L. A. Selby-Bigge, 2nd ed., revised by P. H. Nidditch (Oxford: Clarendon Press, 1978), 254. For a sympathetic account of Hume's discussion of personal identity, see James Giles, "The No-Self Theory: Hume,

Buddhism, and Personal Identity," *Philosophy East and West* 43, no. 2 (1993): 175–200. In explicating Hume, I generally frame his position in terms of contemporary terminology (e.g., saying *concept* where Hume would say *idea*).

18. Hume, *Treatise of Human Nature,* 252.

19. Ibid.

20. Ibid., 251–52.

21. Hume is arguing for a constructionist view of the *concept* of self-identity, and tries to explain both how and why we construct and apply this concept to the things that we do. He is not guilty of an objectionable confusion between a constructionist view of objects and of concepts (e.g., the tendency to overlook the difference between saying that the idea of "ocean" is a social construction and saying the same about the body of water that is the Pacific Ocean). See Ian Hacking, *The Social Construction of What?* (Cambridge: Harvard University Press, 2000).

22. Schemata are simple knowledge structures representing the relevant basic dimensions of an entity that it classifies. Gregory L. Murphy, *The Big Book of Concepts* (Cambridge: MIT Press, 2002), 47. This point about identity conditions should not be confused with the related point that different concepts for object *types* divide into two broad domains.

23. Hume notes that teleological explanations often guide imagination in this process (*Treatise of Human Nature,* 257). The teleological strategy is typical for organizing "nonobject" domains according to context dependent relations. Murphy, *Big Book of Concepts,* 229.

24. Hume, *Treatise of Human Nature,* 254.

25. For an extended discussion of issues surrounding musical works and their identity, see Stephen Davies, *Musical Works and Performances: A Philosophical Exploration* (Oxford: Clarendon Press, 2001).

26. Almost from birth, infants remember and distinguish melodic contours, but not distinct melodies (which requires learning scale systems). Dowling, "Development of Music Perception," 607–8.

27. *Fantasia* is a Walt Disney animated film originally released in 1940. In a forerunner to music videos, visual interpretations accompany orchestral works (edited and conducted by Leopold Stokowski). For example, Igor Stravinsky's *The Rite of Spring* serves as background music for a battle between two dinosaurs. An abbreviated adaptation of Beethoven's sixth symphony (the Pastoral) receives a kitsch interpretation involving satyrs, nymphs, and other creatures from Greek mythology.

28. Trevarthen, "Origins of Musical Identity," 21.

29. Ibid., 26.

30. Hume, *Treatise of Human Nature,* 179. Hume's argument emphasizes the instinctive ability to make inferences based on past experiences.

31. For an overview of recent research findings, see Dowling, "Development of Music Perception," 603–25.

32. Employing the terminology of Jean Piaget, this period of cognitive development is often referred to as formal operational thought. My summary draws from Laurence D. Steinberg, *Adolescence,* 6th ed. (Blacklick: McGraw-Hill, 2001), David R. Schaffer,

Developmental Psychology: Childhood and Adolescence, 6th ed. (Belmont: Wadsworth, 2002), and Kathleen S. Berger, *The Developing Person: Through the Life Span,* 5th ed. (New York: Worth, 2000).

33. Carol I. Diener and Carol S. Dweck, "An Analysis of Learned Helplessness: II. The Processing of Success," *Journal of Personality and Social Psychology* 39, no. 5 (1980): 940–52.

34. Hanslick, *On the Musically Beautiful,* 30, 31, 29, 31, respectively.

35. Ibid., 64.

36. Ibid.

37. Barbara Tillmann and Emmanuel Bigand, "The Relative Importance of Local and Global Structures in Music Perception," *Journal of Aesthetics and Art Criticism* 62, no. 2 (2004): 211–22. These findings would explain those of Narmour, "Hierarchical Expectation," 441–72.

38. Hanslick, *On the Musically Beautiful,* 29.

39. The preceding remarks are an attempt to amplify Tia DeNora's comments on music's "emblematic capacity" in relation to memory. See *Music in Everyday Life* (Cambridge: Cambridge University Press, 2000), 63–68.

40. I am not suggesting that listeners consciously think of music as satisfying this symbolic function. It is no surprise that most adolescents explain music's value by citing its relevance to their emotional needs (Tarrant, North, and Hargreaves, "Youth Identity and Music," 135). Yet we cannot assume that adolescents grasp *all* of the functions performed by music (hence the argument by Tarrant, North, and Hargreaves that it performs an important function in securing group identity by conveying metainformation about listeners).

41. DeNora similarly discusses music's role as "a mirror for self-perception," but she is interested in how "a particular musical mirror" is used for "the articulation of self-identity—for its spinning out for a tale for self and other" (*Music in Everyday Life,* 69–70). In contrast, I am proposing that music also functions as a "mirror" of a more abstract concept.

Selected Bibliography

Alperson, Philip, ed. *What Is Music?* New York: Haven, 1988.

Anderson, Elizabeth. *Value in Ethics and Economics.* Cambridge: Harvard University Press, 1993.

Attali, Jacques. *Noise: The Political Economy of Music.* Translated by Brian Massumi. Minneapolis: University of Minnesota Press, 1985.

Barthes, Roland. *The Pleasure of the Text.* Translated by Richard Miller. New York: Hill and Wang, 1975.

Beardsley, Monroe C. *Aesthetics: Problems in the Philosophy of Criticism.* 2nd ed. Indianapolis: Hackett, 1981.

Bérubé, Michael, ed. *The Aesthetics of Cultural Studies.* Oxford: Blackwell, 2005.

Berleant, Arnold. *Aesthetics and Environment: Variations on a Theme.* Aldershot: Ashgate, 2005.

———. *Art as Engagement.* Philadelphia: Temple University Press, 1991.

———. *Rethinking Aesthetics: Rouge Essays on Aesthetics and the Arts.* Aldershot: Ashgate, 2004.

Bourdieu, Pierre. *Distinction: A Social Critique of the Judgement of Taste.* Translated by Richard Nice. Cambridge: Harvard University Press, 1984.

Brady, Emily, and Jerrold Levinson, eds. *Aesthetic Concepts.* Oxford: Clarendon Press, 2001.

Budd, Malcolm. *Music and the Emotions: The Philosophical Theories.* London: Routledge & Kegan Paul, 1985.

———. *Values of Art: Pictures, Poetry and Music.* London: Penguin, 1995.

Campbell, Patricia Shehan. *Songs in Their Heads: Music and Its Meaning in Children's Lives.* Oxford: Oxford University Press, 1998.

Carroll, Noël. *Engaging the Moving Image.* New Haven: Yale University Press, 2003.

———. *Philosophy of Art: A Contemporary Introduction.* London: Routledge, 1999.

———. *Philosophical Problems of Classical Film Theory.* Princeton, NJ: Princeton University Press, 1988.

———, ed. *Theories of Art Today.* Madison: University of Wisconsin Press, 2000.

Clayton, Martin, Trevor Herbert, and Richard Middleton, eds. *The Cultural Study of Music: A Critical Introduction.* London: Routledge, 2003.

Collingwood, R. G. *The Principles of Art.* Oxford: Oxford University Press, 1958.

Cook, Nicholas. *Music, Imagination, and Culture.* Oxford: Clarendon Press, 1990.

Cook, Nicholas, and Mark Everist, eds. *Rethinking Music*. Oxford: Oxford University Press, 1999.

Copland, Aaron. *Music and Imagination*. Cambridge: Harvard University Press, 1952.

Covach, John, and Graeme M. Boone, eds. *Understanding Rock: Essays in Musical Analysis*. Oxford: Oxford University Press, 1997.

Crafts, Susan D., Daniel Cavicchi, and Charles Keil. *My Music*. Hanover, NH: Wesleyan University Press, 1993.

Dahlhaus, Carl. *Analysis and Value Judgment*. Translated by Siegmund Levarie. New York: Pendragon, 1983.

Davies, Martin, and Tony Stone, eds. *Mental Simulation: Evaluations and Applications*. Oxford: Blackwell, 1995.

Davies, Stephen. *Musical Meaning and Expression*. Ithaca, NY: Cornell University Press, 1994.

———. *Musical Works and Performances: A Philosophical Exploration*. Oxford: Clarendon Press, 2001.

Deliège, Irène, and John Sloboda, eds. *Musical Beginnings: Origins and Development of Musical Competence*. Oxford: Oxford University Press, 1996.

———, eds. *Perception and Cognition of Music*. Hove, East Sussex: Psychology Press, 1997.

DeNora, Tia. *Music in Everyday Life*. Cambridge: Cambridge University Press, 2000.

Deutsch, Diana, ed. *The Psychology of Music*. 2nd ed. San Diego: Academic Press, 1999.

Dewey, John. *Art as Experience*. New York: Capricorn Books, 1958.

Dickie, George. *Art and the Aesthetic: An Institutional Analysis*. Ithaca, NY: Cornell University Press, 1974.

———. *Evaluating Art*. Philadelphia: Temple University Press, 1988.

Diffey, T. J. *The Republic of Art and Other Essays*. New York: Peter Lang, 1991.

Dolfsma, Wilfred. *Valuing Pop Music: Institutions, VALUES, and Economics*. Delft, Netherlands: Eburon, 1999.

Ducasse, Curt J. *The Philosophy of Art*. New York: Dial Press, 1929.

Dylan, Bob. *Chronicles: Volume One*. New York: Simon and Schuster, 2004.

Echard, William. *Neil Young and the Poetics of Energy*. Bloomington: Indiana University Press, 2005.

Evans, Martyn. *Listening to Music*. London: Macmillan, 1990.

Fast, Susan. *In the Houses of the Holy: Led Zeppelin and the Power of Rock Music*. Oxford: Oxford University Press, 2001.

Foster, Hal, ed. *The Anti-Aesthetic: Essays on Postmodern Culture*. Port Townsend, WA: Bay Press, 1983.

French, Peter A., Theodore E. Uehling, Jr., and Howard K. Wettstein, eds. *Philosophy and the Arts*. Notre Dame, IN: University of Notre Dame Press, 1991.

Frith, Simon. *Performing Rites: On the Value of Popular Music*. Cambridge: Harvard University Press, 1996.

Frith, Simon, and Andrew Goodwin, eds. *On Record: Rock, Pop, and the Written Word*. New York: Pantheon, 1990.

Frow, John. *Cultural Studies & Cultural Value*. Oxford: Oxford University Press, 1995.

Fusilli, Jim. *Pet Sounds*. London: Continuum, 2005.

Gaut, Berys, and Dominic McIver Lopes, eds. *The Routledge Companion to Aesthetics*. London: Routledge, 2001.

Godlovitch, Stan. *Musical Performance: A Philosophical Study*. London: Routledge, 1998.

Goehr, Lydia. *The Imaginary Museum of Musical Works*. Oxford: Clarendon Press, 1992.

Goldman, Alan H. *Aesthetic Value*. Boulder, CO: Westview Press, 1995.

Gracyk, Theodore. *I Wanna Be Me: Rock Music and the Politics of Identity*. Philadelphia: Temple University Press, 2001.

————. *Rhythm and Noise: An Aesthetics of Rock*. Durham, NC: Duke University Press, 1996.

Green, Lucy. *Music on Deaf Ears*. Manchester: Manchester University Press, 1988.

Guillory, John. *Cultural Capital: The Problem of Literary Canon Formation*. Chicago: University of Chicago Press, 1993.

Gurney, Edmund. *The Power of Sound*. London: Smith, Elder, 1880. Reprint, New York: Basic Books, 1966.

Handy, William C. *Father of the Blues: An Autobiography*. New York: Macmillan, 1941.

Hanslick, Eduard. *On the Musically Beautiful*. Translated by Geoffrey Payzant. Indianapolis: Hackett, 1986.

Harrington, Austin. *Art and Social Theory: Sociological Arguments in Aesthetics*. Cambridge: Polity, 2004.

Hatten, Robert S. *Musical Meaning in Beethoven: Markedness, Correlation, and Interpretation*. Bloomington: Indiana University Press, 1994.

Hebdige, Dick. *Subculture: The Meaning of Style*. London: Methuen, 1979.

Herbst, Peter, ed. *The Rolling Stone Interviews*. New York: St. Martin's Press, Rolling Stone Press, 1981.

Horner, Bruce, and Thomas Swiss, eds. *Key Terms in Popular Music and Culture*. Oxford: Blackwell, 1999.

Hume, David. *The Philosophical Works*. Edited by Thomas Hill Green and Thomas Hodge Grose. 4 vols. London: Smith, Elder, 1882. Reprint, Darmstadt: Scientia Verlag Aalen, 1964.

————. *A Treatise of Human Nature*. Edited by L. A. Selby-Bigge. 2nd ed., revised by P. H. Nidditch. Oxford: Clarendon Press, 1978.

Iseminger, Gary. *The Aesthetic Function of Art*. Ithaca, NY: Cornell University Press, 2004.

Isenberg, Arnold. *Aesthetics and the Theory of Criticism*. Edited by William Callaghan, Leigh Cauman, Carl Hempel, Sidney Morgenbesser, Mary Mothersill, Ernest Nagel, and Theodore Norman. Chicago: University of Chicago Press, 1973.

Johnson, Julian. *Who Needs Classical Music? Cultural Choice and Musical Value*. Oxford: Oxford University Press, 2002.

Jones, Mari Riess, and Susan Holleran, eds. *Cognitive Bases of Musical Communication*. Washington, DC: American Psychological Association, 1992.

Juslin, Patrik N., and John A. Sloboda, eds. *Music and Emotions: Theory and Research*. Oxford: Oxford University Press, 2001.

Kant, Immanuel. *Critique of Aesthetic Judgement*. Translated by James Creed Meredith. Oxford: Oxford University Press, 1911.

Kelly, Karen, and Evelyn McDonnell, eds. *Stars Don't Stand Still in the Sky: Music and Myth*. New York: New York University Press, 1999.

Kemal, Salim, and Ivan Gaskell, eds. *Performance and Authenticity in the Arts*. Cambridge: Cambridge University Press, 1999.

Keyes, Cheryl L. *Rap Music and Street Consciousness*. Urbana: University of Illinois Press, 2001.

Kieran, Matthew, ed. *Contemporary Debates in Aesthetics and the Philosophy of Art*. Oxford: Blackwell, 2006.

Kitwana, Bakari. *Why White Kids Love Hip-Hop: Wankstas, Wiggers, Wannabes, and the New Reality of Race in America*. New York: Basic Civitas Books, 2005.

Kivy, Peter. *The Fine Art of Repetition: Essays in the Philosophy of Music*. Cambridge: Cambridge University Press, 1993.

———. *Introduction to a Philosophy of Music*. Oxford: Clarendon Press, 2002.

———. *Music Alone: Philosophical Reflections on the Purely Musical Experience*. Ithaca, NY: Cornell University Press, 1990.

———. *Philosophies of the Arts: An Essay in Differences*. New York: Cambridge University Press, 1997.

Korsmeyer, Carolyn. *Making Sense of Taste: Food and Philosophy*. Ithaca, NY: Cornell University Press, 1999.

Kramer, Lawrence. *Musical Meaning: Toward a Critical History*. Berkeley and Los Angeles: University of California Press, 2002.

Krausz, Michael, ed. *The Interpretation of Music: Philosophical Essays*. Oxford: Clarendon Press, 1995.

Kymlicka, Will. *Liberalism, Community, and Culture*. Oxford: Clarendon Press, 1989.

Levinson, Jerrold. *Music, Art, and Metaphysics*. Ithaca, NY: Cornell University Press, 1990.

———. *Music in the Moment*. Ithaca, NY: Cornell University Press, 1997.

———. *The Pleasures of Aesthetics: Philosophical Essays*. Ithaca, NY: Cornell University Press, 1996.

———, ed. *The Oxford Handbook of Aesthetics*. Oxford: Oxford University Press, 2003.

Light, Andrew, and Jonathan M. Smith, eds. *The Aesthetics of Everyday Life*. New York: Columbia University Press, 2005.

Lipman, Samuel. *Music and More: Essays, 1975–1991*. Evanston, IL: Northwestern University Press, 1992.

Lockhead, Judy, and Joseph Auner, eds. *Postmodern Music/Postmodern Thought*. London: Routledge, 2002.

MacDonald, Raymond, David Hargreaves, and Dorothy Miell, eds. *Musical Identities*. Oxford: Oxford University Press, 2002.

Marcus, Greil. *Like a Rolling Stone: Bob Dylan at the Crossroads*. New York: Public Affairs, 2005.

———. *Ranters & Crowd Pleasers: Punk in Pop Music, 1977–92*. New York: Doubleday, 1993.

Meyer, Leonard B. *Emotion and Meaning in Music*. Chicago: University of Chicago Press, 1956.

———. *Explaining Music: Essays and Explorations.* Berkeley and Los Angeles: University of California Press, 1973.

Middleton, Richard, ed. *Reading Pop: Approaches to Textual Analysis in Popular Music.* New York: Oxford University Press, 2000.

Moore, Allan F. *Rock: The Primary Text: Developing a Musicology of Rock.* 2nd ed. New York: Ashgate, 2001.

———, ed. *Analyzing Popular Music.* Cambridge: Cambridge University Press, 2003.

Mortensen, Preben. *Art in the Social Order: The Making of the Modern Conception of Art.* Albany: State University of New York Press, 1997.

Mothersill, Mary. *Beauty Restored.* Oxford: Clarendon Press, 1984.

Novitz, David. *The Boundaries of Art.* Philadelphia: Temple University Press, 1992.

Pearson, Barry Lee, and Bill McCulloch. *Robert Johnson: Lost and Found.* Urbana: University of Illinois Press, 2003.

Postrel, Virginia. *The Substance of Style: How the Rise of Aesthetic Value Is Remaking Commerce, Culture, and Consciousness.* New York: HarperCollins, 2003.

Prall, David W. *Aesthetic Judgment.* New York: Thomas Y. Crowell, 1929. Reprint, New York: Apollo Edition, 1967.

Quinn, Eithne. *Nuthin' But a "G" Thang: The Culture and Commerce of Gangsta Rap.* New York: Columbia University Press, 2005.

Ridley, Aaron. *Music, Value and the Passions.* Ithaca, NY: Cornell University Press, 1995.

———. *The Philosophy of Music: Theme and Variations.* Edinburgh: Edinburgh University Press, 2004.

Robinson, Jenefer, ed. *Music and Meaning.* Ithaca, NY: Cornell University Press, 1997.

Rose, Tricia. *Black Noise: Rap Music and Black Culture in Contemporary America.* Hanover, NH: Wesleyan University Press, 1994.

Sartwell, Crispin. *Six Names of Beauty.* London: Routledge, 2004.

Scarborough, Dorothy. *On the Trail of Negro Folk-Songs.* Cambridge: Harvard University Press, 1925.

Schaper, Eva, ed. *Pleasure, Preference and Value.* Cambridge: Cambridge University Press, 1983.

Schwarz, David, Anahid Kassabian, and Lawrence Siegel, eds. *Keeping Score: Music, Disciplinarity, Culture.* Charlottesville: University Press of Virginia, 1997.

Scott, Derek B, ed. *Music, Culture, and Society: A Reader.* Oxford: Oxford University Press, 2000.

Scruton, Roger. *The Aesthetics of Music.* Oxford: Oxford University Press, 1997.

Searle, John. *Construction of Social Reality.* New York: Free Press, 1995.

———. *Speech Acts: An Essay in the Philosophy of Language.* Cambridge: Cambridge University Press, 1969.

Sharpe, R. A. *Philosophy of Music: An Introduction.* Montreal: McGill-Queen's University Press, 2004.

Shuker, Roy. *Understanding Popular Music.* 2nd ed. London: Routledge, 2001.

Shusterman, Richard. *Pragmatist Aesthetics: Living Beauty, Rethinking Art.* Oxford: Blackwell, 1992.

Sibley, Frank. *Approach to Aesthetics: Collected Papers on Philosophical Aesthetics.* Edited by

John Benson, Betty Redfern, and Jeremy Roxbee Cox. Oxford: Clarendon Press, 2001.

Sircello, Guy. *A New Theory of Beauty*. Princeton, NJ: Princeton University Press, 1975.

Small, Christopher. *Musicking: The Meanings of Performing and Listening*. Middletown, CN: Wesleyan University Press, 1998.

———. *Music of the Common Tongue: Survival and Celebration of Afro-American Music*. Middletown, CN: Wesleyan University Press, 1998.

Smith, Barbara Herrnstein. *Contingencies of Value: Alternative Perspectives for Critical Theory*. Cambridge: Harvard University Press, 1988.

Stecker, Robert. *Artworks: Definitions, Meaning and Value*. University Park: Pennsylvania State University Press, 1997.

Sterne, Jonathan. *The Audible Past: Cultural Origins of Sound Reproduction*. Durham, NC: Duke University Press, 2003.

Subotnik, Rose R. *Developing Variations: Style and Ideology in Western Music*. Minneapolis: University of Minnesota Press, 1991.

Swiss, Thomas, John Sloop, and Andrew Herman, eds. *Mapping the Beat: Popular Music and Contemporary Theory*. Blackwell, 1998.

van der Merwe, Peter. *Origins of the Popular Style: The Antecedents of Twentieth-Century Popular Music*. Oxford: Clarendon Press, 1989.

Wald, Elijah. *Escaping the Delta: Robert Johnson and the Invention of the Blues*. New York: Amistad, 2004.

Walser, Robert. *Running With the Devil: Power, Gender, and Madness in Heavy Metal Music*. Hanover, NH: Wesleyan University Press, 1993.

Wicke, Peter. *Rock Music: Culture, Aesthetics and Sociology*. Translated by Rachel Fogg. Cambridge: Cambridge University Press, 1990.

Wilson, Frank R., and Franz L. Roehmann, eds. *Music and Child Development*. St. Louis: Biology of Making, 1990.

Wolff, Janet. *Aesthetics and the Sociology of Art*. 2nd ed. Ann Arbor: University of Michigan Press, 1993.

Wolterstorff, Nicholas. *Works and Worlds of Art*. Oxford: Clarendon Press, 1980.

Zak, Albin J., III. *The Poetics of Rock: Cutting Tracks, Making Records*. Berkeley and Los Angeles: University of California Press, 2001.

Zangwill, Nick. *The Metaphysics of Beauty*. Ithaca, NY: Cornell University Press, 2001.

Zbikowski, Lawrence M. *Conceptualizing Music: Cognitive Structure, Theory, and Analysis*. New York: Oxford University Press, 2002.

Index

Abba, 118
absolute music, 30, 117, 131
active listening. *See* exclusivity thesis
adolescence, 8, 15, 51–52, 53–57, 180, 184, 188–90; Dutch response to rock and roll and, 51–57; fragmentation of self during, 181, 185–86; listening skills and, 138; uses of music in, 53–55, 59–60, 121, 177–79, 181, 222n13, 224n40
Adorno, Theodor, 43, 196n16
aeolian cadences, 3, 195n7
aesthetic attitude, appreciation vs., 212n26
aesthetic cognitivism, 114–18, 155, 203n24; defined, 48–49
aesthetic distance, 28–30, 37–38, 135, 146
aesthetic evaluation, 2, 3, 5, 38, 69, 191–94; aesthetic cognitivism and, 114–15; aesthetic properties and, 39, 77, 86–99, 103; appreciation vs., 103–4, 109, 111–13, 118–19, 212n19; as contextual, 4, 19, 23, 36–37, 50, 95–98, 122–23; as disinterested, 30, 62; as elitist and reactionary, 33; of experiences, 104–6; functionality and, 122–23; as holistic, 90–91; Frith on, 27; human agency and, 95; internal perspective and, 106–7; principles and, 73–77, 86–89, 91–94, 110–11; social relevance and, 48–50. *See also* aesthetic value; principles, evaluative

aestheticism, 30, 33, 193
aesthetic predicates, 88, 193; aesthetic properties and, 39, 74, 77, 194
aesthetic principles. *See* principles, evaluative
aesthetic properties, 78, 83, 87, 129, 134, 139; aesthetic cognitivism and, 114–16; aesthetic predicates and, 39, 74, 77, 194; appreciation and, 103, 109, 114, 118; as contextual, 36, 84–85, 90, 93–99, 108, 118, 148, 159, 194; defined, 39; emergence from nonaesthetic, 89–91, 93, 96–99, 111, 148, 159, 206n57, 211n8; evaluative principles and, 74–76, 194; as experiential, 39, 85, 94, 116, 126, 158; expressive properties and, 92–93, 156; middle-level, 91–92; musical categories and, 95–98, 154; of nature, 115; particularism and, 77; polarity of, 88–89, 92–93, 209n42; variety of, 132, 193, 202n82. *See also* resultance base
aesthetics. *See* aesthetic theory
aesthetics, new, 14, 36–40, 119, 192, 193
aesthetic theory: of art, 13–14, 28, 198n12; Bourdieu's response to, 28–29; as Eurocentric, 34–35, 50; popular culture and, 2, 14; recent developments in, 14, 38, 62; sociological critique of, 1–2, 6, 14, 33–34, 48, 50–51; sociology and, 59, 73

231